Punishing the Black Body

Race in the Atlantic World, 1700–1900

SERIES EDITORS

Richard S. Newman, *Rochester Institute of Technology*
Patrick Rael, *Bowdoin College*
Manisha Sinha, *University of Massachusetts, Amherst*

ADVISORY BOARD

Edward Baptist, *Cornell University*
Christopher Brown, *Columbia University*
Vincent Carretta, *University of Maryland*
Laurent Dubois, *Duke University*
Erica Armstrong Dunbar, *University of Delaware and the Library Company of Philadelphia*
Douglas Egerton, *LeMoyne College*
Leslie Harris, *Emory University*
Joanne Pope Melish, *University of Kentucky*
Sue Peabody, *Washington State University, Vancouver*
Erik Seeman, *State University of New York, Buffalo*
John Stauffer, *Harvard University*

Punishing the Black Body

MARKING SOCIAL AND RACIAL STRUCTURES IN BARBADOS AND JAMAICA

Dawn P. Harris

The University of Georgia Press
ATHENS

Paperback edition, 2020
© 2017 by the University of Georgia Press
Athens, Georgia 30602
www.ugapress.org
All rights reserved
Designed by Kaelin Chappell Broaddus
Set in Fournier by Graphic Composition, Inc.

Most University of Georgia Press titles are
available from popular e-book vendors.

Printed digitally

Library of Congress Cataloging-in-Publication Data

Names: Harris, Dawn P., author.
Title: Punishing the black body : marking social and racial
    structures in Barbados and Jamaica / Dawn P. Harris.
Description: Athens : The University of Georgia Press, 2017. |
    Series: Race in the Atlantic world, 1700–1900 |
    Includes bibliographical references and index.
Identifiers: LCCN 2017014289| ISBN 9780820351728
    (hardback : alk. paper) | ISBN 9780820351711 (ebook)
Subjects: LCSH: Punishment—Barbados—History—19th century. |
    Punishment—Jamaica—History—19th century. |
    Blacks—Barbados—Social conditions—19th century. |
    Blacks—Jamaica—Social conditions—19th century.
Classification: LCC HV5699.B37 H37 2017 |
    DDC 364.6089/9607292—dc23
    LC record available at https://lccn.loc.gov/2017014289
ISBN 9780820357881 (paperback : alk. paper)

To my late grandmother, Evelyn Harris,
who told me that I could do anything.

To my mother, who believes that I can do anything.

To my daughters, who show me endless possibilities
and remind me of all the things that I can do.

History without bodies is unimaginable.

—LESLIE A. ADELSON

CONTENTS

ACKNOWLEDGMENTS

Books, like people, need a village to raise them. I owe a debt of gratitude to David V. Trotman at York University in Toronto, who helped me craft what began as a small idea into something much larger.

Like Professor Trotman, Michele A. Johnson, also at York University, read multiple versions of this work and prompted me to answer questions even when I felt I had no more answers.

My debt of gratitude also extends outside of Canada, to the United States, where Rutgers professor Dr. Mary E. Hawkesworth helped me flesh out inchoate ideas, offered critical insight, and pushed me out of my comfort zone.

My thanks also to Dr. E. Anthony Hurley, my former colleague at Stony Brook University, who listened to more iterations of this work than he probably wanted to. His advice was invaluable.

Finally, I owe a debt of gratitude to the staff at the University of Georgia Press. It is through their help and patience that this book has come to fruition.

Punishing the Black Body

Colonial Body Politics

*Linking the Punished Body to the
British West Indian Social Order*

Almost every apprentice that sent to workhouse by magistrate,
have to dance treadmill, except the sick in the hospital. It was
miserable to see when the mill going, the people bawling and
crying most dreadful—so they can't dance, so the driver keep on
flogging; them holla out, "massa me no able! my 'tomach, oh! me
da dead, oh!"—but no use, the driver never stop—the bawling
make it rather worse, them make the mill go faster—the more you
holla the more the mill go, and the driver keep on flogging away
at all them not able to keep up; them flog the people as if them
was flogging Cow.

  —JAMES WILLIAMS, *A Narrative of Events*

Back then there were laws to keep people from doing cruel things
to animals, but there was no laws to protect us from cruelty.
Now I'm no lawyer, but what I know is that I've seen a lot of our
people get sent to the jail-house, get whipped and suffer other
things if they happen to mark an animal with a whip, but I have
never seen nor hear of a white man being punish for anything he
do to one of us. Massa was king and king do no wrong.

  —SAMUEL SMITH (quoted in Smith, *To Shoot Hard Labour*)

  The quotations above, taken from the apprentice James Williams's 1837
narrative and from the recollections of Samuel Smith, a workingman of Antigua,
provide a glimpse of the experiences of the laborers whose lives were affected
by the British abolition of slavery in 1834. Both recollections demonstrate the
ambiguity of systems that promised freedom even as they continued to operate,
in some ways, like the institution of slavery. Williams's and Smith's accounts of

their experiences show us that statistics, ledgers, notary records, and laws cannot give us the sum of the changes wrought by abolition. Instead, such quotations illustrate the human dimension of the post-slavery period by placing the former slaves and their experiences front and center. Moreover, Smith's and Williams's recollections show that the post-slavery period represented a condition that could be measured by how it was *felt* by ordinary citizens. Importantly, these two quotations also establish the salience of punishment in Caribbean history—particularly in its ability to further demarcate the extant social and racial boundaries.

What is perhaps surprising is that in spite of the importance of punishment to the "making" of the Caribbean, scholarly discussions on punishment have tended to be either subsumed under explorations of larger topics or intricately interwoven with other themes. In fact, for a long time David Trotman's *Crime in Trinidad*, published in 1986, Ian Duffield's article in *Slavery and Abolition*, published that same year, and Patrick Bryan's chapter on "law and order" in the 1991 publication *The Jamaican People* were some of the few writings in which sustained discussions of punishment could be found.[1] More recently, articles and monographs by such scholars as Mary Turner, Henrice Altink, Jonathan Dalby, and Sheena Boa, illustrate a transformation in British Caribbean historiography.[2] "Histories from below" have now become a part of the canon rather than existing on its periphery. Additionally, contributions by Turner, Altink, Boa, Diana Paton, and Cecilia A. Green provide textual evidence of the inroads that social forces like the women's movement have made within academic institutions and in scholarship. Turner's "11 O'clock Flog: Women, Work, and Labour Law in the British Caribbean," Altink's "Slavery by Another Name: Apprenticed Women in Jamaican Workhouses in the Period 1834–38," and Boa's "Experiences of Women Estate Workers during the Apprenticeship Period in St. Vincent, 1834–38: The Transition from Slavery to Freedom" specifically focus on the lived experiences of women—a group that traditionally had been excluded from the historical narrative.

Paton's groundbreaking 2004 text *No Bond but the Law* and more recent articles by Green also help fill this lacuna.[3] Additionally, the recent works by Green signal a new trajectory on the work on punishment. Whereas many of the earlier works dealt with punishment during slavery, Green's scholarly contributions tackle a more modern form of punitive discipline—namely, imprisonment.

New Ways of Looking at Old Histories

In 2005, the year after Paton's *No Bond but the Law* was published, prisoners at Glendairy Prison in Barbados rioted.[4] Although not directly related, these events—a riot by disaffected prisoners and the release of Paton's seminal text—both sparked dialogues about appropriate punishments for lawbreakers and forced a conversation about the relationship between punishment and a nation's embrace of modern values.

The destruction of Barbados's major prison forced that nation's citizens and leaders to take a close look at the criminal Other. Because those incarcerated were no longer out of sight—and thus could not be "out of mind"—they provoked a national crisis and forced Barbadians to ask questions about criminals, punishment, and the boundaries erected between those considered to be "defiled" and the "pure." These questions were steeped in the corporal, the personal, and the national: Where will we house these criminal bodies? How will we protect the bodies of law-abiding people from criminals? How do we punish bodies of criminals if the technology of punishment no longer exists? How do we uphold a policy of human rights when dealing with those who have contravened the human rights of others? There were no easy answers to these questions, but they did force a public conversation about punishment and the punished beyond the abstract. Indeed, the destruction of Glendairy Prison brought issues of punishment, justice, and crime vigorously into national discourses.[5]

Similarly, Paton's publication, after its eruption in the discursive landscape, has encouraged historians of the Caribbean to think about how punishment can be used to assess a nation's maturation.[6] Paton makes clear from the outset in her book that there was a "longstanding and intimate relationship between [Jamaican] state formation and private punishment." Paton further distils her argument by making the important point that "antislavery and the penal reform movement emerged at roughly the same time and made many of the same assumptions about human nature and the best way to organize society." Moreover, Paton argues against discourses that draw sharp dichotomies between slave punishments and those that occurred in the post-emancipation period. Instead she argues for a nuanced analysis that acknowledges, for example, "that whipping was carried out on the authority of the state both before and after the end of slavery; that slavery relied on prisons; and that slaveholders made direct use of imprisonment, both on and off their estates."[7]

This book, *Punishing the Black Body: Marking Social and Racial Structures in Barbados and Jamaica*, continues the recent interventions in the scholarship on punishment in the colonial Caribbean. It does this by opening another area of inquiry and looking closely at the ways in which the *physical bodies* of individuals were appropriated by colonial states and their agents to demarcate social boundaries—boundaries that were critical to the maintenance of white colonials' social, political, and economic dominance.

Pointedly, this work picks up on a part of Paton's analysis. Highlighting the deficiencies in using Foucault's *Discipline and Punish* to understand punishment in Jamaica, Paton notes that contrasts between "slavery and the whip on the one hand, and the prison on the other, consistently broke down in practice." She notes further that "even when prisons did not rely on floggings—even when the deliberate infliction of pain was not explicitly part of a penalty— punishment remained 'corporal' in that the bodies of prisoners continued to be constrained."[8] In explaining why these continuities were evident on an island that claimed to be embracing full equality for all, my work adds another layer to analyses of punishment by illustrating that the continuities were by deliberate design. Whereas Paton disagrees with Patrick Bryan's assertion that attitudes that were held during slavery prevailed in the post-emancipation period, *Punishing the Black Body* shows that the corporal punishments levied after 1834 reflected jaundiced attitudes about black people and the black body and indicated a desire to preserve the socio-racial hierarchy similar to what had existed during slavery.[9]

To produce an analysis that pays attention to the experiences of the various subaltern classes in Jamaica and Barbados, this book employs an interdisciplinary methodology. Along with using conventional historical sources such as data from Captain J. W. Pringle's nineteenth-century sojourn in the British West Indies, it also draws on information on social conditions in Barbados and Jamaica found in Colonial Office correspondence, travelogues, personal accounts, and "Blue Books" (so named because of their blue covers, these contained statistics and other official reports of the British government) to provide valuable historical context.

I have also used tools, besides ones used typically by historians, to reconstruct the narrative of punishment. Plantation societies and colonialism are rife with paradoxes, as becomes clear when attempting to make sense of societies organized along racial and color lines, particularly when colonialism never seemed to account for the fact that these so-called disparate races would mate and produce offspring. To effectively deal with such paradoxes I have found it necessary to go beyond the historical data and have drawn on the tools of critical race theorists and feminist theorists.

Retaining an interdisciplinary methodology, I have also drawn upon the theories of the body that have been advanced by scholars like Elizabeth Grosz, Judith Butler, and Kathleen Canning.[10] Thus, this work sees the exercise of disciplinary and punitive tactics in nineteenth-century Barbados and Jamaica as forms of "body writing" that bound their inhabitants, as Grosz writes, "often in quite different ways according to sex, class, race, cultural and age codifications, to social positions and relations."[11] Moreover, in telling the history of discipline and punishment via the body, this work draws on the voices of those implicated in the variegated landscapes of disciplinary and punitive practices. Thus the body is analyzed, as Grosz says, as "both object (for others) and a lived reality (for the subject), it is never simply object nor simply subject."[12] By performing such an analysis, this work asserts that through theorizing the body as both a discursive and material artifact, from the vantage point of others and subjects, we can gain a fuller understanding of the colonial Caribbean as a region that was created by bodies as much as it was created by ideas about bodies.

By looking at the black body "as a useful category of historical analysis," to borrow the subtitle of Joan W. Scott's influential work on gender published in 1986, *Punishing the Black Body* does something that earlier histories of the Caribbean have not done.[13] It uses theories of the body that have been the preserve of scholars in other disciplines, such as women's studies and sociology, to show how something (the body) that was so crucial to the making of the Caribbean and its history can be studied. Arguably, the fact that the body was not studied might be attributed to its very visibility. That is to say, the body's obtrusive presence might have made its study seem almost redundant.

However, by training a keen lens on the physical body, this book shows that using the body to examine the workings of the colonial Caribbean is neither redundant nor foolish. Indeed, by paying attention to the ways in which bodies have been co-opted by the state and its agents, I demonstrate that physical bodies are never neutral entities. Instead, bodies are often imbued with and ascribed meanings that have a significant impact on the ways in which individuals experience the world around them. Additionally, my analysis shows how ideas about the black body—what the black body meant, what it could and could not do, and how it could be used—and, by extension, blackness, informed the ways in which men and women were treated in the colonial Caribbean. In addition, by co-opting the black body (whether as an instrument of work or as a receptacle of punishment) colonists helped to create and sustain particular "knowledges" that helped them to organize the societies that they were constructing outside of the metropole.

The Utility of a Comparative Perspective: Were Barbados and Jamaica Opposites?

"It may excite some surprise that I should have selected so small a portion of the globe as the island of Barbados as the field of my researches." So begins Robert H. Schomburgk in the preface to his 1848 *History of Barbados*. Schomburgk continued to stake his claim for Barbados to be recognized as an important subject for historical study, stating,

> It might be supposed that the history of that colony could scarcely offer any incidents of general interest; but I believe that the events recorded in the following pages will prove that such a supposition is incorrect, and that the history of Barbados is by no means barren of events which have materially affected the British Empire. If the navigation laws led to England's supremacy on the seas, that small island was the cause which led to the navigation laws. But this is not the only point of importance attached to its history; it was here and in St. Christopher's that England founded its first colonies in the southern part of America; it was here that the first sugar-cane was planted upon the soil of the British dominions; it was here that many of those attached to the royal cause, during England's civil wars and the interregnum which ensued, sought and found an asylum, until the chivalric opposition of that small spot to the mandates of Cromwell roused his ire and vengeance.[14]

In 1627, when the English occupied an uninhabited Barbados, they might not have been aware of the way in which this small, flat island would be thrust onto the world's stage, nor could they foretell the praise that would be heaped on the island by the likes of Schomburgk.[15] As the site of the "sugar revolution," this small island proved to be the David in the Atlantic world. Its small size did not prevent it from outpacing much larger areas, both economically and in terms of its geopolitical importance.

Even so, Barbados was an island of intractability. Unlike much of the Caribbean, it was to remain the sole possession of the British Crown, with contemporary historian Gordon K. Lewis remarking that it was "[e]ven more intractably English than Jamaica."[16] Its unwavering ties to England had an impact on the culture, attitudes, and institutions that developed on the island. Indeed, many writers saw this to be detrimental as it produced a white plantocracy "proverbial for its reactionary conceit," as Lewis puts it. According to Lewis, Barbados— along with the Bahamas and Bermuda—"became notorious for its entrenched system of racialist prejudice."[17]

Intractability was also evident in the economy that developed and in the opportunities afforded to the island's inhabitants to engage in activities outside the sugar plantation. As a case in point, whereas Jamaica had a system of livestock farms ("pens"), Barbados was an "almost pure sugar plantation economy."[18] This, along with Barbados's ties to England, produced a society with a rigid, caste-like class system. Lewis described Barbadian society as possessing a "familiar hierarchy": at the top, a white "economic oligarchy, along with the professional echelons of law, church, and state; in the middle, the various grades, nicely demarcated by income indices, of the 'middle classes'; at the bottom, the heavily Negro proletariat."[19]

Jamaica, as the third largest island in the Caribbean behind Cuba and Hispaniola, had a history that was different from that of Barbados. Seized from the Spanish by the British in 1655, Jamaica bore many remnants of this former colonial relationship in names like Savanna La Mar and St. Jago de la Vega (modern-day Spanish Town).[20] In addition, whereas many of Barbados's planter class remained resident on that island, many of the planters who created estates in Jamaica preferred to reside in England, a living testament to William A. Green's assertion that the British West Indian colonies were created to "produce wealth, not contentment."[21] Jamaica's large absentee population was also evidenced in the fact that men outnumbered women, whereas the majority of the population of Barbados was female by the end of the seventeenth century.[22]

Thus, the disciplinary and punitive climates in nineteenth-century Barbados and Jamaica invite interesting comparisons. First, the geographical and demographic contrasts between two of Britain's most important colonies suggest, on the surface, that the punitive and disciplinary technologies and ideologies embraced in the islands would have been different.[23] As a case in point, Barbados's high labor-to-land ratio suggests that its plantocracy would have exerted a greater hold over the bodies of the laborers than would have been possible in Jamaica. On the other hand was Jamaica's vaster and more mountainous terrain that proved favorable to the development of a somewhat autonomous peasantry and populations of Maroons who were beyond the boundaries of the plantation and the gaze of the plantocracy.

Barbados's high population density suggests also that the bodies of Barbadian laborers could have been more easily "disciplined"—that is, restricted to space and place and subject to the vagaries of the plantocracy in ways in which Jamaicans would not have been. In fact, so well known was the idea that Barbadians were "under heavy manners" because of their island's high population density, particularly in contrast to Jamaicans' autonomy, that it was remarked upon by plantation proprietor, attorney, and justice of the peace William Carr during testimony he gave to the commission that investigated the suppression of the 1865 Morant Bay Rebellion. When asked if he would be glad if he had a steady supply of Creole laborers, particularly for whom he would not have to provide food, Carr explicitly stated that they "would not do it," as the workers in Jamaica were "not like those in Barbadoes" and were "not dependent upon estates for their livelihood."[24] Bearing Carr's comments in mind, this book investigates whether disciplinary and punitive discourses and practices were influenced by factors external to the body, factors not normally associated with punishment and discipline, like demography and geography.

The ways in which the valences of demography and topography impinged on punitive and disciplinary practices are brought into sharp relief in another sense as Jamaica's vast, arable tracts of land and its low labor-to-land ratio were rationales for the importation of overseas laborers from India, China, and Portuguese territories. The presence of new types of workers in Jamaica, I argue, exerted pressures within and upon Jamaican society that were negotiated within the discursive, legal, and punitive systems—pressures and negotiations that beg for sustained scholarly attention.

Jamaica's influence on both the Caribbean region and the metropole also makes it an attractive case study. Commentators as diverse as contemporary historian William A. Green and members of the nineteenth-century Anti-Slavery Committee in England have remarked upon Jamaica's influence in the region and noted how the "Jamaican situation" often became the blueprint for how to conduct affairs in the rest of the region (or how *not* to conduct them). Indeed, when making their case against the apprenticeship system, members of the Anti-Slavery Committee used data from Jamaica "to watch closely the progress of that pernicious system . . . [and] to facilitate public inquiry into the manner in which the intentions of the Imperial Act had been carried into effect by Colonial Legislatures, Authorities, and Planters, and likewise by the Home Government." This "especial attention to the laws and practices of Jamaica" was attributed to the fact that it contained "more than a third part of the entire negro population of the West Indies."[25]

More than a hundred years after members of the Anti-Slavery Committee made these claims, Green joined the fray and reiterated the extent of Jamaica's historical and historiographical clout. Indeed, he pointed out that "by virtue of its size and importance, Jamaica carried most of the legislative colonies with it on every significant controversial question." To drive home this point, Green added:

> At the best of times imperial policy was devised to meet the requirements of Jamaica; in the worst of times it was contrived to break the resistance of that colony. The anti-slavery party concentrated its attention upon Jamaica. The House of Commons Committee on slavery drew almost all of its evidence from Jamaican sources. Henry Taylor's valuable Colonial Office memorandum recommending the abolition of slavery treated the problem solely in terms of Jamaica. To an inordinate degree, public and parliamentary inquiry on the course of the apprenticeship focused upon that island, and the decision to abandon the ap-

prenticeship system two years ahead of schedule, in 1838, was taken in response to conditions prevailing there.[26]

As further evidence of Jamaica's importance in the region, one only has to look at the efforts that were made to ameliorate prison conditions. When Captain J. W. Pringle left England in 1837 to investigate prison abuses in the British West Indies, he did so at the behest of a British government that had obtained information about abuses within the workhouses and prisons in Jamaica. Even though Pringle reached Barbados first, and it would therefore have been "expedient" for him to begin there, he was advised that Jamaica, because of "its extent and population," would be "the principal sphere" of his investigation. Consequently, Pringle was commanded to "incur no unnecessary delay in proceeding to [Jamaica]."[27] Jamaica's importance was reinforced further by what Sir George Grey outlined in his instructions to Pringle before the latter left for the British West Indies. If Pringle could not complete his investigations in all of the colonies by the time that he was supposed to return to England in April 1838, he should, "after carefully completing the investigation of the prisons in Jamaica, omit such of the other colonies as [he might] not be able to comprise within the period allotted."[28]

More pointedly, examination of practices and discourses of punishment in nineteenth-century Barbados and Jamaica shows that raced, gendered, and classed bodies were as essential to punishment in these two islands as was the execution of punishment itself. This is substantiated further when one considers the thought-provoking questions posed by Gwendolyn Midlo Hall in *Social Control in Slave Plantation Societies: A Comparison of St. Domingue and Cuba*: "How was order maintained on a sustained enough basis for these slave societies to function? How were hundreds of slaves, who were being worked to death on isolated, rural estates and who were armed with machetes, convinced, for at least a significant length of time, not to murder their masters and overseers?"[29] Hall posed these questions after asserting that the various security measures like pass laws and laws prohibiting the assembly of slaves were enforced sporadically. For social order to be maintained, argued Hall, "the person of the white had been made inviolate."[30]

By showing how punishment was apprehended and articulated in a dual context, comparing Barbados and Jamaica, this work diverges from the extant historiographies on the Caribbean, particularly those like Paton's that have served as the advance guard for regional histories on punishment. *Punishing the Black Body* does this by investigating how two of Britain's most important possessions experienced a history of punishment in which there were sometimes glaring differences between the two. Because it takes this comparative approach, *Punishing the Black Body* brings these differences between Barbados and Jamaica into sharp relief. For instance, by using Barbados's land and labor issues as a counterpoint to Jamaica's, I show that punishment and its ideologies and manifestations should be read and understood through wider societal forces that impinge upon them.

My examination of disciplinary and punitive practices in Barbados and Jamaica also revealed similarities between the two islands. This comparative approach, looking keenly at the punished body, raises questions about Barbados's and Jamaica's calling themselves nations of free men and women. For instance, in spite of the supposed quiet compliance of Barbados's inhabitants and Jamaica's seemingly bold and incorrigible populace, punitive approaches on the two islands remained eerily similar, thus reinforcing the notion that the plantation economy and ideas about the place of certain bodies in this economy continued to exert a strong grip even as promises were made to break cleanly with the past.

Although this book concentrates on Barbados and Jamaica, I have also found it useful to draw on examples from other parts of the Caribbean. Additionally, consonant with the argument espoused by Douglas Hay and Paul Craven in their introduction to *Masters, Servants, and Magistrates in Britain and the Empire, 1562–1955,* I have found that much of the penal legislation and punitive practices in Jamaica and Barbados were borrowed either from the metropole or from other British colonies.[31] These borrowings help illustrate that there was much commonality in the ways in which the bodies of all subaltern and colonized laborers were regarded by those in power. They also illustrate that Jamaican and Barbadian apparitions of British legal discourses and punitive practices "developed distinctive structures of [their] own," in the words of Hay and Craven, and that they were "also often administered in highly oppressive and exploitative ways, particularly where workers were not of British or European origin."[32] These disparate sources have helped illuminate ideas about punishment in the wider Caribbean context and reinforce the peripatetic nature of disciplinary and punitive practices as they traveled—via colonial representatives, missives, dispatches, ordinances, and laws—from the metropole to the British West Indies.

Finally, this book is a platform to reexamine the meaning of power and how we define the powerful and the powerless. In the cases of post-slavery Jamaica and Barbados, power was guarded selfishly by colonial elites, but it was not theirs alone. This book demonstrates that subaltern individuals like James Williams, Nancy Murray, Rosey Sample, and Elizabeth Faulkner could appropriate power and use it for themselves. Moreover, the examples of Williams, Murray,

Sample, and Faulkner challenge the idea that punishment was something done to inert bodies. In fact, even as they "took" their punishments—with their bodies providing the tableau upon which these punishments were realized—these individuals also resisted and rewrote the narratives that attempted to define and stringently limit their place in the plantation economy.

Chapter Overview

Chapter 1 establishes the importance of the body as a site of disciplinary and punitive practices in Jamaica and Barbados. It notes that attacks against the bodies of the enslaved set the scene for the punitive climate that was to predominate in the post-emancipation period. It also shows that these punishments were crucial in maintaining the dominance of the planter class and of the socio-racial structures that existed in the colonial Caribbean.

Within the context of the apprenticeship system and referring to data from a variety of sources, including correspondence from stipendiary magistrates (British judges sent to the colonies) and James Williams's narrative, chapter 2 illustrates that "the relationship between the material world and its discursive signification [was] contested on and through the signified and signifying ground of women's [and men's] bodies," in the words of Leslie A. Adelson.[33] Although one might assume that the abolition of slavery and an embracement of a condition of "perfect legal equality" should have occasioned a corresponding loosening of a hold on the body in a disciplinary context, I argue that this was not the case. Data show that the use of corporeal punishments was the norm during the apprenticeship period.

Using the figure of James Williams, the black plantation constable, and examining the actions of other lesser-known apprentices, chapter 2 also explores the ways in which apprentices exercised some power over themselves and shaped, to some degree, their experiences in austere environments. It shows that disciplinary and punitive power were not held solely by colonial and imperial authorities. Instead, this chapter displays the contradictions that inhered within the plantation economy that sometimes resulted in a blurring of the boundaries between different social groups. Thus, the black plantation constable is depicted punishing individuals who occupy the same enslaved status he occupies—even as his tenuous authority to punish is the product of a predatory plantation economy and thus remains circumscribed by a superior white patriarchal authority. This chapter also shows how apprentices could reclaim their personal sovereignty and challenge the very system that attempted to transform them into docile bodies.

Chapter 2 uses the legally and socially ambiguous setting of the apprentice-ship period to analyze disciplinary and punitive practices in Barbados and Ja-maica.³⁴ Chapter 3 examines emancipation—and the ensuing era that was sup-posed to bring about an emphatic change in the social condition of the former slaves—to assess the nature of punishment. Through examination of various acts passed between 1838 and 1900, the conclusion reached in this chapter is that the body—the black body in particular—remained the idée fixe of Jamaican and Barbadian legislators. Along with looking at the legal rhetoric of punish-ment, chapter 3 also examines some of the major social ruptures within these two territories, the legal and punitive responses to these ruptures, and how these responses reveal ideas about bodies, discipline, and punishment. For instance, it uses indentured immigration and the Morant Bay Rebellion in Jamaica to assess how disciplinary and punitive ideologies responded to different kinds of social pressures in the two territories under study.

Chapters 4 and 5 examine spaces and places of confinement in Barbados and Jamaica, respectively. These chapters reinforce the idea that the disciplined body remained central to the execution of punishment in these two colonies, a recur-ring motif in the earlier chapters. Evidence presented in these chapters shows that although the body was constrained within the walls of institutions like work-houses and jails, this did not prevent the confined from receiving supplementary corporal punishments.

Chapter 4, on spaces of confinement in Barbados, departs from the earlier chapters that focused on the more obviously punitive forms of legislation and punitive practices after 1834. It looks at how disciplinary technologies were often aimed at the consolidation of the plantation economy, producing docile, com-pliant laborers, and reinforcing white plantocratic hegemony. By illustrating the importance of disciplinary tactics to the maintenance of the plantation economy, chapter 4 shows how "system[s] of rules [were] used to maintain . . . control" over laborers—control that ensured a surplus pool of readily available and eas-ily exploitable workers for the benefit of the plantation economy.³⁵

In looking at the disciplinary tactics employed by colonial and imperial offi-cials, chapter 4 also complicates the idea of confinement by showing how ideas about *where* bodies belonged could also help entrap or restrict bodies within certain spaces. It examines confinement as a condition that occurred within ar-chitectural spaces like jails, but it also looks at how discourses, most notably laws, helped to create virtual "carceral states" outside of the jail by restricting the mobility of individuals. By examining the Act to Regulate the Emigration of Labourers from This Island, passed in Barbados on November 30, 1836, in addition to systems of control in Glendairy Prison and the other district prisons, chapter 4 argues that such spaces and places were sites for the veritable control of Barbados's working class. Moreover, by applying a Foucauldian framework to an analysis of the 1836 Emigration Act, the chapter argues that this law created a disciplinary topography out of the Barbadian legislative and geographical landscapes as a result of the surveillance, policing, and information-gathering techniques that were central to the act's enforcement. Chapter 4 shows also how the discursive and literal topography created by this act invoked Jeremy Bentham's Panopticon, even at times reflecting its ideals.

Chapter 5 examines how surveillance was used to stem the occurrence of "moral mischief" in spaces of penal confinement in nineteenth-century Jamaica. It does this by drawing on data mainly from Captain J. W. Pringle's 1837 report on prison conditions in the British Caribbean and the report from a commission of March 1873 created because of what Liberal member of Parliament Lord Kimberley saw as a "still defective" penal system. Both reports were precipitated by revelations that were considered to be deleterious to the proper functioning of prisons. The evidence from these reports is used to argue that penal spaces in nineteenth-century Jamaica were entrusted with the task of unmaking the alterity of those defined as criminal and transforming these individuals into upstanding citizens who fit seamlessly into their ordained location in the socio-political hierarchy (albeit at the bottom).

What was the relationship between the public and punishment in Barbados and Jamaica between 1834 and 1900? This is the question tackled in chapter 6. This is done by delineating technologies of discipline and punishment as performances of power in which members of the plantation economy actively witnessed and participated. By examining forms of punishment like hair-cropping and hanging, this chapter contends that the shaming and terrorizing of the punished and the controlling of what the masses consumed—what they were able to see and hear—were key elements of the enactment of discipline and punishment in Barbados and Jamaica.[36]

Punishment and the gendered body is the topic explored in chapter 7. Although the presence of white men, black men, and black women has been accounted for in the discourse of punishment, up to this point white women have been virtually absent. However, this chapter shows that the sheer invisibility of the bodies of white women in the data on punishment can be used to illuminate their lives, and it shows too how they fit into the realm of discipline and punishment. Moreover, by employing a gendered analysis, this chapter reveals that ideas that were held about bodies in nineteenth-century Jamaica and Barbados were not immutable. What were cast as apparently stable notions about the corporeal differences between whites and blacks and men and women were often called into question when punishment met gendered, raced bodies.

This book contributes to the literature on the post-emancipation West Indies by providing an important comparative look at the experiences of Jamaicans and Barbadians. It shows that the role entrusted to the body in the drama of punishment can shed light on the experiences of all of the inhabitants of nineteenth-century Barbados and Jamaica, whether colonial officials or laity, apprentices or workers, spectators or participants. By using the lenses of discipline and punishment to look at nineteenth-century Barbados and Jamaica, this work also shows that these phenomena helped to uphold the socio-racial hierarchies that characterized the post-slavery Caribbean.

CHAPTER I

Six-Legged Women and Derby's Dose

The White Imagination and Narratives of Bad Bodies and Good Punishments

On the 4th, Derby was again caught, this time by the watchman as he attempted to take corn out of Col Barclay's Long Pond cornpiece. He was severely chopped with a machete, his right ear, cheek, and jaw almost cut off. On the 27th of the same month, Egypt was whipped and given "Derby's dose" [that is Derby was made to shit in his mouth] for eating cane. On Thursday, 5th October, Hector and Joe and Mr Watt's Pomona were similarly punished for the same misdemeanour.

— THOMAS THISTLEWOOD (in Hall, *In Miserable Slavery*; brackets in original)

For not only must the black man be black; he must be black in relation to the white man.

— FRANTZ FANON, *Black Skin, White Masks*

Creating a Pathological Blackness

In the Caribbean area today, those thought to be transgressing social boundaries and those considered socially inferior, whether because of their social class or even their age, are often kept in line with an admonition to "know your place." The basic ethos of this well-known directive also undergirded Caribbean colonial societies. Thus, during slavery, punishments were also notable for their aims, whether implied or stated outright, to make the enslaved "know their place." Being lashed with a whip, rubbed in molasses, or pickled with lime and pepper were punishments carried out to reinforce the social position of the recipient. It was through such punitive tactics that blacks' place in society was crystallized and the place of the whites guaranteed. In fact, punishment became a potent symbol that marked the enslaved as slaves, while also demarcating—and solidifying—the boundaries between the races.

Bearing this in mind, this chapter looks at the ways in which corporal punishments helped to shore up the slave-based plantation economy by marking black bodies as inferior. It also demonstrates that although these punishments were enacted during slavery, they formed part and parcel of a wider process—involving ideologies and tangible practices—that simultaneously created and debased blackness as a social identity. These punishments could not have been enacted without a sensibility that, according to historian Trevor Burnard, drew "on earlier Iberian notions of Africans as culturally inferior and marked by their race as savages and idolaters with subhuman, bestial characteristics."[1] It was this sensibility of African grotesquerie, honed even before the plantation model was grafted into the fabric of the seventeenth-century Caribbean, that helped to shape the experiences of the enslaved, including influencing the types of punishments that were meted out to them.

According to this racialized sensibility, there were unassailable differences between Africans and Europeans, with the former possessing an inferiority that firmly cemented their lower status in the social order. In addition, the differences that Europeans noted were often corporeal. For example, when arguing for the existence of a black person as a typology, European colonists paid attention to Africans' hair, bodies, and, of course, complexions. The physical differences that they noticed on the bodies of Africans indicated internal, mental, and psychic differences, some European observers and colonists insisted.

In addition, although ideas about Africans and their bodies often bordered on the ridiculous, their disseminators were successful in reinforcing the narrative of Africans' inferiority in ways that seemed to justify their treatment as brute laborers and punished beings. Colonialists believed that the bodies of the enslaved were shrouded in blackness, which they saw not only as a color but also as evidence of a congenital and moral failing. Not only were Africans afflicted with this epidermal malediction, their differences also rendered them not quite human.

Pejorative ideas about the bodies of Africans—and, by extension, the enslaved—are readily captured in the works of many contemporary observers, most notably the Cornwall-born planter Edward Long, who went to Jamaica in 1757 after the death of his father.[2] In his memoirs, Long posited that the blacks found "on that part of the African continent, called Guiney" differed from whites "in respect to their bodies, viz. the dark membrane which communicates that black colour to their skins."[3] Their hair, according to Long, was not hair at all. Instead, it was a "covering of wool, like the bestial fleece."

Long expanded on his views that there were other fundamental and corporeal differences that set Africans apart from whites besides the color of their skin and the "wool" that covered them. He noted, for example, that Africans had a "bestial or fetid smell, which they all have in a greater or less degree."[4] When one notes Long's use of words like "wool," "fleece," "bestial," and "fetid," along with his emphasis on the supposed stark differences between Africans and Europeans, it is perhaps not surprising to see that he was able to reach the conclusion that "the oran-outang and some races of black men are very nearly allied."[5] In addition, though he acknowledged that his opinion might be "ludicrous," Long did not censor himself and instead stated that "an oran-outang husband would [not] be any dishonour to an Hottentot female."[6] Through these descriptions, this Jamaican planter had aligned Africans with animals, taking them out of the human realm completely—and by extension out of civilization. If the Africans were animals, nonhuman, then they were even further removed from the sphere occupied by Europeans.

Moreover, Long's racialization and pejorative reduction of Africans, though starting with the corporeal, trickled insidiously to other areas of "African" life. In Long's estimation, Africans were "void of genius" and seemed "almost incapable of making any progress in civility or science." He opined further that "in so vast a continent as that of Africa and in so great a variety of climates and provinces" there were no differences among the various peoples with regard to "their qualifications of body and mind; strength, agility, industry, and dexterity, on the one hand; ingenuity, learning, arts, and sciences, on the other." Long concluded that "a general uniformity runs through all these various regions of people; so that, if any difference be found, it is only in degrees of the same qualities; and, what is more strange, those of the worst kind; it being a common known proverb, that all people on the globe have some good as well as ill qualities, except the Africans."[7]

The problems that Long noted with those of African origin did not end with his theorization about the supposed similarities between primates and "some races" of blacks or about blacks' primitivism and amorality. Indeed, Long's theorization extended even further and branched out to the realm of labor, with "enslaveability" being etched into the bodies of the enslaved.[8]

Thus, by sleight of pen, Long had signed away the humanity of Africans, refused to extend the sanctity of womanhood to African women (as it was apportioned naturally to white women, particularly those who were from the middle and upper classes), and contributed to a narrative that justified the maltreatment and subjection of Africans. In his estimation, the blackness that was attached to the bodies of Africans, therefore, was a congenital defect that could never be erased. Instead, it could only be tamed through careful management.

Not all European observers held ideas about Africans like those held by Long. In fact, there were cases where positive ideas about Africans were intermixed with their fetishization. In this regard, for example, whereas seventeenth-century plantation owner Richard Ligon found that the white indentured servants who labored alongside the enslaved during the early phases of Barbados's plantation economy did not have "spirits" that could withstand enslavement, he seemed not to feel that way about blacks.[9] Perhaps Ligon's conclusion had to do with how he regarded Africans. Ligon observed: "But 'tis a very lovely sight to see a hundred hansom Negroes, men and women, with everyone a grasse-green bunch of these fruits on their heads, every bunch twice as big as their heads, all coming in a train one after another, the black and green so well becoming one another. . . . They are happy people, whom so little contents. Very good servants, if they are not spoyled by the English."[10]

The idea that blacks seemed perfectly suited to servitude is also found when one examines Ligon's seeming fascination with their bodies. Upon observing enslaved blacks in Barbados, Ligon noted that the men were very "well timber'd." In clarifying what he meant by this he again paid acute attention to the bodies of these individuals. Enslaved black men were "broad between the shoulders, full breasted, well filleted, and clean leg'd and may hold good with Albert Dürer's rules, who allowes twice the length of the head, to the breadth of the shoulders, and twice the length of the face, to the breadth of the hips, and according to this rule these men are shaped."[11] Ligon's observations are more than cursory glances. In observing their handsomeness, Ligon's fascination is arguably akin to the attention one would pay to an object, observing it for defects or even characteristics that make it worthy of a task for which it was created.

Ligon paid equal attention to the form of the bodies of enslaved women. He described them as having "twice the length of the face to the breadth of the shoulders, and twice the length of her own head to the breadth of the hips." This made them "faulty" according to Ligon, as he saw "very few of them . . . whose hips have been broader than their shoulders, unless they have been very fat."[12] Ligon added: "The young Maids have ordinarily very large breasts, which stand strutting out so hard and firm, as no leaping, jumping, or stirring, will cause them to shake any more, than the brawns of their arms. But when they come to be old, and have had five or six Children, their breasts hang down below their Navels so that when they stoop at their common work of weeding, they hang down almost down to the ground, that at a distance, you would think they had six legs." In explaining why the breasts of young maids would change so drastically in their old age, Ligon cited African cultural practices as the culprit: "And the reason of this is, they tye the cloaths about their Children's backs, which comes upon their breasts, which by pressing very hard causes them to heng down to that length."[13] What stands out in Ligon's description of the "hard"-breasted young woman is that she is transmogrified as she ages and has children. If one were to believe Ligon's description and assume that what he saw would also have been perceived by other observers, from a distance enslaved black women could have been mistaken for six-legged creatures. In a sense, black women had insidiously and fantastically joined the realm of monsters and monstrosities.

This way of thinking about Africans and, by extension, creating a pejorative narrative about a debased blackness, has a long history, as has been noted by modern scholars like Jennifer L. Morgan. In her 2004 publication *Laboring Women*, Morgan notes, for example, that there was an entire discourse about the bodies of Africans, African women in particular, that found its way along a circuit traversed by slave owners, traveling writers, and others with a vested interest in seeing Africans only as debased and enslaved. As Morgan notes of this "European racial ideology," with reference specifically to African women:

> By the time the English made their way to the West Indies, decades of ideas and information about brown and black women predated the actual encounter. In many ways, the encounter had already taken place in parlors and reading rooms on English soil, assuring that colonists would arrive with a battery of assumptions and predispositions about race, femininity, sexuality, and civilization. Confronted with an Africa they needed to exploit, European writers turned to black women as evidence of a cultural inferiority that ultimately became encoded as racial difference.[14]

This "'fabulous fiction' of black women's identities" was used to justify black women's use as brute labor on plantations in the Americas.[15] Additionally, this debasement of Africans and blackness and the alignment of Africans with animals contributed to the ideological wellspring from which the punishment of the enslaved was drawn. I also argue that this pejorative delineation of Africans, along with the concomitant valorization of a European identity, made it very easy for enslaved blacks to be punished in a draconian fashion.

Thus, during slavery, the punishment of Africans and their descendants was never only a physical act. Instead, the punishment of the enslaved was bound up in a complex scheme of physicality and racialization, of the palpable and the ideological. The punishment of the enslaved was also part of a process that helped to create and instantiate the socio-racial order upon which the slave societies in the West Indies depended for their survival. This socio-racial order meant that the class system in the colonial Caribbean was organized along racial and phenotypic lines, with whites occupying the apex of the social hierarchy and those of mixed-race and black ancestry occupying the middle and lower rungs of the hierarchy respectively.[16] This was the "order" that colonial officials were attempting to preserve through punishment and the debasement of the black body.

For punishments to effectively feed this socio-racial order, they were by necessity a central component of a multipronged process that was tied to the dehumanization of the enslaved and their categorization as a separate species. Additionally, the punishment of the enslaved was tied to the white population's sense of being and personhood. Punishment, therefore, formed a core part of the process whereby the enslaved were differentiated from the colonialists.

Making the Enslaved Know Their Place

One of the exigencies of the colonial project that helped to fuel the slave-based plantation economies in the Americas was an us-versus-them ideology.[17] Essentially, the colonial Caribbean—particularly during years of the slave-based plantation economy—was fortified by the exploitation and hierarchization of differences among its inhabitants and the concomitant elision of any similarities that these groups might have shared. This simultaneous spotlighting and erasure was very important in separating colonists—the "us" in the colonial narrative—from those they would come to dominate—the subaltern "them."

One way this us-versus-them ideology was cemented was in the legal codes that sprang up in Barbados and Jamaica in the seventeenth century. In Barbados, examples of these legal codes included legislation governing "Christians and heathens," "servants and Negroes," and "masters and servants," which set in motion a gradual process of racialization that inextricably linked African bodies to slavery.[18] Even though the marriage between blackness and enslavement occurred in a piecemeal fashion, there were strong indicators in the early seventeenth century that enslavement was linked to non-Europeans, as historian Edward B. Rugemer points out. As evidence, Rugemer cites the machinations of the 1636 "Barbados Council [that] resolved that 'Negroes and Indians, that came here to be sold, should serve for Life, unless a Contract was made before to the contrary.'"[19]

An examination of the laws relating to white servants in Jamaica provides further evidence in support of the processual linking of African bodies to enslavement, while at the same time making the us-versus-them ideology even more knotty. In fact, although the title of the 1681 "Act for Regulating Servants" appears to be "racially neutral," a reading of the law reveals that there were clear *and* "racial" distinctions between who was enslaved and who was free. This law mandated that "all and every Master or Mistress of Slaves, for the first Five Working Slaves, shall be obliged to keep One White Man-Servant, Overseer, or hired Man for Three Months at least."[20] The distinctions between whites—whether servants or employers—and enslaved blacks was further reinforced in "An Act for the Better Order and Government of Slaves" that was passed in Jamaica in 1696. Not only did this law stipulate that slaves could not leave a plantation without a "ticket" but also that in lieu of a ticket a slave could be accompanied by a white servant. In reinforcing the socio-racial hierarchy by placing a higher value on white lives, Section 2 of this act stipulated further: "And if any Slave shall offer any Violence, by striking or otherwise, to any white Person, such Slave shall be punished at the Discretion of Two Justices and Three Freeholders, who may inflict Death or any other Punishment, according to their Discretion; provided such Striking or Conflict be not by Command of his or their Owners Persons, or Goods."[21] Jamaica's Consolidated Slave Act of 1787 reiterated that whiteness was a valorized social identity in the stipulation that not only were the enslaved to be "in due obedience to their owners" but also "in due subordination to the white people in general."[22]

Many observers—contemporary and modern—have pointed out that white indentured servants had experiences akin to those of slaves, and some have even argued that it was the system of white indenture that provided the blueprint for what would become "African slavery." Writing about his experiences in Barbados in the seventeenth century, for example, Richard Ligon in *A True and Exact History of the Island of Barbadoes* noted the particularly miserable lot of the white indentured servants vis-à-vis the enslaved in the early years of the plantation economy. Providing a colorful commentary on the way the society was organized, Ligon stated: "The Island is divided into three sorts of men, viz., the Masters, Servants, and Slaves. The Slaves are kept and preserv'd with greater care than the servants, who are theirs but for five years, according to the law of the island. So that for the time, the servants have the worser lives, for they are put to very hard labour, ill lodging, and their dyet very sleight." Ligon recalled examples where white indentured servants were beaten by the overseer if they complained, and he cited one particularly harrowing incident whereby a servant was beaten with a cane "about the head, till the blood [had] followed, for a fault that [was] not worth the speaking of."[23]

Echoing Ligon much later in her 2013 publication *Everyday Life in the Early English Caribbean*, Jenny Shaw cited examples of the Englishmen Marcellus Rivers and Oxenbridge Foyle who, banished to Barbados for participating in a royalist uprising, likened their experiences as indentured servants to those of Africans who had been kidnapped, sold, and enslaved.[24] Although Shaw noted the tendentious nature of the claims put forward by Rivers and Foyle, she also pointed out that "the specific rights of English subjects remained an important topic of discussion when it came to decisions about who *was* suitable for enslavement" [emphasis in original].[25]

According to Shaw, the shared experiences of white servants and black slaves did not end with how they were transported to the Caribbean. Even while working on the plantations, Shaw pointed out, the experiences of white servants and black slaves were similar—even in the realm of punishment. Shaw quoted French priest Antoine Biet, who traveled in the Caribbean in the mid-seventeenth century and noted that blacks who wandered beyond the plantation could be given fifty blows with a cudgel, compared with Irish servants who, if found "wander[ing] up and down from Plantation to Plantation as vagabonds refusing to Labour," were to be "whipt according to the Law."[26]

Consonant with the view that white indenture bore similarities to enslavement, historians Eric Williams and Hilary Beckles separately argued that it was this system of white indenture that provided the ideological and structural blueprint upon which seventeenth-century slave-based plantation economies would be constructed.[27] In his book *From Columbus to Castro*, for example, Williams noted that white indenture provided the essential building blocks for colonial societies propelled by cupidity:

> The lack of squeamishness showed in the forced labour of whites was a good training for the forced labor of blacks. The transportation of white servants established a precedent for the transportation of Negro slaves. The practice developed and tolerated in the kidnapping of whites laid the foundation for the kidnapping of Negroes. Bristol, Honfleur and other ports turned without difficulty from the servant trade to the slave trade. Barbados, a word of terror to the white servant, became to the Negro, as a slave trader wrote in 1693, "a more dreadful apprehension . . . than we can have of hell."[28]

With the consolidation of the plantation economy, however, combined with the plantation's hunger for a large, captive workforce, an us-versus-them ideology that had been invoked to highlight differences among whites was now used to highlight the differences—real and imagined—between Africans and Europeans and, by extension, to establish these groups' diametrically opposed positions in the social hierarchy. Consequently, the expansion and entrenchment of the plantation economy was marked by both the movement of the bodies of whites away from the plantation field and their realignment in discourses of punishment.[29] This movement of whites from field labor and their replacement by African workers accentuated one of the fundamental ways that white indenture differed from the enslavement of blacks. Namely, within white indenture lay the promise of freedom and even the possibility of upward social mobility. By contrast, slavery rendered blacks as innately inferior and their status as chattel infinite.[30] Moreover, with black slavery and "white mastery" cemented, both in laws and elsewhere in the social structure, punitive acts became ways in which the disparate statuses of blacks and whites were reinforced.[31]

Like the aforementioned Edward Long, traveling writer Janet Schaw also claimed to possess supposedly unassailable knowledge about blacks and believed that draconian punishments were needed to manage them. While on a journey to Basseterre, St. Kitts, in the mid-1770s, Schaw, upon observing enslaved laborers, had this to say: "The Negroes who are all in troops are sorted so as to match each other in size and strength. Every ten Negroes have a driver, who walks behind them, holding in his hand a short whip and a long one." Acknowledging that the whip was used for "horrid" purposes, Schaw assured her readers that blacks *had* to be punished with the whip. In justifying the use of the whip against the enslaved, Schaw wrote: "When one comes to be better acquainted with the nature of the Negroes, the horrour [*sic*] of it must wear off. It is the suffering of the human mind that constitutes the greatest misery of punishment, but with them it is merely corporeal. As to the brutes it inflicts no wound on their mind, whose Natures seem to bear it, and whose sufferings are not attended with shame or pain beyond the present moment."[32]

It must be noted that however persuasive, the ideas, musings, and jaundiced opinions of Schaw, Ligon, Long, and other colonial observers were not enough to prop up a system that would systematically debase Africans. Such rhetoric would have to find expression in more compelling forces and, as historian Elsa Goveia points out, the West Indian slave laws were able to do just that. Goveia asserts that "under the English slave system in the West Indies, the slave was not regarded as a subject, but rather as property."[33] Slave laws made the ludicrous musings of colonialists a preamble to the legal objectification of the enslaved.

The fact that the enslaved were seen as property—and expendable property at that—was reinforced in the slave laws. As noted by Michael Craton in *Empire, Enslavement, and Freedom in the Caribbean*, punishments like mutilation, execution by slow burning, or allowing the enslaved to starve to death while hanging from gibbets were carried out against enslaved people who had committed the most serious crimes.[34] By contrast, white people who had killed a slave were merely fined.

The discrepancies between how the enslaved were punished vis-à-vis whites were also noticed by Netherlands-born soldier John Gabriel Stedman. During his voyage to Suriname in the 1770s, Stedman condemned the racist application of colonial laws when he noted that "partiality" was shown to a "European" who was whipped for stealing, whereas "the poor african" was put to death for a similar crime. Relating a story told to him by a "decent looking Man," Stedman also detailed other punishments that were meted out to enslaved individuals in Suriname. Black men were reportedly "hang'd alive by the ribs, between which with a knife was first made an incision, and then clinch'd an Iron hook with a Chain," while another was quartered with four "strong horses" being fastened to each of his limbs, and then "Iron Sprigs [were driven] home underneath every one of his nails, on hand and feet." Other slaves were reported to have been broken on the rack and others roasted alive while "chain'd to Stakes."[35] There are recurring motifs in all of these punishments: the need to humiliate the enslaved and reinforce their position as chattel; the quest to reinforce the power of the plantocracy and establish the hegemony of the plantation economy; and, of course, the fact that the punishments all harmed the physical body.

Essentially, the ease with which enslaved individuals were punished was possible because of the same process that reduced Africans to things. Yet this process was never simple. It contained many antinomies in that even as the enslaved were reduced to things, colonialists also could not deny their humanity.

Plantocrats' desire to objectify blacks was unrelenting. It was demonstrated in slaveholder Thomas Thistlewood's ordering of one slave to defecate in the mouth of another—after all, one does not fill human mouths with waste. This action was also meant to reinforce the blackness of the enslaved and Thistlewood's whiteness—and to amplify the power associated with this whiteness. When Thistlewood ordered the punishment of the slave named Egypt, he was emphasizing Egypt's blackness and his servitude. When Thistlewood ordered the slave named Derby to defecate in Egypt's mouth, he was emphasizing Derby's blackness and Thistlewood's power over both Egypt and Derby. Thistlewood's reach, his power, therefore, extended beyond his own body and even carried over into a realm that at first blush appears beyond reach. In addition, Thistlewood made a private act a public one, thus defiling the private-public dichotomy as easily as he had Egypt's mouth.[36]

Yet, for all the power that this action seemed to credit to Thistlewood, it also unwittingly reveals the tenuousness and falseness of his power. That is to say, the act of commanding Derby and Egypt to participate in such a vile and inhumane performance served to reinforce the humanness of the enslaved, as there is no need to erase the essence of a thing, and a thing cannot be humiliated. Perhaps unwittingly, Thistlewood staked his whiteness, and the power that accrued from it, on blackness and the debasement of the black body, and by extension he high-lighted blacks' humanity.

As historian Vincent Brown notes, this debasement of the black body through punishment occurred not only when the enslaved were alive but also when they were dead. Brown notes that "as early as the mid-seventeenth century, British West Indian planters hoped that mutilating the dead would impress Africans not only with their power over life, but with their influence on the afterlife."[37] Brown cited the case of one planter, Colonel Walrond, who, in an attempt to dis-courage his slaves from copying a group of three or four slaves who had commit-ted suicide, ordered that one of the heads of the dead slaves be hung up on a pole for everyone to see. With the head hanging from the pole, Walrond marched all of his slaves around to show them the head, while mocking the idea that Africans thought that at their death they would return to Africa.[38] By this action, Walrond was attempting, through the use of a mutilated dead body, to establish not only his power but also the power of the plantation. In addition, and perhaps ironi-cally, he was attempting to challenge African belief systems by using mutilated *African* bodies—thus making the black body the problem *and* the solution.

Brown referred to this phenomenon as the plantocracy's attempt to exert "spiritual terror" over the enslaved, and while this is true, what it also showed was the hold that blackness had over whites' abilities to define themselves. Al-though Brown noted that "Caribbean slave masters used spectacular terror to deter Africans from self-destruction," what must also be acknowledged is that this "spectacular terror" was needed to cement their claims to a white identity.[39] The "spectacular terror" to which Brown referred was essential to demarcate what constituted whiteness as much as it was to draw a line around what consti-tuted blackness.

Enslaved women were not exempt from attempts to strip away their humanity through punishment, nor were they immune from having their bodies appro-priated and used to give meaning to whiteness and blackness. As was the case for enslaved men, the punishment of enslaved women was intimately tied to the installation of a white authority over their bodies. Author and academic Mari-etta Morrissey notes that enslaved men and women were generally punished the same way and that there appeared to be "little difference in the severity with which men and women were punished," although she does acknowledge that "men may have been brutalized more frequently."[40]

This last supposition should give us pause, however. The evidence that exists about slave women's lives suggests that we should look at punishment as not only an exercise in white racial power but also as white *masculine* power. If we look at punishment through this intersectional lens, then we can see that women could be punished as members of the class of enslaved workers *and* as women—thereby allowing us to make a more nuanced argument about the brutality of slavery and whether the female slave had an easier lot. As members of the slave class, women would be flogged or whipped for quotidian infractions, and those who were accused of being rebels were often executed just like men. In addition, womanhood and motherhood did little to shield women from draconian punishments. As Morrissey notes, even pregnant women were severely punished. She writes that French West Indies' slave owners "followed the custom of whipping the pregnant woman by staking her to the ground, hollowing an area in the ground for her unborn child."[41] Pregnant women in Jamaica were also maltreated, as noted by contemporary observer Matthew Gregory Lewis, an English novelist who owned property in Jamaica. He stated that although he had been in Jamaica for less than six months, he had observed, on two separate occasions, pregnant women being kicked by white bookkeepers.[42]

Evidence from other sources further reinforces the notion that being female hardly spared women the brutalities of slavery. For example, Mary Prince, a slave from Bermuda, recounted instances of being severely punished for minor infractions. As a case in point, Prince was whipped "long and severely" when her mistress blamed her for breaking a jar. In addition, perhaps in an effort to demonstrate that she was not alone in her suffering, Prince also related the tale of "a French Black" named Hetty who was beaten so badly that she eventually died. Prince recounted a beating that Hetty received the first night that the two women met:

> I got a sad fright, that night. I was just going to sleep, when I heard a noise in my mistress's room; and she presently called out to inquire if some work was finished that she had ordered Hetty to do. "No, Ma'am, not yet," was Hetty's answer from below. On hearing this, my master started up from his bed, and just as he was, in his shirt, ran down stairs with a long cow-skin [whip] in his hand. I heard immediately after, the cracking of the thong, and the house rang to the shrieks of poor Hetty, who kept crying out, "Oh, Massa! Massa! me dead. Massa! Have mercy upon me—don't kill me outright."[43]

In this instance the master appears to have had complete power over her body, as Hetty begged her master not to kill her. The fact that there is no report of Hetty's master being admonished or disciplined for this beating speaks to the power he held as a slave owner.

After this, Hetty endured another beating. This time it occurred when Hetty was pregnant, and Prince was certain that it was this beating that helped to hasten her death. During this flogging, Hetty was stripped naked and tied to a tree.

Then, according to Prince, their master "flogged her as hard as he could lick, both with the whip and cow-skin, till she was all over streaming with blood." The punishment did not end there. Their master "rested" and apparently after getting his "second wind," he beat Hetty "again and again." Prince recalled that "her shrieks were terrible."[44]

Henry Coor, an Englishman living in Jamaica in the eighteenth century, likewise recalled draconian punishments being meted out to enslaved women. English academic Barbara Bush notes in *Slave Women in Caribbean Society, 1650–1838* that while giving evidence in 1790 before a House of Commons committee investigating the slave trade, Coor reported having seen a master "nail the ear of a house wench to a tree post" because she had broken a plate.[45]

Similar brutalities were also visited upon the enslaved in the Spanish Caribbean, as the example of Juan Manzano's mother illustrates. Manzano, born into slavery in Cuba in 1797, and eventually to become one of Cuba's most famous poets, detailed in his *Autobiografía de un esclavo* how his mother was punished when she was trying to protect him from being beaten. Manzano recounted his mother's punishment:

> My mother's mistake was that she assaulted the overseer when she saw he was about to kill me and, while he was dealing with her, I was able to stand up. When the watchmen arrived from the yard where the coffee beans are dried, they led us away and I saw my mother put in the sacrificial place for the first time in her life. . . .
>
> Bewildered, seeing my mother in this position, I could neither cry nor think nor flee. I was trembling as the four blacks shamelessly overpowered her and threw her on the ground to whip her. I prayed to God. For her sake I endured everything. But when I heard the first crack of the whip I became a lion, a tiger, the fiercest beast.[46]

The plantation also held power over enslaved women as sexual beings and as sources of white male sexual pleasure, a power that was often expressed through punishment. The ideology that defined black women as things and as property was the same ideology that undergirded the reactions of overseers who would punish women for refusing to have sex with them. According to this line of thinking, enslaved women, as property, did not have the right to refuse white male sexual advances. If they did refuse, they could be punished. One such example was recorded by slave owner Thomas Thistlewood: "Wednesday, 5th May 1756: p.m. Egypt Susanah & Mazerine whipped for refusal last Saturday night, by Mr. Cope's order. Little Phibbah told Mrs. Cope last Saturday night's affair. Mrs. Cope also examined the sheets and found them amiss."[47]

Many actors were drawn into this drama that reinforced the racial and gender hierarchies within the plantation economy, while also reinforcing black women's objectification. First, Mr. Cope and Mr. McDonald (the second party in this exchange) illustrated the expendability of enslaved black women's sexual labor as the refusal of sex by Egypt Susanah and Mazerine did not cancel the sexual affair. Instead Mr. McDonald was able to have sex with Eve, "to whom he gave 6 bitts," while Mr. Cope was able to make Tom "fetch Beck from the Negro houses for himself." Tom, who was both slave and pimp, was subjected to the whims of the plantocracy even as he was also party to black women's sexual exploitation. Then there was "Little Phibbah," who was being schooled in the socio-racial and sexual culture of the plantation economy and was able to tell Mrs. Cope about an affair to which she was not privy, thus potentially implicating two black women and potentially getting them into trouble. Eve, Beck, Egypt Susanah, and Mazerine are enslaved women who were caught up in a sexually exploitative circuitry from which the only escape was a total change in their social status. As black women, they shared fates—not just working lives—that were inextricably linked to their status. In addition, within the plantation society, black women's bodies were subject to multiple forms of disciplinary and punitive regimes. Yes, they could be punished in more traditional ways like being whipped for disobedience, but they were also disciplined as sexual beings with their bodies conditioned for sexual intercourse, with anyone, at any time, on command.

As these examples illustrate, the plantation had a strong hold over the bodies of enslaved women as laborers, as mothers, as women, and as members of the plantation society. Because women were sexualized objects and commodities within the plantation economy, they were subject to punitive measures that men were not subjected to.

Conclusion

The study of the punitive ideologies and technologies that were present in the Caribbean during slavery cannot be divorced from an examination of the ways in which blackness and the bodies of Africans were conceptualized then by whites. The symbiotic relationship between punishments and the socio-racial order must be noted as it was the socio-racial divide that made draconian punishments possible, while the punishment reinforced the divide. This was true during slavery and as talks of emancipation intensified and a new era, that of apprenticeship, loomed.[48]

Thus, on the eve of the apprenticeship scheme that started in 1834 in the British Caribbean, colonialists already had an ideological wellspring upon which they could draw to craft the punishments that would partly characterize this new era. Not only did colonialists—and others who had a vested interest in the continuation of the economic and socio-racial structures from slavery—already have strong ideas, honed during slavery, about punishments and what constituted effective ones, they also held hardened and pejorative ideas about the bodies of blacks—and how they were to be controlled via punishments.

Although it is accurate to note that the punishments employed after 1834 tended to become less extreme and less sadistic, and punishments like "Derby's dose" appear to have been relegated to the pages of Thistlewood's diary, it is also true that there were draconian punishments continued after slavery. As the following chapters show, after 1834, colonialists seemed unable to move beyond their conceptions of punishment as a tool to be administered in a racist and classist fashion. As a result, in spite of changes in the laws, punishment continued to be an important tool that helped shore up the socio-racial organization of the plantation economy.

CHAPTER 2

The Persistence of Corporeality

*The Apprentice's Punished Body and the
Maintenance of the Socio-racial Structure
in Barbados and Jamaica, 1834–1838*

Chains are the portion of revolted man,
Stripes and a dungeon! and his body
Serves the triple purpose!

—WILLIAM COWPER (*The Task*)

The period that started in 1834 provides a fitting point of departure to examine the changes in the methods of discipline and punishment in post-slavery
Jamaica and Barbados and the place of the black body in punishment. Imperial and colonial legislators saw this as a transitional phase whereby the former
slaves, known as apprentices, were to be readied for their roles as free laborers. This meant, among other things, an introduction to wage labor, religious
instruction, and the promotion of "Christian values" like marriage. Although it
is not clear how the former slave masters were to be prepared to live in a society
constituted largely of free black men and women, there was the implication that,
by dint of the former slaves being schooled in the ways of freedom, the former
masters were also being readied for changes in social relations.

In spite of its legislative and corporeal promises, however, the apprenticeship system fell short primarily because of congenital failings. Namely, from
its conception there were central reformative issues that were missing from apprenticeship: an assessment of what whiteness and blackness meant in a changing colonial society and how white and black bodies should take on new meanings in the post-slavery society. If this reassessment had been done, then the
black body should have no longer signaled a lack of personal sovereignty. No
longer should the punishment of blacks have been tied to their perceived congenital failings, and no longer should an individual's corporeality have determined their social condition. However, the apprenticeship system held on to
the motif of the governed and disciplined black body. Indeed, at its core, the

apprenticeship system was a labor system and thus able only to consider the former slaves—regardless of how they were renamed—as merely that, ex-*slaves* whose labor was being renegotiated but whose bodies and bodily labor were to remain under the vigilance of plantation authorities.

For the most part, evidence shows that the punishments associated with contravening the laws of apprenticeship remained largely corporeal and that, as in slavery, these punishments were disproportionately meted out to blacks. Furthermore, the data show convincingly that the changes specifically relating to discipline and punishment in the years after 1834 often reflected Jamaica's and Barbados's past engagement with slavery, were often the result of several concessions to the proprietary classes, and in most cases reflected racist and paternalistic attitudes about black inferiority and consequently the black body.[1] What is also evident is that the apprentice's punished body became a way of redrawing the socio-racial boundaries that had existed during slavery and that continued to exist during the apprenticeship era.

Apprenticeship in Post-slavery Jamaica and Barbados

Most observers—contemporary and modern—have spoken or written about the post-emancipation Caribbean only in regard to what happened in terms of changes in the laws, changes in the economic health of the societies, or in terms of the changed status of the former slaves, but none have assessed apprenticeship in terms of how it was felt on the body. If one of the defining characteristics of enslavement was the loss of sovereignty over the body and the punishment of the enslaved, then surely apprenticeship would have felt differently to the newly freed.

On its face, 1834 promised to usher in new relations in the British West Indies, particularly in Barbados and Jamaica. Related to this, apprenticeship suggested that the newly freed were now in full possession of their bodies and that their relationship to their own bodies would change. Indeed, with the introduction of the apprenticeship scheme, there was a legislative break with slavery and ideas about punishments, especially as these punishments related to the formerly enslaved. In legislative and nominal terms, the former slaves were now defined as apprentices, and new legislation like that governing relations between masters and servants defined the roles that each interested party was required to uphold and enumerated the punishments to be administered for contravening these roles.

The British Parliament and its passage of the Abolition Act of 1833 brought the apprenticeship scheme into effect. This act proclaimed that on August 1,

1834, all enslaved children under the age of six were to be freed, while enslaved persons six and older were to be classified as either "predial" (agricultural) or "non-predial" apprentices, a social and legal designation that was dependent on the type of labor that they had performed twelve months before the passage of this act. The apprenticeship system, slated originally to last for six years—non-predials were to be freed in 1838 and predials in 1840—stipulated that apprentices could, through manumission, gain complete freedom. This period was also marked by legislation that outlined the changes that were to be made with regard to discipline and punishment. These changes, however, were essentially compromised by the fact that the imperial government left the final form of the Abolition Act to be crafted by the various colonial legislatures to take into account the needs of their individual territories.[2] To ensure that the colonial legislatures complied, according to historian William A. Green, a compensation package of £20 million would not be "made in a colony until its legislature had produced an emancipation Act in conformity with the framework of the imperial measure, incorporating rules and regulations which were acceptable to the Crown."[3]

In spite of these concessions to the proprietary classes, there were still some revolutionary aspects to the Abolition Act. One of the more significant characterizations of the apprenticeship system was a change in *who* could punish.[4] For instance, Section 21 of the Jamaica Abolition Act provided that:

> it shall not be lawful for any person or persons entitled to the services of any such apprenticed labourer, or any other person or persons other than such justices of the peace holding such special commissions as aforesaid, to punish any such apprenticed labourer for any offence by him or her committed, or alleged to have been committed, by the whipping, beating, or imprisonment of his or her person, or by any other personal or other correction or punishment whatsoever, or by any addition to the hours of labour herein-before limited; *nor shall any Court, Judge, or Justice of the Peace, punish any such apprenticed labourer, being a female, for any offence by her committed, by whipping or beating her person.* [emphasis in original][5]

The significance of the appointment of these justices of the peace was summed up further by the Marquis of Sligo, who served as governor of Jamaica from April 1834 until August 1836. In a speech addressed to the "Newly Made Apprentices of Jamaica," Sligo informed them of their newly minted rights, stating, "Neither your master, your overseer, your bookkeeper, your driver nor any person can strike you, or put you into the stocks, nor can you be punished at all except by the order of a special magistrate."[6] Seemingly placing the apprentices on the same footing as all free men and women and asserting that they too could seek legal recourse if their rights were infringed upon, Sligo added: "If any person, without such authority, shall raise a hand to you, or put you into the stocks, he will be liable to be *severely* punished himself" [emphasis added]. In the same breath, however, Sligo showed that the law was not in fact equitable and that the apprentice was worth considerably less than the employer. He revealed an insidious philosophy of paternalism and condescension that inhered in the laws in the British West Indies. Sligo pointed out to the apprentices that if they "behave[d] badly" their master or any special constable could put them in a cell or any "place of confinement" for up to a day. When a magistrate finally visited the property, the complaint against the apprentice would be brought before the magistrate who would then decide if the apprentice should be punished for misconduct. Likewise, masters could also be punished if they had "improperly confined" their apprentices.[7] From an examination of Sligo's address, however, it can be seen that the laws specifically regarding apprenticeship were never created equally. Laborers were still placed in a position of inferiority vis-à-vis their employers, a fact that is revealed when one examines data that show how employers were punished for offenses that they committed against their apprentices.[8]

Like the Jamaica Abolition Act, the Barbados Abolition Act also removed the power to punish from the former slave masters and entrusted this power to stipendiary magistrates, also known as special magistrates, who were sent to the colonies from Britain to oversee the apprenticeship system and protect the apprentices from abuse. Clause 86 of the Barbados Act "for the Abolition of Slavery, for the Government of Apprenticed Labourers, and for Ascertaining the Reciprocal Duties between Them and Their Employers" stipulated that an employer convicted of inflicting corporal punishment on an apprentice could be fined up to five pounds sterling.[9] If this fine were not paid within fourteen days, the employer was liable to be imprisoned for a period of up to one month. This latter punishment is one of the few examples where the law explicitly stated that members of the ruling classes were liable to be punished in a manner that implicated the white body as a site of punishment, particularly for offenses committed against the labouring classes.[10] However, this coup should not be seen as complete because, even though whites could be imprisoned, the evidence suggests that they were mostly sentenced monetary fines for infractions of the apprenticeship laws. Moreover, even penal confinement seems tame when one considers that apprentices could be whipped for flouting apprenticeship laws.

In spite of the obvious shortcomings of the Jamaica and Barbados Abolition Acts, with their failure to extend penalties for bad behavior on employers and apprentices equally, the change in who could administer punishment under the apprenticeship scheme was significant. It indicated that legislators in Britain were attempting to provide a more evenhanded and progressive justice than what had hitherto been operational in the Caribbean with its planter-dominated legislatures and planter-directed justice. It can be said, therefore, that on the surface, the appointment of these stipendiary magistrates held great promise for the apprenticeship scheme and for apprentices, male and female alike. On paper it was suggested that the brutality that had characterized these two societies up to this point would be a thing of the past, even as ideas were reinforced regarding the superiority of imperial justice to that administered by the colonies locally.

Having not been direct participants in enslavement and most not having lived in the societies in which they were to act as arbiters, the stipendiary magistrates seemed untainted by British West Indian societies that had long steeped in slavery. To ensure further that the one hundred stipendiary magistrates who were sent to the colonies were unlikely to be swayed by any blandishments, the British government was responsible for paying them a salary of three hundred pounds sterling a year.[11]

In spite of the Crown's efforts to administer justice fairly and without bias through the appointment of these magistrates, to the diametrically opposed camps of abolitionists and pro-slavery groups they seemed like prime targets to further their interests. To some degree, the abolitionists thought of the stipendiary magistrates as tragic heroes who had been appointed to help provide a new, humane beginning for the apprentices in what was a very flawed system. Although they saw the magistrates as the protectors of the apprentices and persecutors of the planters, those in the abolitionist camp felt that these tasks would be impossible to achieve since the conditions weighed so heavily against them. They also saw the magistrates as overworked and underpaid, and they were keenly aware that the difficult working conditions made the magistrates more liable to manipulation by the planters, who could offer them the material blandishments that the apprentices could not.[12]

Strikingly, both the pro-slavery and abolitionist factions thought that the position was filled with pitfalls and problems. Each regarded the stipendiary magistrates as sycophants and as outsiders who were meddling in affairs that did not concern them. On the other hand, however, the proprietary classes saw the stipendiary magistrates as kin since they often shared similar cultural and ethnic identities. One of the most pointed descriptions of the prickly position was summed up by John Bowen Colthurst, who served as stipendiary magistrate in Barbados and St. Vincent between 1835 and 1838. He lamented: "What a difficult and critical task is mine! First, to maintain the rights of the negroes, without irritating the planters; next, to calm their tempers and combat their prejudices, at the same time upholding their reasonable and legal claims on their apprentices; and, above all, to bring about, if practicable, a kind feeling between parties, at present cordially hating each other."[13]

Carrying the different burdens and expectations of an imperial government, abolitionists, pro-slavery groups, planters, and apprentices, it is easy to see the difficulties stipendiary magistrates faced as arbitrators of the apprenticeship system. When their work is examined, the findings tend to bear this out and reflect the thorny position they occupied. For instance, whereas some stipendiary magistrates interpreted the Abolition Act in somewhat compassionate terms and consequently used relatively lenient forms of punishments like fines, there were others who saw floggings, stints on the treadmill, and confinement in dungeons, jails, and houses of correction as the best methods to deal with those who had broken the law.[14] In fact, this second type of stipendiary magistrate was often caricatured and vilified in the media in England and the British Caribbean. For example, in an 1838 article, one abolitionist concluded that the appointment of the stipendiary magistrates had been a failure and that, instead of protecting apprentices, the magistrates had done just the opposite. The writer of this article described the magistrates as "half pay officers, inured in flogging, and accustomed to enforc[ing] the sternest discipline." When these men died or quit their jobs, continued the source, "the governors were permitted to fill their places with plantation managers, mercantile clerks, discharged wharfingers, and men of notoriously depraved habits."[15] Examples of magistrates like Captain Clarke of St. James, Jamaica, seemed to confirm this writer's withering assessment of the stipendiary magistrates and the office that they occupied. W. L. Burn, author of the 1937 *Emancipation and Apprenticeship in the British West Indies*, also provided evidence in support of this view when he described an incident involving Clarke, whose alleged failure to be evenhanded drove the apprentices from Leyden Plantation "*en masse* to Montego Bay" to lodge a complaint against him. Clarke responded to this by sending members of the military to Leyden, soldiers who subsequently flogged two of the ringleaders who had helped to lodge the complaint.[16]

Having said this, it should not be thought that all stipendiary magistrates were men who favored the lash over less corporeal forms of punishment. Stipendiary magistrates like E. D. Baynes of Jamaica were intent on improving disciplinary and social conditions for the apprentices. There was also the example of Stipendiary Magistrate Norcott, of Montego Bay, Jamaica, "who refused to order any sentences of flogging at all," and the case of Richard Hill, who, like Norcott, was not prone to prescribe lashing and was said to order "almost none." According to Burn, these two stipendiary magistrates became renowned for their pattern of leniency toward apprentices, to the extent where, in the case of Hill, "crowds thronged the 'Bay' from all over St. James in search of this delightful justice."[17]

There were other magistrates who were neither harsh "planters' men" nor men who favored the apprentices. Some can be said to have adopted a more phlegmatic approach to overseeing the apprenticeship scheme. For instance, there was the case of Macleod, whom Sligo described as "well-intentioned but not very strong-minded," and Davies, whom Sligo labeled "weak," "inefficient," and "very slow."[18] Then there was the extreme case of Stipendiary Magistrate Jones, who was reported to have "taken up his residence with an overseer on one of Sir Alexander Grant's estates, where he lived at little or no expense." Jones's notoriety did not end there as he was reported to have been "habitually in a state of beastly intoxication."[19] Still, one cannot help but laud the perspicacity of the British government for seeing that the apprenticeship scheme required independent arbitrators.

Along with demonstrating that the imperial authorities were giving a nod to a measure of evenhandedness, the appointment of stipendiary magistrates also helped to illustrate that the power structure in Jamaica and Barbados was undergoing radical changes. Men and women who had been defined legislatively as property, labeled as "chattel," and treated accordingly, were at the foothills of claiming a legal right over themselves and their bodies. Furthermore, their former masters were being forced to accept that their most tangible indicators of power—the power to punish and their claims over the bodies of blacks—had been taken away from them. That these stipendiary magistrates were not always white—as the appointments of the aforementioned Hill, who was the son of a white father and East Indian mother, and the mulatto R. B. Facey, both of Jamaica, confirm—only helps to highlight the changes that were being made to the existing socio-racial structure.[20] The appointment of nonwhite stipendiary magistrates may be interpreted in a number of ways. It could indicate that the symbol of white authority was being compromised, even though the appointment of black or "coloured" stipendiary magistrates was still rare. The appointment of these men of color reinforces an irony that finds its parallel in slavery: that of the black driver given the power to whip and compel his fellow blacks. Yet one cannot be blind to the fact that the appointment of these stipendiary magistrates may be said to have reinforced white male hegemony on some level since the majority of these magistrates were white men and their appointment had been sanctioned by the imperial authorities. Finally, their appointment also served to amplify male dominance at home and in the metropole.

Besides changes in who could administer punishment, the Abolition Act also called for changes in the severity of punishments and, to some degree, on whom they could be inflicted. For instance, under the Abolition Act "the power of the whip, as a stimulant to labour" was abolished, and women were not to be flogged, although this was upheld as a suitable mode of punishment for male apprentices.[21] At this point one can see different ideological approaches to male and female lawbreakers and ultimately male and female bodies impinging on the laws. This gendered consideration was not new, as similar considerations had been made during slavery. Showing no hint of irony, the Abolition Act sought to give all ex-slaves "the power of claiming to be put in a situation, in which he shall enjoy all the privileges of a free man,—in which he shall feel no taint of his servile condition,—in which he shall be freed from the atrocious system of irresponsible corporeal punishment,—in which he shall not be compelled to see those that are nearest and dearest to him insulted by punishment, or liable to degradation."[22]

These attempts to mitigate punishment were also reflected in clauses outlining the number of lashes that could be administered to apprentices at any one time. One may argue, however, that because it was only blacks who could be whipped, this stipulation did not signal a large-scale ideological shift. The importance of the black body as the focal point in punishment, how the criminal body was conceptualized, and the laborers' position in the worker-employer hierarchy all remained. In this regard, therefore, one does not detect the revolution in disciplinary and punitive praxes in Barbados and Jamaica that apprenticeship promised. Instead the "taint" of the apprentices' former slave status lingered.

It is noteworthy to point out that attempts had been made previously to mitigate disciplinary and punitive measures in Barbados and Jamaica. These mitigations in punishment bore some similarities to the clauses relating to punishment in the Abolition Act, a fact that suggests that the bodies of blacks always already comprised the veritable and discursive tableau where notions about state and plantocratic power were displayed. For instance, in 1826 the Jamaica Assembly had passed a consolidated slave law, with Clause 36 stipulating that slaves were not to receive more than 10 lashes, "except in presence of owner or overseer, & c., nor in such presence more than 39, nor until recovered from former *punishment*, under penalty of £20."[23] Clause 39 of this same law stipulated "no collar, or chains, to be put on slaves, but by order of a magistrate. Justice of peace to cause such collar, & c., to be removed, under a penalty of £100."[24] From a reading of this law, one can see that the attempts to remove some of the punitive power that was held by the planters over laboring bodies was not wholly new, as the appointment of the stipendiary magistrates during the apprenticeship scheme suggests. This example from slavery about the transference of punitive power suggests, moreover, that the governance of the slaves was a commodity that could be exchanged—or at least transferred between authorities designated by the state—even as it reinforced the idea that governance over slave bodies was never held by the individual slaves themselves.

By comparison, Barbados's slave laws appear to have been milder than the Jamaican slave laws. The slave laws passed on October 8, 1827, not only reinforced Barbadian connections with Britain, they also reinforced a gendered understanding of punishment. An example of this law's British connections was illustrated in Clause 46, which stipulated that slaves were to be whipped with instruments like those used in the army and navy, except in those cases where a "milder instrument" was the punitive technology of choice. This clause suggests that there was some equalization of the enslaved with members of the army and navy. Certainly the plantation economy, army, and navy each called for strictly regulated and disciplined individuals.[25]

Along with an imperial connection, Barbados's slave laws also had a gendered dimension. Clause 46 stipulated that female slaves were to be punished "in a *private* and *decent* manner [emphasis added], and when pregnant, to be punished by confinement only." The penalty for breaching this law was ten pounds sterling.[26] From this one can see that at certain times the bodies of female slaves were inscribed with ideologies of decorum and decency, and afforded protection, in spite of the degradation that enslaved women experienced generally. This seeming contradiction in the way in which enslaved women were treated corresponded to the changing needs of the plantation economy. Scholars like Hilary Beckles and David Lambert have noted that developments like the abolition of the slave trade had a direct impact on the ways in which the bodies of black women were regarded.[27] These developments were often translated into "belly woman" policies that shielded enslaved women generally—and pregnant women specifically—from the harshest punishments.[28]

In spite of the self-serving ways in which colonial authorities administered justice and showed mercy, Clause 46's stipulations to shield the punished black female's body from the public gaze invite parallels between conceptions of black femininity vis-à-vis white femininity—especially when one notes that calls to shield the white female body from the male leer, both black and white, were a perennial fixture throughout the colonies. Whereas black women were only accorded protection at specific times and for specific ends, white women and the white female body, by contrast, were regarded as sites of decorum—and thus sites of potential defilement.[29] What these calls reveal is that there were both a racialized and a gendered understanding of the body, a body that was caught up in a plantation economy that required, for its very survival, subjugated black laborers and the strict separation of whites from blacks.

The calls to protect the body of the enslaved woman also give one an idea of the status of the black male body in Barbadian legislative and social discourses of the nineteenth century. In the Barbados slave laws, there was no stipulation to shield the punished male body from the public gaze. This serves to reinforce a theme that was implicit in nineteenth-century discourses about morality, namely that the male body did not, and should not, carry the burden of morality and decorum.[30] This idea has also been supported elsewhere by historian Brian Moore, who noted the same for white women in Guyana and the wider Caribbean. Moore pointed out that white women in Guyana, like white women in the rest of the region, provided a stabilizing and civilizing foil to the "'rowdy, crude, and hard-drinking lifestyle' of the rural plantocracy."[31]

In spite of the attention that was paid to shielding black female bodies in the 1827 slave laws of Barbados, punishments that directly assaulted the bodies of black women and black men continued to be quite common in that country and in Jamaica too in the early nineteenth century. This was consistent with the contemporary view that held that slaves were property and subhuman, and with the general mood prevailing in Britain that corporal punishments not only preserved order but were also a necessary corrective for misbehaving underclasses. Moreover, the evidence provided from the testimony of several apprentices, including James Williams from Jamaica, reports from stipendiary magistrates, correspondence from governors, and legislation in both Jamaica and Barbados show that during the apprenticeship period—as in slavery—the black body retained its preeminence as a site of punishment.[32] Furthermore, the bodies of blacks remained those surfaces upon which ideas about power were crystallized, and in their marked, punished states they alluded to the power that continued to be held by planters over workers. The approaches to punishing the so-called criminal (whether apprentice, free, black, or white) in the colonies were also mediated by ideas about race and social emplacement. This was necessarily so given the importance of class in the metropole and the colonies' emphasis on a pyramidal social structure that placed whites at the apex and blacks at the base.[33]

Evidence from ex-slaves from territories like Antigua that did not adopt the apprenticeship system and instead embraced total emancipation in 1834 helps highlight how ideas about race, punishment, and the laboring body were firmly entrenched in British Caribbean societies and could taint the practice of freedom in the post-emancipation period. The Antiguan example shows that ideas about bodies and their inherent worth continued to impinge on individuals' quality of life in the post-emancipation period. An example is seen in the case of Samuel Smith, an Antiguan workingman born in 1877. In his autobiography he provided rich evidence to show that bodies were multidimensional surfaces, in that pejorative notions about race could be ascribed to them yet these bodies were also the surfaces upon which these ideas could be crystallized: "Back then there were laws to keep people from doing cruel things to animals, but there was no laws to protect us from cruelty. Now I'm no lawyer, but what I know is that I've seen a lot of our people get sent to the jail-house, get whipped and suffer other things if they happen to mark an animal with a whip, but I have never seen nor hear of a white man being punish for anything he do to one of us. Massa was king and king do no wrong."[34]

In explaining social conditions in post-slavery Antigua, Smith stated: "In them days a good portion of the people would go to jail for all kinds of simple things. The cat-o-nine was the worse that could happen to you in the jail-house. And if you be unruly, you would also get a 75lb. ball locked to your waist or ankle by a chain and you would have to try and move around with it."[35]

In another statement that reinforced the importance of race and class to punishment, Smith observed: "It seem to me that the whole jail-house thing was set up to keep us down and make sure the bakkra [white person] always have plenty workers for free. For example, the magistrates use to order a fine he very well knew you couldn't pay and then you would be off to the jail-house. For sure them never make joke with that."[36] He noted further that those imprisoned in the house of correction in Antigua were forced "to shoot hard labour" for the planters, "and that [forced labor] happen to be one of the main reasons that people get put in jail."[37] Smith's poignant recollection, along with invoking race and class, highlighted that in a post-slavery society, labor, bodies, and race were not easily abstracted from each other. His aligning of the "bakkra" with the magistrate (who was supposed to be disinterested) against "workers" signaled that the exigencies of the plantation economy persisted.

Writing in 1986, historian David Trotman echoed Smith's sentiments. Trotman observed that law and punishment, as they were articulated in Trinidad after 1838, were inextricably linked to the operation and survival of the plantation system, pitting worker against employer, and black against white in a discordant dance that had begun in an earlier time. He argued that Trinidadians from the working class were often sentenced to hard labor, a form of punishment that kept a large pool of cheap, easily accessible workers ready for the plantation economy.[38]

Even though black Antiguans were legally free, Smith's account revealed that they continued to be defined and treated differently from whites. His account also showed that punitive tactics that were used against blacks were still brutal and that corporal punishment was still a feature of post-slavery Antigua. These examples from Antigua bring into sharp relief the position of the black body after emancipation, while reinforcing its use as a marker to reinforce the socio-racial order. These examples also substantiate the argument that the black body, even in the post-emancipation period, occupied two of several key spheres in the plantation economy, as a tool of labor and as a site of punishment. Anthropologist Mindie Lazarus-Black also confirmed the gravity of this body-punishment relation when she wrote about delinquent youth in Antigua in the post-emancipation period: "Delinquent children faced forced apprenticeships, corporal punishment, or confinement. Youths convicted of stealing fruits, vegetables, or livestock, of destroying property, or of 'leading an idle and vagrant life, not attending any school or being sufficiently under the care and control of the parent' might be apprenticed for up to three years for their first offence with parental consent."[39] According to Lazarus-Black, "Alternately a magistrate could order a delinquent to be whipped."[40] All of this was a reality, even though it is also a truism to acknowledge that "emancipation altered the class structure and the organization of power in the [British West Indies]."[41]

The examples recounted by Smith and substantiated by Lazarus-Black's findings illustrate that the black body remained an important site of punishment, even as the British West Indian colonies changed from societies that depended on slave labor to those that depended on wage labor. It must also be noted that the roles ascribed to punishment during the apprenticeship period remained similar to those during the period of slavery, which seemed at variance with colonial secretary Lord Glenelg's utterances about freedom—namely, that freedom was to be delivered "in that full and unlimited sense of the term in which it is used in reference to the other objects of the British Crown."[42] Moreover, the examples of punishment in Antigua, when viewed alongside those in post-emancipation Barbados and Jamaica, suggest that there were ideas about punishment and black and laboring bodies that were held by the white ruling classes that transcended national, temporal, and socio-political borders. Thus, instead of apprenticeship being characterized by the disappearance of practices where "[t]he body [was] the major target of penal repression," as viewed through the lens of Foucault, there was continued reliance on physical torture as punishment.[43] For example, historian Claude Levy notes that in 1834 several acts were passed by the Barbadian legislature that increased the number of crimes for which the penalty was death. These legislative proscriptions included "An Act for the Prevention and Punishment of Malicious Injuries to Property," "An Act for the Punishment and Prevention of Larceny," and "An Act for the

Prevention and Punishment of Offences against the Person."[44] Some of the crimes that were listed as capital offenses included arson, rape, attempted murder, "robbery of chattels, money, valuable property," "breaking and entering a church or chapel," sodomy, "exhibiting false signals to ships," and abortion.[45]

Although Levy does not explain why there was this flurry of legislation designating certain crimes as being punishable by death after 1834, one can only deduce that they were created in response to the forthcoming apprenticeship of the former slaves. One could argue that this legislation reflected elite fears that individuals who had been under their control were likely to run amok without the benefit of their governance, and that this legislation was one way of seeing that the strictures under which the slaves lived would remain. This assertion is all the more compelling when one notes that these capital crimes included crimes against property and even larceny. Moreover, some of the crimes for which the judgment of death could be rendered, like arson and destruction of property, are acts that might be interpreted as harmful to the plantation economy. The importance of criminal sanctions against actions that either directly or indirectly threatened the plantation economy was illustrated more tellingly in the "Barbados Gaol Report" of 1835. For instance, the third highest number of persons confined in the Barbados Town Hall jail were those who had been remanded for "desertion of work," an offense that may best be described as a civil offense but which had serious consequences within a plantation economy—particularly in light of the fact that the apprentices theoretically could not be compelled to work like they had been as slaves.[46]

By contrast, the types of punishments meted out to their employers tended to be financial in nature rather than corporeal, even in cases where the crimes that the employers committed were clear and serious violations of the apprenticeship law. An example of this may be seen in the modes of punishment that were described in "An Act for the Abolition of Slavery, for the Government of Apprenticed Labourers, and for Ascertaining and Enforcing the Reciprocal Duties between Them and Their Employers" of Barbados of August 5, 1836.[47] Whereas Clause 35 of this act fined employers not less than five pounds sterling but no more than fifteen pounds sterling for refusing, omitting, or neglecting to provide medical services for their apprentices, Clause 65 clause of the same act stated that

> if any apprenticed labourer, being a watchman or cattle-keeper, shall perform his work indolently, carelessly or negligently, he shall be adjudged to make good the damage that the crops or cattle or property under his charge shall have received by his negligence or misconduct, or he shall be punished for his first of-

fence by whipping, not exceeding 30 stripes[.] And whereas it is expedient to give a discretion to the several special justices of the peace to substitute confinement with hard labour or solitary confinement in lieu of whipping for every such first offence: Be it enacted, that whenever any apprenticed labourer, being a watchman or cattle-keeper, shall be convicted before any special justice of the peace for the first time, of performing his or her work indolently, carelessly or negligently, it shall be lawful for such special justice of the peace, at his discretion, to substitute as a punishment in lieu of whipping for every such first offence as in the said clause is provided, confinement with hard labour, or solitary confinement not exceeding 14 days.[48]

What is most noticeable in the application of punishment and the apprehension of justice in this context is that the definition of crime was tied to the exigencies of the plantation economy. Moreover, those who had a vested interest in seeing that the apprentices were labeled as criminal were the same individuals who were entrusted with the task of defining when an apprentice committed a crime. This assertion is borne out by the fact that defining the apprentices as "indolent" or "negligent" is not quantifiable and instead was wholly dependent on how the masters perceived the apprentices' performance of their duties. This serves also to concretize the notion that the black body was defined only in terms of its importance to the maintenance of the plantation system. And thus blacks could be punished by methods like whipping for carrying out any act that was deemed to threaten the smooth running of the plantation. This can be contrasted to the relatively mild and less corporeal methods of punishment inflicted on white employers for not providing adequate medical care for their apprentices, for instance. When one notes that medical care for apprentices was not given as much weight as workers' execution of their duties, one sees that the black body's importance as a productive tool was firmly established. Punishments had a practical aim: they reinforced black workers' subservient position in the plantation economy and the socio-racial pyramid.

This lack of reciprocity between the fines and penalties inflicted on the apprentice and the master was identified as a key problem that plagued the operation of the Abolition Act. A House of Commons report of 1836, for instance, found that the operation of sanctions tended to be too lenient when employers were punished, as opposed to the "excessive severity" when apprentices were the ones being punished. The committee members identified the problem thusly: "The authority of the special magistrate over the apprentice extends to six months' imprisonment, to fifty stripes, to the right of depriving him of fifteen hours' labour in any week during the whole period of the apprenticeship, and even of indefinitely prolonging that apprenticeship; whereas his authority over the manager extends only to a penalty of £5 currency, or five days' imprisonment, which he is not required, but merely empowered, to inflict."[49]

Sir Lionel Smith, who served as the governor of Barbados during the apprenticeship scheme, also saw the inequities in the punitive system as problematic.[50] However, he saw it as a problem that was occasioned by the *class* of the employers, rather than because of a rapacious system that marked some bodies as worthwhile and others as worthless. In a dispatch to Lord Glenelg on July 26, 1836, Smith wrote that "there is still a great deal of violence and cruelty practiced on the unfortunate apprentices by low whites, which I have not had the means of preventing."[51] Seeing this as a problem that was in the hands of the stipendiary magistrates, Smith assured Glenelg that he had met with them and "remonstrated" with them in an effort to see that they would apply the maximum penalty that could be leveled against the employers when they had been found guilty of abusing their apprentices.[52]

Smith was right to be concerned about the lack of reciprocity between the punishments meted out to apprentices compared to those leveled against their employers. Data from the journals of the stipendiary magistrates for the period January 1 to May 31, 1836, show that Barbadian employers received relatively light sentences, often of a pecuniary nature, for serious abuses committed against their apprentices—a situation that may be contrasted with the fact that apprentices could be sentenced to imprisonment, sometimes with hard labor, for crimes like "indolence" and "neglect of duty."[53] For example, despite the law that established a maximum penalty of fifteen pounds sterling, the highest penalty inflicted on Barbadian employers in the post-apprenticeship period was five pounds sterling, as was seen in the cases heard in the rural and town divisions of District A combined. Geo. T. Robert, as a case in point, was fined five pounds for tying the apprentice John Thomas by his hands to a beam in the kitchen and beating him on two separate occasions "till he got into fits."[54] Thomas's crime was not returning to the house after his mistress had sent him to get meat. Even if one were to argue that Thomas's crime constituted desertion or running away, in that he had failed to return to his employers after being sent on an errand and instead had to be "brought" home, it does not minimize the fact that Robert had committed a grave crime by disobeying Clause 86 of the Barbados Abolition Act that had taken away his right to inflict corporal punishment on his apprentices. What was also significant about this case was that in awarding the punishment to Robert, the stipendiary magistrate certainly showed whose side he was on. The magistrate acknowledged that even though it was "the worst case" that had come before him since he had arrived on the island and that he "should have sent

[it] to the [periodic court] sessions," all of the evidence had to be disregarded since "the boy [Thomas] is a very bad character and a runaway."[55] Thus, like Robert, the stipendiary magistrate also undermined the spirit of the Abolition Act and reinforced the idea that harsh, physical punishments were the only way to deal with "very bad" characters. Additionally, by dint of his ruling, the magistrate had upheld the socio-racial hierarchy.

Robert was not the only employer who received a comparatively light sentence for violent abuses against apprentices. The returns (official reports) of the stipendiary magistrates for January 1 to May 31, 1836, had an ambiguous classification system for the range of abuses committed by employers against their apprentices. While several of the explanations in the "Substance of Complaint" field are quite detailed, there are others that make a distinction between whether an employer "assaulted" his or her apprentices, as opposed to when they had committed acts of "unlawful punishment."[56] In many cases the nuances distinguished by the stipendiary magistrates are not clear, as some of the assaults committed by the employers were carried out as punitive acts. For example, William Cragg was fined one pound for horsewhipping his apprentice Hugh for not picking up stones properly. By comparison, Budding Dash was fined one pound for assault and battery committed against his apprentice James, and Geo. Boryne was fined six shillings and three pence for "[i]nflicting unlawful punishment" on the apprentice Joseph.[57] While all three of these acts could surely be designated as acts of assault and battery, only one of them is described that way in the "Substance of Complaint" field. Moreover, Cragg also inflicted unlawful punishment on his apprentice, yet his crime is not given that label.

Barbadian female employers also received similar types of pecuniary punishments for assaults committed against their apprentices, thus giving lie to the notion that women were, by dint of being women, less violent than men. Essentially, their participation in these punitive acts reinforces their culpability in sustaining the parasitic structure of the labor system and the socio-racial hierarchy that existed in the wider society. There are, for example, the cases of A. Ashurst, who beat Polly Anne on her head with a rock and was fined two pounds sterling, and Mrs. G. F. Gilkes, who was fined fifty shillings for assaulting the apprentice Harriet.[58] The apprentice Sarah appeared in the District A rural division court to lodge a complaint against Susanna Lucas, who was alleged to have struck her over her eye on February 8, 1836. Lucas was found guilty and was fined ten shillings.[59] The criminal actions of these women who were fined for assaulting *other* women, along with illustrating how diffuse power was in the plantation economy, in some sense also showed that a superior (white) womanhood was being asserted. In this latter instance, white women, who, like black women, could be subject to the patriarchal authority of the plantation system and of white men, were responsible for subjecting and assaulting black women.[60]

It would be misleading to state that all of the employers who abused their apprentices only had to pay fines if found guilty. A more serious form of punishment meted out to employers was that the abused apprentice could be discharged from his or her service. An example of this was seen in the case of S. Massiah, who was charged in the District A town division in Barbados on May 17, 1836, for beating R. Charity with a horsewhip. The courts responded by having Charity discharged from Massiah's employ.[61] Although on the one hand it may seem that Charity was vindicated, when one looks at this act of punishment from a larger point of view, it may be argued that this form of punishment may not have been as subversive as it may seem on the surface. In a country which was notorious for having a steady supply of workers even when neighboring countries like Trinidad and British Guiana suffered labor shortages, it could be said that the discharge of an apprentice from an employer who was known to abuse his or her apprentices only left a void for another apprentice to fill. At the same time, with few avenues left to find an alternative form of employment, particularly one that would have taken him away from the plantation, Charity might have subsequently had a difficult time trying to make a living.

There were other problems with the system of sanctions that governed the apprenticeship system. Not only would apprentices continue to feel the brunt of apprenticeship on their bodies, but also the socio-racial pyramid that had been evident during slavery would persist, and punishment would be one way of ensuring its persistence. Special Magistrate Gilmore D'Ames Gregg of Jamaica gave a lively summation that explained the gravity of the situation, not only the lack of equal justice in sentencing but also in showing that the feelings that obtained in the British West Indies were inimical to the equitable operation of the apprenticeship system:

> Is the spirit of the Abolition Law complied with? Surely, there are none residing in this country that will say the spirit of the Abolition Law is fully entered into. Few, very few say this! Why, is it just as reasonable to expect that the London pick-pocket will leave off his old trade because the House of Commons have passed a law declaring pick-pocketing illegal, as to expect that persons, who for 50 years have governed with arbitrary power, will, because it is the law of the land, become not only mild in their government, but that they will fully enter into the spirit of the law. It is not uncommon to hear it said, whenever the special magistrate has occasion to fine for a violation of the law, that he

(the person fined) will the next time take d——d [*sic*] good care and give the d——d black scoundrel a d——d good hiding, and then pay his [five pounds] contentedly for it. This reminds one of the story of the sailor, who was fined by a court one guinea for having knocked out a Jew's eye, who, on being informed of the sentence, threw down two, saying, There, but I must have the other eye.[62]

Gregg's assertion reveals a number of things about discipline and punishment in Jamaica—and these also held steadfast in Barbados. For one thing, his analysis of the system of punishment in Jamaica reinforces a basic premise of this study. Namely, black bodies were, as a matter of course, subject to corporeal and assaultive punishments to an extent not visited onto white bodies, and these punished black bodies were routinely used to shore up the socio-racial divide. Furthermore, Gregg's comments highlight the discrepancies in punishments meted out to blacks and whites when either of these groups violated the laws of the land. Finally, although the anecdote of the "black scoundrel" might be apocryphal, it shows that black bodies were still seen as commodities, with five pounds being the going rate for its use.

That the body retained its importance as a site of punishment for blacks in the post-1834 period is demonstrated further in Sections 29, 41, and 44 of the Jamaica Abolition Act. Section 29 of this act stipulated that apprentices convicted of insubordination to their employers were liable to be sentenced to hard labor in a house of correction or penal gang for up to two weeks, or to receive "stripes"—lashes—not exceeding thirty-nine in number. For criminal offenses too, the body of the apprentice remained the major locus of punishment. Section 44 of the Jamaica Abolition Act stipulated that for "inferior misdemeanors" and crimes committed by apprentices either against each other or against their employers, if convicted after undergoing legal proceedings headed by the stipendiary magistrates, the offending apprentice could receive either fifty lashes, three months imprisonment with hard labor, or twenty days in solitary confinement. For crimes like insolence, neglect, or improper performance of work, the Jamaica Abolition Act, like the Barbados Abolition Act, stipulated that at his discretion, the stipendiary magistrate could sentence the offender to be flogged either as a punishment in itself or along with hard labor, "for such number of hours or days, in his or her own time, for the benefit of the person intitled [*sic*] to his or her services, as the justice of the case may seem to require, not exceeding fifteen hours in any one week."[63]

In fact, corporal punishment remained quite common throughout the apprenticeship system. Its frequent occurrence was alluded to in correspondence from stipendiary magistrates in the British Caribbean to officials in the Colonial Office. For example, in a circular to Lord Glenelg dated May 16, 1837, C. H. Darling wrote: "I am directed by his Excellency to repeat the injunction, which has been so strongly urged upon the special magistracy from the very commencement of the apprenticeship system, and pointedly impressed upon them in numerous individual instances by his Excellency himself, that the use of corporal punishment should be restricted as much as possible, and in fact rigidly confined to offences of a disgraceful or highly aggravated nature." The letter makes it clear that not only was flogging used regularly to punish, but that there was also a more sinister motive behind this mode of punishment. Darling goes on: "I am further to desire, that [corporal punishment] may on no account be inflicted on offenders who are not entirely recovered from the effect of previous punishment, and that you take care that in all cases, the apprentices are perfectly cured before they are removed from the hospital, and required to resume their work."[64] Rather than being used to deter or reform, and instead of being leveled against egregious crimes, the impression is given that corporal punishment was employed deliberately to inflict pain and suffering on the apprentices and to reinforce their subaltern status. Although Darling did not explain the motives behind the use of corporal punishment in this context, its impact was unmistakable. Corporal punishment reinforced the differences between the apprentices and their employers, blacks and whites, and their disparate social statuses. By applying a draconian form of punishment on the bodies of the apprentices for seemingly trivial offenses, the special magistrates in question had broken Lord Stanley's promise that the apprentices were to "feel no taint of [their] servile condition" and that they were to "be freed from the atrocious system of irresponsible corporeal punishment."[65] Instead, apprenticeship was definitely a condition that apprentices felt on their bodies.

Ironically, even as corporal punishment dehumanized apprentices and reinforced their subaltern status, it served also to reinforce the humanity of those it marked and challenged the idea of total corporeal domination. This was visible in the Jamaica Abolition Act, for instance. In an unwitting acknowledgment of black femininity, Section 41 of this act stipulated that for all offenses where flogging would be the punishment awarded normally, when these offenses were committed by women, these women were to be sentenced instead to solitary confinement for a period not exceeding ten days.[66] Still, in spite of the aforementioned acknowledgment of black humanity, particularly to black womanhood, one must affirm that the general theme that undergirded Section 41 of the Jamaica Abolition Act was that the black body was the de facto site of punishment and that the punishment meted out to blacks had to be comprehensive. By banishing the bodies of females to solitary confinement, both real and intangible boundaries were erected between the free and the unfree, the criminal and the law-abiding, and criminal men and criminal women. Not only were these females denied their freedom, but in addition their isolation from other inmates may have intensified the punishment.

From a reading of first-person accounts, it is clear that punishment in post-emancipation Jamaica remained draconian. One of the most notable accounts was provided by James Williams. His recollection of his punishments during his apprenticeship resulted in a monograph that generated heated controversies about the question of truth, representation, and the production of knowledge—controversies that were present not only in the nineteenth century, when his narrative was originally published, but that have also continued to this day. In spite of these controversies, however, Williams's narrative is an important account of apprenticeship in Jamaica, not only because it is in his own voice, but also because it gives detailed accounts of the experiences of apprentices from plantations in St. Ann, Jamaica. Additionally, Williams's narrative can be placed with the activities of anti-slavery activists since it too contested planter hegemony (by its very existence) and because it was a document that provided evidence of abuses committed by the planters in contravention of both the spirit and the law of the Abolition Act. Moreover, the fact that Williams's narrative prompted the British government to order the governor, Sir Lionel Smith, to investigate the alleged abuses illustrates that the narrative had challenged the seeming omnipotence of the plantocracy.[67] Although some of Williams's contemporaries, such as the planter and Barbadian attorney general Henry Sharpe, challenged the veracity of his allegations, the inquiry that resulted from his narrative upheld his claims about the apprenticeship system as it operated in Jamaica. Sharpe questioned whether Williams's experiences spoke to the experiences of all the apprentices in Jamaica and the actions of the "whole proprietary body of Jamaica." He found it difficult to conceive "that a person could bear such cruelties as this man [Williams] experienced, and survive to tell his tale."[68]

Sharpe's incredulity notwithstanding, Williams's testimony served as an important counter-narrative that allowed the apprenticeship scheme to be viewed through the eyes of the apprentices and not just from Colonial Office correspondence and colonial legislation. Essentially, Williams's narrative forced officials—and twentieth- and twenty-first-century readers—to consider that the apprentices *felt* apprenticeship on their bodies. Moreover, his narrative served to remind officials that apprenticeship was about people and not just the economic health of the colonies. In his narrative, the apprentices were sentient protagonists who lived in a society where the use of the whip and the treadmill was common. Williams also depicted a system of punishment that in many cases did not privilege gender or age, a phenomenon that seems at variance with those instances where the state offered clemency because of these two factors.

Williams's narrative, though detailing draconian corporal punishments against apprentices, also brought to light the paradoxes that inhered within the apprenticeship system itself, even as it highlighted examples of subaltern agency. In the latter respect, it showed examples of apprentices challenging punishments meted out to them, complaining to stipendiary magistrates about their employers, and in some cases even making claims about their personal sovereignty. Indeed, the agentic behavior of the apprentices gained such notoriety that W. L. Burn in 1937 saw the use of the law by the apprentices as evidence of them exhibiting a proclivity toward "litigiousness," writing of "their tendency to haunt the Stipendiary Magistrates' court in large gangs."[69] Burn's interpretation notwithstanding, the activities of the apprentices in Williams's narrative lend credence to Stipendiary Magistrate Patrick Dunne's contention that the apprentices were "fully aware of their rights, and tenacious in upholding them."[70]

At the time of his narrative, which was first published in 1837 in Britain, eighteen-year-old Williams was apprenticed to Penshurst plantation in St. Ann, Jamaica. In his recollection he cataloged a number of abuses that had been meted out to him, abuses that both directly and indirectly assaulted his body, ranging from flogging to being confined in dungeons at Knapdale and Carlton, a cage in Brown's Town, and a workhouse in St. Ann. One particularly brutal account of punishment involved Williams being sentenced to receive thirty-nine lashes by the stipendiary magistrate Dr. Thompson. According to Williams, this beating was so severe that it cut his back and left it bloody. Williams gave this as the reason for this punishment: "When them try me, massa said, that one Friday, I was going all round the house with big stone in my hand, looking for him and his sister, to knock them down." Williams denied this accusation and argued: "I was mending stone wall round the house by massa's order; I was only a half-grown boy that time. I told magistrate, I never do such thing, and offer to bring evidence about it; he refuse to hear me or my witness; would not let me speak."[71]

What is significant about this account is that it showed that Williams was well aware of his legal rights and was knowledgeable about the legal process. By calling on witnesses to testify on his behalf, for instance, Williams showed that he was not naïve about the manner in which he should go about proving his innocence. In fact, even though he was not allowed to speak, one can see that in attempting to call witnesses, and in attempting to speak, Williams was cognizant of the power of the spoken word and its potential to exonerate him. In this account too we see Williams asserting not only his legal rights as an apprentice but also his rights as a human being, which unequivocally illustrate that he was making claims to his person. Also, his description of himself as a "half-grown boy" illustrates that, in his mind and at that time, he was willing to use age as his defense. Williams implied too that the magistrate who conducted the trial was unreasonable as not only did he refuse to *listen* to the mitigating evidence, he also refused to let Williams speak. Yet what Williams's narrative shows—both from the details embedded within it, through his attempted defense of himself against Mr. Senior and his sister, and from the very fact of its publication—is that, in spite of the restrictions placed upon him as an apprentice and in his silencing, he could use his body to assert his own power, and at the same time he could contest the power that the elites sought to exert over him.

Williams's narrative is valuable for its insights on the nuances of punishment. Not only did it reveal that punishment continued to be used to reinforce the socio-racial hierarchies in the plantation economy, it also showed that one form of punishment could simultaneously be both an indirect and a direct assault on the body. Apprentices who were confined in the workhouses in Jamaica often found that they were the recipients of what may be classified as "augmented punishments." Augmented punishments can be defined as those that supplemented the punishment of confinement, and these were mostly in the form of stints on the treadmill. In an evocative and harrowing account—perhaps in an effort to pique the emotions of the British public—Williams told of punishments that brutalized men and women, regardless of their age and health, and that did not take into account the severity of the crime committed. Recalling his confinement in the St. Ann's Bay workhouse, Williams told the story of "one old woman with grey head," who, not being able to "dance the [treadmill] at all," was severely flogged by the driver. According to Williams, this woman was whipped until her clothes were "cut off," and "when she came down [from the treadmill] all her back covered with blood."[72] In fact, as Williams pointed out in his testimony, this elderly woman was put on the treadmill for an entire week and flogged every time that she could not "dance."[73]

Noting the indiscriminate and ubiquitous use of the treadmill, Williams continued: "When them come off the mill, you see all their foot cut up behind with the Cat [multi-tailed whip], and all the skin bruise off the shin with the mill-steps, and them have to go down to the sea-side to wash away the blood."[74] In this account, Williams forced his readers to notice the bodies of the punished apprentices. He abstracted bruised and skinned shins, bleeding backs, and feet that had been cut up and focused on the humanity of the punished individual. By pointing out that one woman had "grey head" Williams was invoking shame on a system and on individuals who refused to revere age and gender.

Williams was not the only apprentice whose voice challenged the punishments inflicted upon apprentices. Edward Lawrence, an apprentice at Penshurst who was punished for insolence at the same time that Williams was punished, had his own narrative to tell: "I remember having been flogged at Penshurst, by order of Dr. Thompson; James Williams and myself were flogged. At the same time Henry James and Thomas Brown were flogged, and two boys, named Thomas Mills and William Graham, were switched. I do not know how many lashes James Williams received, but he was one that was flogged by the constable, Alexander Mills, and not by the police. . . . The police flogged Adam Brown and Henry James . . . Henry James's flogging was very severe, his stomach was bruised by the cart-wheel to which he was tied to receive his punishment."[75]

Thomas Brown recalled: "On the same day that Dr. Thompson came, I was flogged by Alexander Mills, and got 30 lashes; the flogging was not severe. Alexander Mills flogged James Williams; his flogging was not severe. I heard master complain that the flogging by the constable was too light, and upon that Dr. Thompson ordered the police to flog the rest, that is, Henry James and Adam Brown."[76] What these testimonies from Lawrence and Brown show is the commonness of flogging, and they help also to substantiate Williams's claims about the brutalities that apprentices at Penshurst encountered. In neither account does the speaker express any shock at the punishment that he received. In all of the examples of apprentices being punished, the body is notable not just because it is the site of punishment but also because its marking helps to reinforce the very structure of the society.

The punishments given to the apprentices at Penshurst Estate were not always in the form of quantifiable, direct attacks on their bodies, yet these punishments were able to reinforce the subaltern status of the punished individuals. Confinement, another type of punishment that was used widely during the apprenticeship period, did not always leave the indelible marks associated with corporal punishment, yet it too may be characterized as an assault against the black body. Again, evidence from Williams's narrative provides crucial support for this point. In his narrative he described his confinement for ten days in the dungeon at Knapdale, a punishment that he had suffered for not "turning out" the sheep on time. This time it was Captain Dillon, another magistrate, who had sentenced Williams to the punishment of confinement. In a vivid account of his place of confinement, Williams described the dungeon as dark, cold, damp and recalled that his "little bit of a cell [was] hardly big enough for me to lie full-length." The diet was meager, helping to augment the severity of the punishment. Williams and Adam Brown, confined with Williams, received just a pint of water and "two little coco or plantain" daily for the duration of their confinement, which, according to Williams, left them weak and "hardly able to stand up."[77]

Besides James Williams and the other apprentices at Penshurst, apprentices from other estates provided evidence that shows that the apprenticeship system as it operated in Jamaica had vestiges, at least, of the brutality of slavery. For instance, there is the case of John James, an apprentice from Owen Plantation who appeared before a commission to enquire into abuses that he had suffered at the hands of his employer. James, who was described in the evidentiary minutes as a boy "apparently 12 or 13 years of age," recounted how his employer "fummed" him with pimento switches. He also described how the employer, Mr. Nesbett, had pulled off his "frock" and tied him to a tree; all of this punishment was for running away.[78] Thus, James's body was not only physically assaulted by being whipped, there was also a psychic assault with the humiliation of being stripped and tied to a tree for all to see. James's case exposes a conundrum: in a free society, can leaving a job be considered running away, something warranting punishment?

In an indictment of the failure of the stipendiary magistrates to protect him as their office required, James told the commissioners that Mr. Nesbett, his "busha," had flogged him on a number of occasions for running away, and that even though he had complained to Stipendiary Magistrate T. H. Dillon, who "sometimes comes to Owen," he had never been carried before him, nor had he [Dillon] ever ordered James to be "switched." Instead, Nesbett had often flogged James "of his own free will."[79]

There is further evidence that apprentices from Recess Plantation in the parish of St. Thomas in the Vale, Jamaica, complained to two magistrates about their punishment and the state of the plantation's dungeon and the hospital, which they described as "one and the same place." This site was described as a "damp cellar under ground, without window, without flooring, without privy, and with nothing but the bare ground to lie upon." The dungeon was also alleged to have contained "a place of torture" called a "coffin case." The apprentices testified that "in this loathsome dungeon, the sick people were closely imprisoned along with those who were expressly put in for punishment—that men and women, boys and girls, were indiscriminately huddled together night and day; and, that neither the sick nor the delinquents were provided with any sort of sustenance during their imprisonment."[80] In response to these accusations, the governor of Jamaica, Lord Sligo, directed stipendiary magistrates Palmer and Harris to visit the property in question, which was owned by a Mr. Giles, to verify the complaints of the apprentices. Upon their arrival at Recess Plantation, it was alleged that both Mr. Giles and his wife obstructed the magistrates from inspecting the hospital and dungeon. Although bills of indictment were eventually laid against Mr. Giles for preventing Palmer and Harris from carrying out their investigation, these bills were said to have been ignored by the grand jury.[81] Further, Giles had then brought a case against Harris and Palmer for "trespass on his premises, assault, false imprisonment, [and] riot."[82]

From these accounts of apprentices being abused by their masters and the failure of the stipendiary magistrates to effectively deal with these abuses, the impression given is that power and punishment were administered only in a top-down, linear fashion. At first glance, these examples seem to tell a story of powerful white men punishing weakened—although not weak—laborers. Yet a close reading of the data reveals that the exercise of punishment was much more complex and multilayered and that power and the power to punish were distributed in a circuitous fashion. Furthermore, power was not a monolithic behemoth but was a quality that could be found in various degrees and forms and exerted by individuals whom one would not have defined as powerful players in the apprenticeship system. It is for this reason that the apprenticeship period was also noteworthy for producing characters who reinforced the very contradictions and complexities that the system engendered. One example of these contradictions came in the position of the estate constable, which in 1834 bore many similarities to that of the slave driver who was often entrusted with the task of punishing enslaved individuals who refused to know their place.[83] One such example of this continuity—and an illustration of the diffuse nature of power—was Constable William Clarke of Queenhithe Plantation in Jamaica. The evidence shows that Clarke, a black man, flogged apprentices from the Dry Harbour Plantation in Brown's Town, St. Ann. As in the accounts of Williams, Lawrence, Brown, and James, this punishment was physical and brutal, aimed to humiliate and inflict pain. According to one account, an apprentice named Donald Grant was "tied to the horse stable and . . . catted [flogged with a cat-o'-nine-tails] by William Clarke."[84] Clarke was paid half a dollar by James Smith, the proprietor of Dry Harbour, for giving Grant twenty-five lashes. The severity of Grant's beating was evident in Clarke's testimony: "Mr. Smith told me to lay it well on, but I did not do so as his flesh was weak, and every knot on the cut was a bump as big as my finger, and whaled the flesh; his back bled after I was done, and was much swelled. Mr. Rawlinson [the stipendiary magistrate] came up after the flogging; he looked at the back, and said that he must be taken back to Dry Harbour to his work immediately."[85] Grant's body is hyper-visible in this testimony. It is described as "weak" and bleeding. Even though Clarke refers to Grant's "flesh," his testimony does not allow observers to see it as just a corporal mass. Instead, it is delineated as flesh that responds to a beating by forming a knot and swelling. Because it bleeds, swells, and knots, Clarke empathized with Grant, as encapsulated by his refusal to "lay it well on." In contrast, the stipendiary magistrate did not see past Grant's body as a laboring tool and instead sent Grant immediately back to work. How could two men read Grant's body so differently? Why did one empathize and see pain and weakness and the other see someone who was fit to work? Could it be that Rawlinson saw Grant as nothing more than a cog in the wheel of a plantation that held precedence over his body? Grant had committed what amounted to a heinous crime against the plantation: he had been away from Dry Harbour for sixty-six days, disobeying Rawlinson's command to go back to work, a crime that was probably exacerbated by his declaration that he was a "free man."[86]

Clarke's testimony is revealing. First, it shows that sometimes those who administered punishment were not the powerful actors that a casual glance at the evidence would suggest. Instead, through the person of Clarke, we see that sometimes those who administered punishment were just puppets in a system where they also occupied subaltern positions. Second, Clarke's testimony reveals a compassion and humanism that is generally not associated with those who wielded the whip. This empathy is evident in Clarke's reluctance to "lay it well on" after seeing Grant's severely bruised back. Third, perhaps most importantly, it reveals that Grant and Stipendiary Magistrate Rawlinson had different opinions and definitions about Grant's so-called freedom. Whereas Grant had tried to establish a claim to his body by running away and making a verbal assertion about his status, Rawlinson was quick to reinforce (by ordering the whipping) that the plantation and Grant's employer had a prior and superior claim over Grant's body. Finally, from this episode one can see that although the Abolition Act of 1833 had declared blacks free, as apprentices they were still not in full possession of their person—a socio-political reality that could be reinforced emphatically through the administration of corporal punishment.

Although Grant's punishment was later ruled to be draconian, and Rawlinson, the special magistrate at Brown's Town in St. Ann, was suspended for this and other abuses, Rawlinson's punishment lends credence to the view expressed by scholars of crime and punishment who have argued that whites who broke the law received comparatively milder punishments than ordered for blacks and others of color who broke the law. An example of this view is that of historian David V. Trotman, who writes on crime in Trinidad from emancipation to the turn of the twentieth century. Writing about the disparities in committals (jail sentences) between those of the working class who broke the law compared with those from the upper classes who committed white-collar crimes, Trotman reveals an inherently flawed justice system that he attributes to "the inequalities of a [legal] system based on race, class, and colour."[87]

The examples of James and Grant being punished for running away, although showing that apprentices could be severely punished for flouting apprenticeship laws, are also revealing for what they say about the ways in which agentic behavior could be exercised within an authoritarian system. Indeed, James's and Grant's actions of running away may be likened to those acts of marronage that occurred during slavery, which challenged the hold on the body that was exerted by that system. By attempting to remove their bodies from a system that sought to claim sovereignty over them, James and Grant were showing the untenability of the somatic claims being made by the imperial and colonial governments.

Like their male counterparts, female apprentices also received brutal punishments that targeted their bodies, as was seen in the cases of Mary Ann Bell of Penshurst Plantation and Nancy Webb of Knapdale in St. Ann, Jamaica. For example, Bell was sent to the workhouse and treadmill by the aforementioned Stipendiary Magistrate Rawlinson while "quite heavy in the family way."[88] Webb, who was also sent to the workhouse and sentenced to "dance the treadmill," stated on September 26, 1837, that she had been hung by her wrists to the straps on the treadmill because she "could not keep step at all." In a detailed recollection of her punishment, Webb stated that her legs had "dragged and knocked against the wheel, so that the blood could be traced all along the steps."[89] From this account, one can see that the treadmill was used as an instrument of torture. This has also been substantiated in evidence provided by British abolitionists Joseph Sturge and Thomas Harvey, who recorded their observations about disciplinary and punitive practices in the colonies while on a visit to the British West Indies in 1837. In the highly publicized book that came out of this visit, *The West Indies in 1837*, these two members of the Society of Friends told about the horrors of apprenticeship. During a visit to a workhouse in St. Ann, for example, they had seen both "recent and old" blood on the steps of the treadmill, blood that "had been shed so profusely, that even the sand of the floor was thickly sprinkled with it." To emphasize the questionable aims and tendentiousness of punishment inside the prisons, Sturge and Harvey noted that "[t]he driver of the penal gang, superintendent of the treadmill, and other similar officers, in this, as well as in other workhouses, are taken out of the gang of life convicts." To Sturge and Harvey, the ramifications of such decisions were grave: "It is fearful to contemplate the abuses committed by these petty tyrants, who, being sentenced to imprisonment for life, are thus almost irresponsible, and beyond the reach of the law."[90]

Along with these personal and eyewitness accounts of punishment, there is also statistical evidence that confirms the view that punishment that targeted the body remained widespread throughout the apprenticeship system, as it had been during slavery. Indeed, the statistical evidence shows that flogging was only one example in a range of corporal punishments that were in use after 1834. Data gathered for Jamaica from August 1, 1834, to August 1, 1835, show that there were other methods of punishment employed during the apprenticeship scheme, although corporal punishment was one of the most favored types (see tables 1 and 2 in the appendix). Indeed, as can be seen in table 1, "repayment of time" was the form of punishment most widely used, followed by flogging.[91]

The story in Barbados was similar (see tables 3 and 4 in the appendix). Punishments recorded against apprentices on that island for the period August 1, 1837, to September 30, 1837, show that in the employer-employee relationship, Barbadian apprentices were punished severely for actions that appeared to threaten the smooth operation of the plantation economy.[92] For instance, as indicated in table 3, there were 1,549 convictions for "indolence" and only 95 acquittals. The large number of convictions for indolence vis-à-vis other offenses causes pause because this "crime" was not quantifiable, yet its frequent prosecution suggests that Barbadian employers were successful in making the courts see it as such. However, one could also argue that so-called acts of indolence might have been forms of malingering, that is, outright resistance to the corporeal demands of the plantation system, and, in calling resistance "indolence," Barbadian legislators and planters were renaming and thereby subverting an action that could threaten the viability of the plantation economy. This argument is all the more compelling when one notes that the punishment for indolence was imprisonment for a maximum of four weeks and a minimum of three days.[93] After their time of imprisonment apprentices still had to repay the work time that was lost to said confinement. In labeling such a high number of offenses as forms of indolence, planters and the courts were also inscribing ideologies of laziness onto the bodies of black apprentices. The result was that a pathological typing of the apprentices, specifically as "indolent" workers and generally as "indolent" individuals, was established. This marking was then used to justify the punishment of apprentices if they did not execute their duties in a manner that was deemed acceptable.

By comparison, employers received relatively light punishments for offenses that were sometimes of a very serious nature. These discrepancies reinforce the skewed nature of the relationships between Barbadian employers and employees and laws and punishment during the apprenticeship period. In many ways, the master-slave relationship had merely been renamed the employer-apprentice relationship, and punitive measures served as the bridge that allowed for the maintenance of the pre-apprenticeship socio-racial hierarchies. The data for employers convicted for crimes committed against their apprentices presents a telling contrast to the figures of the apprentices convicted. All told, there were 52 convictions for employers in the same two-month period, compared with 2,897 for apprentices (see table 4 in the appendix).

The quantitative and qualitative evidence presented here can be interpreted in a number of ways. First, the data suggest that the aims of discipline and punishment in Jamaica and Barbados were manifold. Whether aimed directly at the body, through floggings or "dancing on the treadmill"—which sometimes left scars, made marks, or caused pain—or indirectly at the body, as exemplified by confinement in dungeons, jails, or houses of correction, which functioned to limit the mobility of the body, they were used to bring about the subjection of the laboring population.

Moreover, the disciplinary and punitive measures employed were also meant to humiliate the working class and at the same time reinforce their social position. In essence, these kinds of brutal punishments that were administered by the ruling bodies onto the subaltern bodies seem in many ways to represent the Parthian shot of an increasingly anachronistic plantocracy. From the statistical evidence presented in tables 1, 3, and 4 one also gains some idea of how crime was defined. With regard to the definitions of crimes committed by the apprentices, the tables suggest that the crimes for which apprentices in Barbados and Jamaica were convicted were subjective, and it was left entirely up to the employer to define when conduct in the workplace was insolent, indolent, or neglectful. In addition, the fact that Jamaican apprentices were convicted 6,024 times over a year (table 1) for being disobedient while Barbadian apprentices were convicted only 309 times over two months (table 3), a rate over three times greater, raises interesting questions. Is this wide discrepancy due to the fact that the data for Jamaica were collected in 1834 and 1835, when the island's apprentices were still learning the new rules, whereas the Barbadian data come from two to three years later, meaning apprentices in those cases had had more time to become acquainted with the rules, which made them less likely to contravene them? Or do these figures merely reflect the differential apprentice population size of the islands? While either of these questions might contain answers that help to explain these statistical differences, a more compelling explanation might combine both suppositions, along with the assertion that perhaps Jamaican and Barbadian legislators and plantocrats simply defined "disobedience" differently. It is likely also that Jamaican apprentices were indeed more "disobedient" than Barbadian apprentices and that they refused to accept the terms under which they were apprenticed as they were secure in knowing that if they were fortunate enough to escape from their employers and their apprenticeship, Jamaica had an abundance of arable land from which they could make a living. Barbadian apprentices, on the other hand, would have been aware of the scarcity of arable unoccupied land and might have found it not in their best interest to act with the bravado of their Jamaican peers.

Whatever the answers to these questions, an analysis of "crimes" and their punishments tells us a lot about ideas about the body and bodies in post-1834 Jamaica and Barbados. For instance, in Barbados, corporal punishment was one of the most popular punitive measures used by stipendiary magistrates to punish workers for infractions of the law. In fact, concern grew about the misuse and prevalence of flogging in Barbados. This is borne out in a dispatch from Lord Glenelg to Governor MacGregor, whose jurisdiction was Barbados and the Windward Islands after Lionel Smith's departure: "On receiving the monthly returns of punishments inflicted by order of the special magistrates in the West Indies, I observe with regret, that in some of the colonies under your government the average amount of corporal punishment has not been reduced. It has been the anxious hope of Her Majesty's Government, that under the judicious administration of the Apprenticeship Law, this mode of punishment would be gradually disused, and that it would become needless to resort to it as a means of enforcing the duties attached to that condition."[94]

In spite of the sentiment expressed by Glenelg, the degree to which corporal punishment was used in the British West Indies remained a matter of debate. Still, Glenelg could point out that in some of the colonies, notably Jamaica, Barbados, British Guiana, Grenada, and the Leeward Islands—with the exception of Dominica—the number of floggings inflicted had been very greatly reduced. Yet he noted that the opposite situation obtained in St. Vincent, Tobago, and Trinidad, where there was "no appearance of a progressive diminution," and for St. Lucia, where, "though there has been a considerable reduction within the last year, the monthly average of floggings still continues larger than it was during the first year of the apprenticeship."[95]

Still, we must not be blind to the fact that corporal punishment remained the norm rather than the exception in Jamaica and Barbados between 1834 and 1838. For example, from table 5 in the appendix we can see that the total number of lashes ordered by stipendiary magistrates in Jamaica between April and June 1836 was 15,037, with the average number of floggings administered being about 247. Some of the highest numbers of floggings administered included 1,181 by Richard St. John, 1,521 by Henry Moresby, 1,093 by J. R. Thomas, and 943 by W. H. Sowley. The lowest numbers include 20 lashes by R. Chamberlayne Jr. and Henry Kent, and 25 by W. H. Brownson. Out of a total of sixty-one stipendiary magistrates, only eight did not order any floggings.

Transportation and the Presence of the Absent Body

Along with floggings and sentences like hard labor and dancing the tread-mill, transportation (banishment) was one other punishment where the body could be said to be the target. Transportation is a particularly interesting corporal punishment because it was in the *absence* of the punished body—because of its removal from the country where the crime was committed—that its potency was highlighted. Additionally, the frequent usage of this method of punishment, combined with spirited discussions about its use and efficacy, highlight how ideas about racialized bodies were always central to punishment in the British West Indies.

On the surface, transportation as punishment in Barbados and Jamaica during the apprenticeship period seems to suggest a number of things about imperial and colonial ideas about bodies and punishment. Its use, one might argue, implied that certain bodies were dispensable to the plantation economy, particularly when one considers that the economies of Barbados and Jamaica were labor-intensive. That this form of punishment was not used as frequently as other types of punishment makes this dispensability thesis all the more compelling. At the same time, the use of transportation suggested that there was a criminal type that authorities believed could not be reformed by domestic forms of punishment, thus lending credence to the idea of an incorrigible criminal type. Finally, the use of transportation as a punishment of choice suggests on the surface that there were types of crimes that were deemed so egregious that complete removal of the perpetrators was the only solution. This seems supported by the fact that Barbadian legislation for the "prevention of riotous assemblies" stipulated a penalty of transportation for its infringement.[96] A careful examination of transportation, however, reveals that its use was part of a draconian deployment of punishment and an exercise in plantocratic hegemony.

Ian Duffield, writing on the subject of West Indian convicts transported to Australia, noted that between 1834 and 1839 twenty-eight Barbadians and fifteen Jamaicans were sent to Australia for a variety of crimes ranging from the trivial to the serious.[97] For example, William Prince, a field laborer from Barbados, was transported to New South Wales for life for stealing a sheep.[98] His countryman George Ironmonger, who was described as a "tolerable" shoemaker, shared the same fate for stealing clothes.[99] Of the Jamaicans who were sentenced to transportation, there was the example of William Evins, who was described as a good cooper. He was transported to New South Wales in 1834 for stealing a horse. That crimes of theft were often harshly punished was also seen in the examples of James Robin and Quashie, alias Russell, who were sentenced to transportation for life for stealing a handkerchief and receiving stolen goods, respectively.[100]

The fact that stealing, a relatively trivial crime, was punished so harshly also invites one to ask what was it about these bodies of individuals and the idea of property that motivated the state to respond in this manner. This question is best answered by looking at the idea of property in the metropole to ascertain if a similar philosophy could have been transferred to nineteenth-century Barbados and Jamaica. Roger Norman Buckley, writing specifically about the British army in the West Indies, makes a compelling case that there was a "deification of property" in eighteenth-century Britain that resulted in capital sentences being leveled against property crimes.[101] In response to property crimes in Britain, there was the enactment of the Bloody Code that instituted capital statutes for crimes like burglary and stealing shipwrecked goods.[102] The sentence of transportation for property offenses intimates that there was a similar deification in Barbados and Jamaica. And because blacks had been formerly designated as property themselves, this particular crime and its punishment pit notions of non-human property against notions of dispensable and removable forms of human property.[103] That is to say, property in Barbados and Jamaica was deified insofar as it could be used to shore up the power of the planters—especially through their right to designate property's worth—and to reinforce the subjugated status of blacks. In addition, acts of theft perpetrated by members of the working class might have been viewed by colonial and imperial elites as a symbolic threat to property rights, thus helping to explain why transportation was the punishment of choice to deal with this crime. Thus, for instance, the handkerchief that was stolen by James Robin was not just a small piece of cloth but represented his ability to pilfer from a superior power and contravene, however slightly, the might of the colonial and imperial governments.

Women were not exempt from the punishment of transportation. Matty Beck, a nursemaid and cook from Barbados, was transported to New South Wales for seven years for receiving stolen goods, and Johanna Esmon, also from Barbados, received fourteen years for stealing clothes.[104] Although the data do not show that there were any Jamaican women sentenced to transportation during 1834–37, earlier figures show that in 1831 Priscilla, a housemaid and cook from that island, was transported to New South Wales for seven years for "attempted poisoning."[105] Her crime also substantiates the findings of several historians, including Hilary Beckles, Arlette Gautier, and Barbara Bush, who have noted that enslaved domestics were more likely to attempt to poison their masters than field slaves as an act of resistance. Matthew Lewis writes about the case of a fifteen-year-old "black servant girl" called Minetta who appeared at the slave court in Jamaica for attempting to poison her master. For this crime, Minetta was sentenced to death.[106] However, the statistics about the men and women who were sentenced to transportation reveal a gender disparity. They show that the vast majority of those who were transported were male, thereby giving the impression that females either committed less serious crimes than males or were thought to be relatively harmless when compared with male criminals.

At first glance, some of these examples seem to confirm Duffield's conclusion that those sentenced to transportation were symbols of hyperbolic responses from the ruling classes, fueled by what they saw as a "dangerously restive Black population."[107] Yet, upon closer examination, the examples reveal that transportation's use was more complex and perhaps even more sinister. For example, Lewis noted that of the two ringleaders of a thwarted rebellion in Jamaica, one was hanged while the other was sentenced to transportation.[108] There was also the example of Tom from Jamaica—said to be a farrier, "horsebreaker," cook, servant, and "Doctor Man"—who was sentenced to transportation for a number of serious crimes including murder, rebellion, arson, and participating in a mutiny.[109]

In the main, when transportation was used instead of other forms of punishment, deterrence was not the major aim of those who administered the punishment. The evidence suggests that those individuals who were sentenced to transportation, though sometimes categorized as "incorrigible rogues," were more likely to be dispensable elements of the plantation economy. Indeed, in those cases when it was felt that transportation was being carried out too often against able-bodied males, calls were made for the adoption of alternative methods of punishment. In fact, in a dispatch to Lord Glenelg in 1836, Lionel Smith expressed this very problem with transportation. In response to Glenelg's questions about the transportation of felons from Barbados, Smith not only noted that "[m]any of the ablest bodied men in the island are now transported annually to New South Wales at a great expense to the colony," he also revealed that the Barbadian legislature wanted him to have the authority to commute transportation in appropriate cases for a commensurate number of years to hard labor. Disputing the effectiveness of transportation as a punishment for offenders and a deterrent to possible offenders, Smith contended further: "Certain it is, many desperate characters do not care for transportation, and if your Lordship would approve of a Bill to the effect stated above, much useful labour might be saved to the colony, and a better example of punishment be shown."[110] In a subsequent response, addressed to the new governor of Barbados, E. J. MacGregor, Glenelg showed that he agreed with Smith's solution to the problem, although he emphasized that women, those who were ill, and those deemed to be too young or too old were to be exempt from the proposed hard labor. Furthermore, Glenelg was unconvinced that transportation could ever be an effective form of punishment for black West Indians, and he strongly expressed his feelings in a later dispatch to Governor MacGregor:

> The Negro population can hardly be supposed to possess any definite notions respecting the place to which criminals are sent, or the penalties awaiting them there. Great as is the existing demand for labour in the West Indies, the removal even of criminals would seem to be inexpedient, as subtracting the work which they might perhaps be compelled to perform in the public roads; while the introduction of any considerable number of the Negro race into the Australian colonies is to be deprecated for many reasons, applying to that part of his Majesty's domains, though inapplicable elsewhere.[111]

Indeed, so great was Glenelg's lack of confidence in the effectiveness of transportation that he suggested that it be abolished totally in the Windward Islands in favor of a punishment that not only produced "a more wholesome terror," but that also "subjected the revenues to a smaller charge, and reliev[ed] the Australian colonies from an inconvenience to which they ought not to be subjected."[112]

The idea that transportation was unwieldy and ineffective is supported further by a reading of the various correspondence emanating from the Colonial Office in 1837. In one dispatch to the governors in the British West Indies, Lord Glenelg broached the subject about the inefficacy and unwieldiness of transportation as a mode of punishment. Glenelg stressed the "extreme evils" and "inconveniences" that accrued from transportation. He found that "as applied to the negro race," transportation did not "possess most of the essential qualities of efficient secondary punishment." Glenelg found that those sentenced to transportation often spent a long time in prison awaiting their banishment. Although not explicitly suggesting an alternative, Glenelg did recommend a "more efficient punishment" instead. In addition, he stated that "the introduction of negro convicts into the Australian Colonies is a practice which his Majesty's Government have resolved shall be discontinued."[113] Even before Glenelg expressed his misgivings about transportation, J. Rowe, chief justice of Jamaica in 1836, highlighted the major problems that he had observed with the administration of transportation and, implicitly, its inefficacy. In a letter to Stipendiary Magistrate C. H. Darling, Rowe pointed out that a number of prisoners sentenced to transportation had not yet been removed from the country since it was difficult to obtain ships to take them to England.[114]

Thus, the evidence shows that although Duffield's argument that transportation was used to "control a dangerously restive Black population" is compelling, it does not tell the whole story. Moreover, when one looks at the Jamaican government's response to the Morant Bay Rebellion that occurred much later, in 1865, one can see that colonial authorities often had quick, emphatic, relatively cheap, and somewhat easy punitive measures like hanging available to them when they were actually faced with a dangerous and roused black population. What one can see is that transportation was often used in an ad hoc, menacing fashion. Sheep, handkerchief, and sugar thieves hardly seem worthy of "dangerous classes," and even though rapists, murderers, arsonists, and mutineers do threaten the social fabric, one wonders why incarceration, flogging, or hanging did not seem to be appropriate punishments for these offenses.[115] Therefore, Duffield's later argument about the roles of punishment in the early nineteenth century in Britain is more apt to explain the role that transportation specifically, and punishment in general, played in Barbados and Jamaica during the apprenticeship period. Duffield saw punishment in early nineteenth-century Britain not as something that was static but as a dynamic tool that could be manipulated and administered to further the aims of the elites. He found that in Britain the courts "manipulated terror, justice and mercy, in a sophisticated way, as a means of controlling the masses."[116] Yes, the Barbadian and Jamaican courts and their agents sought to control the masses, but this control was inextricably tied to pejorative ideas about blackness and black bodies. Moreover, transportation helped to support the exigencies of the plantation economy and the wider social structure.

That the majority of those transported from Barbados and Jamaica were working-class blacks is not in question, as Duffield's list of occupations shows. For example, the majority of those transported from Barbados were grooms, house servants, or field laborers, while the majority of the Jamaicans transported were grooms.[117] As can be seen by the large number of transported Jamaicans and Barbadians who were skilled workers, compared with those who were field laborers or house servants, the argument can be made that those who were transported were the more dispensable components of the plantation economy. In addition, when the figures for the transported are examined, one can see that this form of punishment was the least popular of all punitive tactics employed, and it gradually fell into disuse.[118] Moreover, the passage of laws like the 1854 act to substitute other forms of punishment in place of transportation helped to hasten its demise. Citing the "difficulty of transporting offenders beyond the seas," penal confinement was put forward as the ideal successor to transportation.[119]

Even as transportation to the likes of Australia was discouraged, in the latter half of the nineteenth-century the intra-regional transportation of West Indian offenders found support from among some individuals who held the highest positions of authority in the colonies. For instance, John Pope Hennessy, who served as governor-in-chief of Barbados and the Windward Islands, in arguing for the advantages that the Confederation (a political organization intended to unite the Windward Islands and Barbados) would bring, stated in an address to the House of Assembly of Barbados: "I dwelt on the advantage of enabling the Chief Justice to sentence certain classes of criminals to transportation."[120] Hennessy's comment helps to reinforce the assertion that punishment in the British colonies was always mediated by ideas about race and the racialized body. Yes, transportation had proved over the long haul to be onerous for logistical reasons as well as for the colonies' coffers, but ideas about bodies and the places and the roles that they should occupy had also helped to shape the discourse and practices relating to transportation.

Conclusion

At the end of the apprenticeship system in Barbados and Jamaica in 1838, those who took stock of signs of progress by examining the legal system and its corporeal expression through the practical application of punishment must have been left pessimistic. On the one hand, there had been a significant shift in the administration of punishment in that it was moved out of the hands of plantation owners and placed in the hands of the state. Persisting, on the other hand, were the racist and classist ideologies that undergirded the ways punishment was levied. In this regard, although in some quarters there was recognition that punishment and discipline in the post-slavery era should be more "humane," the body—as in slavery—remained the focal point when thinking about, defining, and administering punishment, especially when it came to former slaves.

Moreover, in spite of the legal changes wrought by apprenticeship, the meanings ascribed to the bodies of blacks remained unchanged. As the evidence shows, the bodies of the former slaves continued to be coded as offensive, problematic, and suited primarily for brute labor. One way this was manifested was that the crimes that they committed were classified differently from the crimes committed by free persons. Lurking beneath this differential treatment was a discourse of corporeality that held that the bodies of the former slaves were not like other bodies, that blacks were fundamentally different from whites, and that punishment should be reflective of this.

In sum, therefore, it may be argued that freedom for the apprentices remained ambiguous at best, with their punished bodies providing the slate upon which ideas about their place in society was written. Thus, the era of apprenticeship, rather than serving as that period that signaled Barbados's and Jamaica's break with slavery and the devolution of black bodies to their rightful owners, may be more accurately described as a suture that linked the slavery era to the post-slavery period.

CHAPTER 3

The Entanglements of Freedom

Bodies of Laws and Their Role in the
Reinforcement of the Socio-racial Order

At the expiration of the apprenticeship system, all taint of a
former servile condition is to be forever obliterated, and a
condition of perfect legal equality is to succeed, comprising
within it, all the essential elements of constitutional freedom.

—LONDON ANTI-SLAVERY SOCIETY, *The*
Permanent Laws of the Emancipated Colonies

Do punish the blackguards well.

—LIEUTENANT COLONEL J. ELKINGTON

In his 1962 publication *How to Do Things with Words*, British philosopher
J. L. Austin makes the point that in some situations uttering a sentence "is to
do it."[1] A similar assertion is made in this chapter, which is based on the premise that the proclamation of laws relating to punishment and their codification
helped to reinforce the social position of black, brown, and white bodies, male
and female bodies, and elite and laboring bodies in post-1834 Jamaica and Barbados.[2] Thus, this chapter departs from the preceding chapter, which shows how
the practical application of punishments helped to reinforce the subaltern position of the working classes, to show how legislation could perform a similar
role. In this sense, the laws were "performative utterances" that not only named
crimes and their punishments but also *created* criminal and noncriminal bodies
and cemented pejorative ideas about blacks and their subaltern position in the
socio-racial pyramid.[3]

The idea that legislative utterances demarcated social boundaries while also
marking bodies is viewed first by looking at examples of what may be termed
"social order legislation" that sprang up in response to emancipation. Secondly,
I investigate how these ideas about bodies that were codified in the law were

"uttered," or expressed, on the bodies of those who were unlucky enough to feel the law's punitive application. In this latter regard, this chapter looks at "social ruptures" like emancipation, indenture, and the Morant Bay Rebellion to argue that the language used to name, report on, and respond to these social ruptures and their protagonists often borrowed from the same vocabulary and philosophy evident in legal discourses that designated some bodies as wayward, vagrant, idle, or criminal, among other things.

Performative Sentences

Lord Glenelg, one of the major protagonists in the execution of the Abolition Act, was of the opinion that emancipation held great promise.[4] In a dispatch he sent to the governors of the West Indies in November 1837 he stated: "The great cardinal principle of the law for the abolition of slavery is, that the apprenticeship of the emancipated slaves is to be immediately succeeded by personal freedom, in that full and unlimited sense of the term in which it is used in reference to the other subjects of the British Crown." He added, "The freedom to which I refer must of course, however, be that of men living in civil society, enjoying the franchises and performing the duty of citizens." Glenelg noted that previous colonial codes, now anachronistic, had to be considerably revised "to adapt them to the new state of affairs." He saw this as a task that should be carried out by the local legislatures, an important duty that he thought "should be performed with great circumspection, and in such a manner as, if possible, to prevent the necessity of any collision between the sovereign authority in this kingdom and the local authority in the several colonies."[5]

As simple as this may have seemed, the evidence shows that to throw off the raiment of master and instead wear the garb of an employer was not easy. Although Glenelg's words declared an imminent freedom for blacks, there was a disjuncture between his words and how they were applied on the ground. The narrative of blacks as always already problematic was crystallized in punitive acts, thus making Glenelg's utterances about "personal freedom" for ex-slaves ring hollow. Essentially, post-emancipation legislation and practices of punishment illustrated that there was a dual element to freedom. Freedom in Barbados and Jamaica had been proclaimed in the legal discourse, but it also had to be performed. However, in framing the laws, legislators often operated under the notion that there was a sizeable portion of the population who had to be chastened because of their supposedly congenital base temperaments and their resulting base actions. These ideas shaped how punishment was executed, even as it tainted the Barbadian and Jamaican laws. If it was not clear to all at the time, we now see a tension between utterances of freedom and post-emancipation legislation and punishment. Formerly enslaved people had to live with paradox.

Reading the laws of Barbados and Jamaica in the nineteenth century and examining the lives of those governed by these laws, one can see that emancipation did not bring about the full freedom that Glenelg and his cohorts intended. Indeed, full emancipation only further illuminated the socio-racial hierarchies that had been present during slavery. In the post-slavery period, individuals' positions in the law and their punishment for violations of law were based on a convoluted mix of ideas about their race, ethnicity, class, gender, and the roles that they performed in the plantation economy. Emancipation further highlighted the potency of difference that was pervasive in the British West Indies, with the bodies of black inhabitants providing the flesh upon which these ideas were realized.

With talk of emancipation in Barbados and Jamaica, one of the major concerns of the imperial officials in Britain, like the authorities on these two islands, was maintenance of law and order. This was evident in a dispatch by Glenelg to the governors of the British West Indies. He outlined in detail the new role of the formerly indispensable, if often ineffective, stipendiary magistrates:

> I have to inform you that Her Majesty's Government have felt that the continued employment, for a limited time, of at least a considerable number of the existing special magistrates, would greatly conduce to the peaceable and successful transition of the labouring population to a state of unqualified freedom; and I have, therefore, to convey to you authority, in the event of the termination of the apprenticeship by Act of the Local Legislature in the colony under your government, to retain so many of the special magistrates as you may consider necessary, and as may be willing to serve for a limited period.[6]

Although Glenelg acknowledged that their continued employment was temporary, he saw the stipendiary magistrates "exercising a concurrent jurisdiction with the ordinary magistracy."[7]

In Barbados, this role of stipendiary magistrates as enforcers of law and order was also supplemented by the appointment of black constables in rural areas. Along with reinforcing the predominance of men as the creators and executors of law and order, the appointment of these rural constables also had the effect of diffusing punitive power across the class and color divide. Under new law, two constables were to be appointed to every plantation occupied by one hundred laborers, while one constable was to be appointed to plantations that had less than one hundred workers.[8] One reason behind the appointment of these men of color to the constabulary was that colonial officials felt they would have more

legitimacy and command more authority than white constables.[9] The following quotation illustrates how widely power could be dispersed within draconian
societies, and it also shows that in societies where the black body was deprecated
as a matter of course, it could also be ascribed, at least superficially, with an elevated status that could serve to further subjugate other black bodies:

> This is a very necessary law, and its effects will be most beneficial. In the first
> place, it will tend to encourage and elevate the emancipated apprentice by in-
> vesting him with authority in his own plantation, and by putting him on a foot-
> ing of perfect equality with any other constable in the parish. In the next place,
> it will be the means of preserving the peace in the negro villages on each estate,
> and materially tend to check the spirit of litigation with which the negro charac-
> ter is strongly imbued, by the timely interference of a person to whose personal
> influence among the labourers on the different plantations the authority of this
> appointment will be added.
>
> Lastly, *it will at all times afford a small body of constables ready to act in case
> of any riot or combination for unlawful purposes, who, being taken from among the
> labourers themselves, will, be the most effective and least objectionable force to bring
> against them.* [emphasis added][10]

The role to be carried out by the rural constables was enacted first legally, then
verbally (in their recitation of the oath of office), and finally tangibly, as they
carried out the duties of their office. The oath, which was the second step in this
performance of law and order, went thusly:

> I. A. B., do swear that I will well and truly serve our Sovereign Lady the Queen,
> in the office of rural constable for the plantation or place called [_____] and as a
> constable generally for the parish or parishes of [_____], if need be, without fa-
> vour or affection, malice, or ill-will; and that I will to the best of my power cause
> the peace to be kept and preserved, and prevent all offences against the persons
> and properties of Her Majesty's subjects, and in all respects execute the duties of
> my said office to the best of my knowledge and ability. So help me God.[11]

In taking the oath and pledging to serve the queen, the black rural constable was
a state-approved irruption in the social order. The body of the black constable
was now cloaked in the authority given to him. His black body, stamped with the
state's approval, now symbolized order rather than disorder, and control rather
than impulsivity. Further, and ironically, whereas the stipendiary magistrates
had been criticized in some circles because of their racial affinity with the planters and the fear that they could not administer justice fairly, the rural constable's
racial similarity to the laboring classes was now seen as advantageous.

Yet seeing the appointment of black men to act as constables gives one only a superficial glimpse into the nature of punishment in Barbados. Even as their appointment suggests that emancipation had wrought revolutionary changes, the evidence shows that emancipation was most notable for its paradoxes. For one thing, even as the rural constables in Barbados pledged allegiance to the "Sovereign Lady the Queen," so too did emancipation reveal the ambivalent relationship between the metropole and its developing colonies. The rupture that was emancipation also brought with it calls for the colonies to break away from the mother country, like young children hankering for independence from omnipotent parents. At the onset of emancipation, the London Anti-Slavery Society cautioned legislators in the British West Indies against adopting laws from the mother country in toto. Society members argued that otherwise "the future liberties of the emancipated classes will be sapped, if at all, by unsuitable laws of home manufacture."[12] Indeed, C. T. Metcalfe, the governor of Jamaica in 1841, acknowledged in a dispatch to Lord Stanley that many laws had been passed in that colony "with a view to meet the change that has occurred in social relations of the inhabitants of [Jamaica], and to approximate the statutes of this country to those of England."[13] Metcalfe saw this mimicry in the Jamaican Act, which sought to govern relations between masters and servants. According to him, this particular law was framed "mostly in the same words as the English Act 4th Geo. 4 Ch. 34 Sec. 3."[14]

In spite of the local adaptation of imperial laws, and even as changes were made and laws were introduced that seemed to give a nod to the condition of "perfect legal equality," in many ways punitive practices in the British West Indies in the mid-nineteenth century hearkened back to the days of slavery. An example is seen in the efforts by Jamaican authorities to delimit the boundaries of acceptable behavior. These attempts to define order and punish those who transgressed these boundaries were ongoing concerns throughout the British West Indies even during slavery, but with the complete abolition of slavery they seemed to take on new relevance. In an 1838 dispatch that Glenelg sent from Downing Street to the governors of British Guiana, Trinidad, Saint Lucia, and Mauritius, he made it clear that laws regulating relations between masters and servants and those relating to vagrancy were of the utmost importance.[15]

The controversy between the metropole and its colonies notwithstanding, one area that the two agreed on unequivocally was that of dealing with vagrancy. Glenelg approached the issue from all possible angles. Firstly, he tackled the definition of vagrancy to remove what he perceived as its vagueness. To Glenelg, vagrancy threatened the social order and thus necessitated state intervention. Thus, he proffered a solution that used British legislators' definition of vagrancy, which he saw as germane to post-emancipation Jamaica. Based on Glenelg's assessment, the label "vagrant" was to be affixed to individuals who were "living in a state of vicious and unnecessary idleness, without any honest means of subsistence, and who therefore become burdensome to society as paupers, or dangerous to the public peace by their demeanour, those who seek their living by dishonest arts," practiced "vulgar superstitions," or had the intent to "commit depredations on property." Since the West Indies could no longer rely on the "domestic authority of the employer," Glenelg thought it expedient that an Order in Council would be able to protect the colonial societies against vagrancy. Those branded under this law were to be punished by imprisonment with hard labor, to be carried out either in a space of confinement or in the "public streets or highways."[16]

In post-emancipation Barbados too, laws relating to vagrancy became the measuring stick by which some persons were adjudged punishable. What was also significant about these laws is that they criminalized some of the *spaces* occupied by the black Barbadian laboring classes along with some of their activities. One of the first acts that helped to manufacture a criminal class was the "Act to Punish and Suppress Vagrancy, and to Determine Who Are Vagrants, Rogues, and Vagabonds, and Incorrigible Rogues and Vagabonds."[17] This act not only became the legal barometer that measured a specific kind of criminality, it also provided that those who had the misfortune of falling under its purview could be sentenced to hard labor in a house of correction for up to a year. Despite the entreaties of the London Anti-Slavery Society not to adopt laws from the metropole, the law was an adaptation of "Act 5 Geo. 4, c. 83" of Britain, with its first, second, third, fourth, and fifth clauses corresponding with the third, fourth, fifth, sixth, and seventh clauses of the British act.[18] Such legislation in Barbados was clearly not enacted to ensure justice for former slaves. Rather, it had classist and racist subtexts. Based on this law, only a certain class of blacks could be considered respectable.

> The reason for this alteration is that in the first place there are no such houses of entertainment and reception as those pointed out by the Imperial Act in this colony; and in the next, the evil intended to be provided against by this clause, while it will exist to a considerable extent, will chiefly take place in the negro villages, and they will themselves be the chief victims of it; for while the industrious are at their work the "rogues" will take that opportunity to enter their houses and steal their clothes, or their poultry, pigs, and sheep, in which their property chiefly consists. This system has already commenced, and the respectable class of negroes have great apprehensions on this subject.[19]

Under this act to punish and suppress vagrancy, "pedlars," prostitutes, and generally any person who was defined as able-bodied but who was not engaging in constructive labor could be punished. In the delineation of this act there was the specter of the body. Essentially, individuals were deemed to be flouting the law if their bodies were not being used for what was termed acceptable labor. Perhaps not surprisingly the stipulated punishment was also corporeal in nature: those convicted under this act were to be committed to a house of correction for up to one month.[20]

These concerns with controlling the bodies of the subaltern classes and delimiting the boundaries they could traverse were also exemplified in "An Act for the Punishment of Idle and Disorderly Persons, Rogues and Vagabonds, and Incorrigible Rogues," which was passed in Jamaica on December 5, 1839.[21] Persons who could be prosecuted for breaching this law were defined as persons who were "wholly or in part" able to maintain themselves and their dependents but refused to do so and instead depended on charity. Prostitutes and beggars, who by dint of their activities rendered themselves "disorderly" and "idle," were to be prosecuted under this act. In fact the law was all-encompassing and called for prosecuting almost every misdemeanor imaginable, from breaking and entering, practicing obeah and myalism, and indulging in gaming, to indecent exposure.[22] From the variety of possible transgressions proscribed, one can see that Jamaican legislators attempted to provide for the probable bodily and spiritual transgressions likely to be committed by black Jamaicans in the post-emancipation period. Punishment for contravening this act could be rendered by any justice of the peace, who was empowered to commit the offender to a house of correction for a maximum of ten days. The offender could be apprehended by any constable, police officer, or officer of the peace.

Another example of Jamaican colonial officials' preoccupation with preserving social order and controlling assembled bodies is "An Act for Preventing Tumults and Riotous Assemblies, and for the More Speedily and Effectually Punishing the Rioters."[23] Passed in Jamaica in 1842, this act made it illegal for twelve or more persons to be "riotously" and "tumultuously" assembled together to disturb the public peace. The penalty for infringing this act was harsh. Those convicted were liable, "at the discretion of the court," to be transported for life (or for not less than ten years) or to be imprisoned for any term not exceeding three years.[24] Closely related to the specific crime of riot was the more general offense of "breach of the peace," which historian Jonathan Dalby notes included riot, rebellion, "causing a disturbance," "riotous assembly," and affray. From an examination of the assize court records of Jamaica between 1756 and 1856, Dalby noted that 456 individuals were indicted for breaching the peace.[25] In a similar vein, "An Act for Regulating the Police of the Town of Port Royal, and of Wherries, Canoes, and Other Boats Plying for Fare and Freight, to Authorise the Sale of Certain Lands, and for Other Purposes" also instituted rules to govern individual and group comportment. Individuals in Port Royal who flouted this law by being drunk or behaving in a loose, disorderly, riotous, or indecent manner, especially those who disturbed the public peace between the hours of nine at night and six in the morning, could be fined a maximum of three pounds sterling or be imprisoned in the common jail or house of correction for a maximum of twenty days, with or without hard labor.[26]

Similar laws were passed in Barbados. Under the fourth clause of "An Act for Preventing Tumults and Riotous Assemblies, and for the More Speedy[,] Effectual Punishing of the Rioters," offenders could be sentenced to transportation from fifteen years to life, or they could be imprisoned for up to three years.[27] In this case, the sentence of transportation can be viewed as the excessive reaction of an increasingly anachronistic planter class. Even Glenelg seemed to think that the punishment of transportation was inappropriate in this instance. In reviewing Act 667, "An Act for Preventing Tumults and Riotous Assemblies," he implored Barbadian authorities to refrain from resorting to this sentence as far as possible, saying, "It is not desirable to increase the list of offences for which this penalty may be inflicted."[28]

These post-emancipation laws sought to control potentially disruptive bodies and behavior that seemed to compromise the social order, and they were certainly enforced. In a report submitted by Barbados magistrates in 1839, it is recorded that from June 1 to June 15 twenty-one individuals had been punished by the justices for the parish of St. Michael—Moore, Hendy, and Gill—for a range of crimes, including "disorderly conduct in the streets," keeping more gunpowder in town than was allowed, and theft.[29] Likewise, as the justice for the parish of St. Andrew, Nathaniel Roach punished four people—three men and one woman—for destruction of property, using obscene and vulgar language, and "challenging to fight."[30] Between July 16 and July 31, 1839, the justices for St. Michael punished seventy-eight people after dismissing fourteen of the appeals that were brought before them. The nature of offenses for which these seventy-eight individuals were punished included taking sand away from the beach, assault and battery, theft, and "[l]oose and disorderly conduct in the streets." The punishments inflicted included fines and imprisonment with hard labor. In addition, in the parish of Christ Church, judgments were upheld for fourteen of the twenty-three individuals who lodged appeals before Justice Samson W. Waith. These individuals were to be awarded punishments that included fines, imprisonment with hard labor, and sureties to keep the peace.[31]

The appeals brought before Justice Waith, like James Williams's narrative and the desertion during the apprenticeship system, could be read as acts that challenged the corporality inherent in the system of punishment during the apprenticeship system. This contention is especially compelling when one notes that individuals who lost judgments in the Courts of Appeal in Barbados could be punished in multiple ways for their challenges and outspokenness. The example of Rosey Sample of Barbados is a case in point. Accused by police magistrates Hendy and Moore as being a "loose," idle, and disorderly character who had been fighting in the streets, Sample was sentenced to one month of imprisonment with hard labor in the county jail. Obviously disagreeing with this judgment on some level, Sample lodged an appeal that was heard in the appeals court sitting August 16–31, 1839. The police magistrates' judgment being upheld, Sample's punishment of imprisonment with hard labor was not only sustained, she was also forced to pay the thirteen-shilling cost of the appeal.[32] A similar situation obtained in the case of Sample's countryman Jack Williams, who was also sentenced by Hendy, the superintendent of police, to imprisonment with hard labor "for being riotous and disorderly in the streets." Williams too not only lost his freedom for ten days for being found guilty but also had to pay eleven shillings for his unsuccessful bid to overturn the original judgment against him.[33]

It was not just in the wider society or in the streets of Bridgetown, Barbados, that individuals could be arrested and charged with disorderly conduct. The plantation too provided the setting for the exercise of laws relating to social order. For example, as acting police magistrate, Samson W. Waith was responsible for forcibly removing from the workplace Anco Patience for "disorderly and contumacious behaviour in the Field."[34] In another case, Mary Princess, a laborer on the Alleynedale Hall Estate, was sentenced to be ejected from the estate because of the actions of her husband. According to a report submitted by police magistrate J. T. Corbin, Princess's husband, a laborer on a different estate, had been rude "and otherwise guilty of riotous and disorderly conduct" on the Alleynedale Hall Estate. Obviously interpreting to the extreme the oath that husbands and wives were yoked to each other, and perhaps fearful that if Princess continued to work there that her husband would return to the plantation and be disruptive, R. A. Alleyne, the proprietor of the estate, had declared that she would have to leave the estate in a week's time. Corbin, however, displaying more restraint than Alleyne, recommended "an accommodation," and at the time of his report some two months after the ruling in April, Princess was still working on the estate.[35]

An examination of Jamaica's criminal codes, like the acts that sought to regulate social conduct, also gives important insight into that country's disciplinary philosophy and lends credence to the assertion that while the response to the 1865 Morant Bay Rebellion was excessive, it was representative of a general climate of autocracy that was pervasive in the plantation economy after 1834. By looking at the 1877 "Draft of a Criminal Code and a Code of Criminal Procedure for the Island of Jamaica" it can be seen that the colony continued to rely on corporal punishment well beyond 1838 and long after Glenelg had made lofty promises that people emancipated from slavery would enjoy freedom akin to that of others under the rule of the British Crown.[36] For example, the punishments that could be inflicted under this code included death, imprisonment, flogging (with cat-o'-nine-tails), and whipping (with a rod or cane), along with fines, "disqualification for offices of public trust on conviction for felony," and "liability to police supervision."[37]

Moreover, although these punishments appear to be delineated in gender-neutral tones, elaboration in latter parts of the document show that they were to be administered in a gendered fashion. Even though the pronouns used in referring to punishments that could be given under the 1877 draft criminal code were often gender neutral, the "person" to whom the section on corporal punishment referred, as a case in point, was male—females could not be whipped or flogged under this code. In this sense, it could be argued that the 1877 draft criminal code helped to reinscribe the importance of gender in the organization of post-emancipation Jamaica.

Further, by making a distinction between whipping and flogging, this code made claims about the bodies of children ("juveniles") vis-à-vis adults, even as the act of flogging infantilized adult males. Flogging, the harsher of the two sentences, was not to be inflicted on individuals under sixteen years of age; instead, they were to be whipped. These whippings were to be inflicted "with a light rod or cane."[38] By way of comparison, flogging was to be done with a cat-o'-nine-tails, which was supposed to be "of such a pattern as is for the time approved by the Governor of Jamaica," with the amount of lashes not to exceed fifty.[39]

The mitigation of punishment was based on other factors besides gender and age, most notably race and color, and these too found expression in the draft criminal code. In considering general exemptions to punishment, the draft criminal code questioned whether infancy should be used as a "ground of exemption from criminal liability." This section of the draft criminal code demonstrated that its framer saw crime as something engaged in by "coloured races" as an inherent part of their makeup but something to which whites only succumbed: "Infancy as a ground of exemption from criminal liability appears to require no comment, except that it may be a question for those who are acquainted with coloured races whether any difference in the limits of age should be made in their case on the ground of precocity." To his credit, the framer of the code acknowledged, however, that "there might be some difficulty in the way of applying different rules to white and coloured persons."[40]

It is also important to note that, as set out in this draft criminal code, flogging was "mainly a punishment of torture" whereas whipping was "mainly a punishment of indignity." The draft code explained "firstly, that where the lesser punishment will suffice, it is inexpedient to inflict the greater, and whipping may probably be found as effectual as floggings with any but hardened offenders; secondly, that the public are more likely to be tolerant of the infliction of the less severe punishment; and, thirdly, that it is inexpedient to make the mind of the public familiar with the idea of physical cruelty even to criminals, a reason which may perhaps be regarded as sentimental, but which is not necessarily based on any sympathy with the criminal."[41]

Yet corporal punishment was not as easily resolved as the 1877 draft criminal code suggests. The efficacy and ethics of corporal punishment were always moot. For instance, in the closing pages of this draft, the frequency and effectiveness of corporal punishment were debated. One key argument that was put forward in this regard was that corporal punishment employed too often lost its power to terrorize. However, an alternate view was advanced that "bodily pain must continue to be an object of certain and effective fear even when the particular form of infliction ceases to be novel."[42]

This body-punishment philosophy would continue to drive punitive practices in both Jamaica and Barbados. An examination of the 1892 Obeah and Myalism Acts Amendment Law of Jamaica supports this contention. It stipulates that any person convicted before any resident magistrate could be sentenced to imprisonment with or without hard labor for a maximum of six months.[43] To augment the imprisonment, however, a more direct assault on the body could be rendered in the form of flogging, which could mean a total of thirty-nine lashes being inflicted on the "bare back" with a cat-o'-nine-tails. An amendment was made to this law on April 28, 1892, that limited to nine the number of lashes that could be inflicted on those under sixteen years of age, while those sixteen and over could receive up to eighteen lashes.[44] Those convicted for offenses against the person could receive between ten and thirty-nine lashes with the cat-o'-nine-tails. Those under the age of sixteen years could receive a maximum of eighteen lashes "with a rod composed of tamarind or other switches."[45] Under Jamaica's Law 8 of 1896, the "Juvenile Offenders Law," persons between the ages of ten and sixteen were liable to be whipped, with these whippings being inflicted within five days of the order being given. These lashes could total up to thirty-six with a tamarind rod.[46]

From a reading of the laws, one can see that the importance of the body as a site of punishment continued right up to the end of the nineteenth century, as did some of the earlier concerns about the maintenance of social order. As a case in point, some fifty-six years after full emancipation, "predial larceny" continued to be viewed as a threat, as seen with the passage of Law 38 in Jamaica in 1896, the Praedial Larceny Law. This enacted that any "suspected person" in possession of agricultural produce, from a list including plantains, cassava, annatto, and garden vegetables, was to be detained in custody until an investigation was completed. If convicted of larceny and if found to be vagrant or idle, the accused was sentenced to be whipped.[47]

The harsh punitive approaches adopted in response to predial larceny in Barbados and Jamaica were consistent with how crimes appearing to threaten the plantation economy were dealt with. Writing on nineteenth-century Jamaica, Patrick Bryan sees the law as being at its "most intimidatory" with regard to predial larceny, although he was quick to point out that even though the crime was sometimes attributed to hunger or "ignorance," it would be "naïve to assume that people stole only to supply immediate nourishment." He added that "some evidence points to the marketability of stolen produce as a major incentive to predial larceny, including citrus, logwood and pimento, all export commodities. As a planter, Mr. Gossett emphasized, his grapefruits were never touched until a market for them appeared in the United States."[48] Be that as it may, hunger was a real problem for the laboring classes in Jamaica and Barbados, and this hunger did lead some individuals to commit crimes. Members of the commission appointed to investigate the Morant Bay Rebellion in the 1860s found that social and environmental conditions like hunger and drought had contributed to the increase in predial larceny in Jamaica prior to the outbreak of the rebellion.[49] In any case, punishment for this crime was doled out with a "broad brush" approach, not appearing to account for the fact that some of those engaged in the theft of food crops and livestock could have been motivated by hunger. In Barbados in 1898, Hilary Beckles notes, nineteen people were arrested for having taken part in a "potato raid" on Bowmanston Plantation in St. John, with provisions stolen to provide "several days' sustenance."[50] Beckles defines earlier potato raids as "a form of predial larceny in which workers expressed the ideological notion of 'justified appropriation'"—which he sees as having resulted from poverty.[51]

Whether dealing with crimes like predial larceny or other infractions, the landscape of punishment in Barbados was dynamic. The *Barbados Blue Book* of 1898 shows that along with various corporal punishments, fines were also a popular sanction given to Barbadians who had transgressed the laws. For example, the payment of fines was the most popular judgment rendered in "Offences against Revenue Acts, Highway Acts, Health Acts, and other Acts relating to the social Economy of the Colony." Imprisonment in lieu of fine and peremptory imprisonment were the two most popular punishments after fines. Whipping was fourth and was most widely used against those who had committed predial larceny. In 1898 there were 1,120 Barbadians convicted of predial larceny, and 310 were imprisoned in lieu of fine or surety, 288 were fined, 277 were whipped, and 230 were peremptorily imprisoned. These figures show that 24.7 percent of those convicted under this offense were whipped, with 25.7 percent being fined. W. Herbert Greaves, the attorney general in Barbados, noted that the total punishments of whipping inflicted that year were 684, with boys under the age of sixteen bearing the brunt of these. He noted that imprisonment and whipping were two methods used to punish juvenile offenders. Greaves also noted: "The imposition of a penalty in the large majority of cases is equivalent to imprisonment because in default of payment imprisonment is imposed by the Act under which the order is made, and because the parent is either unable or unwilling to pay the fine. It will, I think, be generally conceded that whipping, inflicted as it is in this Colony with a comparatively slight tamarind whip, is preferable to imprisonment as a means of punishment."[52]

Although the numbers for whipping may seem unremarkable—and Greaves's comments may appear compassionate—when assessed in combination with the sentencing of imprisonment, one can see that punishments that either directly or indirectly assaulted the body were most often employed for offenses described as "prevalent in the sugar-growing and Coolie-importing Colonies . . . of robbing provision grounds and homesteads." By comparison, what can arguably be seen as the more serious crimes of assault and "other Offences against the Person" were fined, with only 169 of the 1,622 convicted under this offense being whipped.[53]

The post-1838 period in Barbados and Jamaica, it is evident, resembled the past. Although laws may have heralded that a change in social relations would follow, it was not a time of legal equality for all without regard to skin color. Whipping was still common, and corporal punishment continued to be handed down in classist, raced, and gendered fashions. In November 1899 the Regulation of Whipping Act was passed in Barbados, but though this act sought to reduce the number of strokes to be inflicted on offenders, its very existence shows that punishment was still apprehended in somatic terms. Under this act it was stipulated that offenders under sixteen years of age were to receive a maximum of twelve strokes for offenses, while those over sixteen could receive up to twenty-four lashes.[54] Although the act did not stipulate what offenses were punishable under its precepts and whether both men and women could be whipped, it made clear that the body-punishment relation continued in Barbados at the dawn of the twentieth century. The story remained quite similar in Jamaica, where the punishment of whipping was still on the books. Law 4 of 1900, the Whipping Law Amendment, stipulated that every person sentenced to be whipped in the district where the offense had been committed was to be whipped in prison. This mode of corporal punishment was for certain cases of larceny and other offenses.[55]

Bodily Ruptures in the Post-emancipation Social Order

Although an examination of the post-emancipation laws shows that ex-slaves continued to be harshly punished for breaking the laws in Jamaica, so were other subaltern groups recruited to the island from Asia, Africa, and Europe between 1845 and 1916, mostly to work on plantations in parishes like St. Thomas in the East, Clarendon, and St. Andrew.[56] Their presence also demonstrated that some Jamaican ex-slaves had been successful in removing themselves from the governance of their former masters. This and other social ruptures, including rebellions, provided another testing ground for the ideologies that undergirded legislation. Moreover, although the ruptures may have been new, there was already a rich vocabulary and a wellspring of practices upon which legislators and the executors of punishment could draw to deal with situations that threatened the smooth running of the plantation economy and concomitantly the fabric of the society. Additionally, the ways colonial officials and state agents responded to these ruptures show that maintenance of order and the socio-racial structure were important.

After the abolition of slavery in 1838, Jamaica, unlike Barbados, experienced a shortage of plantation laborers, as many former slaves moved away from plantations and established their own communities.[57] The answer to the labor crisis, it was thought, lay in the importation of workers who could fill the void.[58] Indentured laborers from India, China, Africa, Europe, and elsewhere immigrated to Jamaica in the post-emancipation period.[59] This influx altered the social landscape of the colony—many of the newcomers stood out as different—and resulted in new laws that regulated relations between employer and worker and even regulated the lives of laborers more generally. As a case in point, in 1850 indenture contracts stipulated that on arrival in the colony the immigrants were to be indentured for a period of three years, and by 1860 the duration of the contracts had been increased to five years.[60] While indentured on a plantation, these workers were to receive lodging, medical attention, and wages from their employers.[61] They were required to work six days a week, nine hours a day, with the exception of Sundays, Good Friday, and Christmas Day. Male indentured workers over sixteen years of age were to be paid a minimum of one shilling per day, whereas those between twelve and sixteen were to be paid nine pence. Female indentured laborers, regardless of age, were to also to be paid nine pence.[62] Most of these immigrants worked on plantations in St. Thomas in the East, Clarendon, and St. Andrew.[63]

East Indian immigrants were especially visible. Governor George Grey alluded to this in a reference to the "desertion and vagrancy of a large number of Coolie labourers" from plantations in that colony, an exodus that concerned local officials.[64] In fact, their condition elicited concern from Grey, who noticed that a significant number of them were destitute and diseased. Although Grey was "fully sensible of the objections which might be urged against the policy of subsisting these persons at the public expense," the "Coolies," he wrote, were "now so generally impoverished, and the evils arising from their inveterate idleness extending so fearfully in all directions, that the question of the immediate moment is what can be done to secure them from starvation."[65] Grey's Dickensian portrait of the Indian workers suggests that Jamaican legislators would have been equally concerned, whether that had to do mostly with "vagrancy" and begging or with the very sight of their distressed bodies.[66]

As an island that, from a reading of its laws, was fixated on social order and as a society that abhorred idleness, post-emancipation Jamaica found itself grappling with the problem of disorder among the same bodies that were supposed to ease the island's economic turmoil. Immigrants' allegedly deleterious impact on Jamaican society was reported in newspapers like the *Falmouth Post* and *Morning Journal*. In the latter, for instance, it was reported that East Indian laborers in St. Thomas in the East were "almost in a state of nudity." This attention to the bodies of the immigrants continues in a quoted description by someone who said that the immigrants were "crowd[ing] the highways and places of public resort, in the last and worst stages of destitution, squalor, filth, disease, and dejection." This image of the "begging Coolies" was said to be evident throughout the island's other parishes.[67]

East Indian immigrant workers certainly broke some of Jamaica's laws regarding offenses against property, as was evident in comments attributed to Stipendiary Magistrate George W. Gordon. In a dispatch to the secretary of the colonies, Gordon noted that a number of "coolie" laborers had been brought before him for stealing. However, the men had been "let loose again on society" because they could not be provided with an interpreter.[68]

Jamaican colonial authorities also found themselves grappling with issues considered peculiar to East Indian workers, the most notable of which was the problem of uxoricide—the murder of wives. Besides crafting a discourse about the jealousy of East Indian males to explain the murders of Indian women by their spouses, the Jamaican government responded also by passing Law 26 of 1896 to deal with the problem.[69] This law stipulated that any person threatening a wife or any other woman was liable to be imprisoned for one month.[70] Further, it empowered any woman who feared for her safety by granting her the right for transfer from her estate. Although this law appeared to offer protection to women, it was a reductionist gesture to a problem that was more complex than a wife being threatened by a spouse. Scholars like Michele Johnson writing on Jamaica, Prabhu P. Mohapatra writing on British Guiana, and David V. Trotman writing on Trinidad advance several reasons to explain uxoricide in the nineteenth-century British West Indies.[71] The skewed male-to-female ratio that put a premium on East Indian women in the society, the patriarchal orientation of the plantation economy that devalued nonwhite women as a matter of course, and the violent and draconian nature of the society are all seen as helping produce a milieu conducive to the prevalence of uxoricide. Considering this, one can see that Law 26 was a mere bandage to a deeper problem. Moreover, the responses to the problem of uxoricide—imprisonment of perpetrators for a mere four weeks—endangered women who had to apply to be removed from their estate, suggesting that the maintenance of the plantation system fueled the law's passage, not the protection of the immigrant women.

Likewise, the presence of Chinese workers also called for greater negotiation within the social and political landscapes of Jamaica. The introduction and popularity of a Chinese lottery certainly challenged the country's laws relating to assembly, gaming, and morality. One could argue, for instance, that the laws that allowed for the prosecution of those deemed vagrant and "loose" could be easily manipulated to include the crowds of "idle vagabonds" and "slatternly women" that the lottery was said to attract.[72]

Even if immigrants were spared persecution and prosecution in the course of pursuing their leisure activities, they could still be easily labeled as criminals in other contexts. The image of destitute, uncontrolled, and unregulated bodies of indentured laborers wandering about the Jamaican landscape and flouting the island's moral codes is not the one that dominates the discourses of the day. More typical is the immigrant body that is very much like the body of the slave and the apprentice, subject to stringent punitive and disciplinary control. Laws relating to indentured workers reinforced the reason for their presence on the island in the first place, and they confirmed the importance of the plantation as that site that gave meaning to their bodies, particularly in relation to other bodies. Punishments of indentured immigrants who committed infractions while on the job were like those experienced by Jamaican slaves and apprentices, as was the fact that the immigrants often "had limited recourse against improper treatment."[73]

Many of the punishments meted out to indentured immigrants were also corporeal, thus illustrating the idea that punitive tactics had a way of homogenizing working bodies in both the pre- and post-emancipation periods along with shoring up the socio-racial hierarchy. This assessment is supported by evidence from Monica Schuler's work that deals with the experiences of African indentured workers in Jamaica. Not only did she show that the employment of whipping for labor offenses was common, she also showed that its use as a method of punishment remained virtually unchallenged even in the post-emancipation period. Schuler described how immigrant laborers from Treadways Plantation were whipped with various instruments including "supple jacks," horsewhips, sticks, and switches. According to her, these examples of whipping were neither isolated nor rare. Schuler noted that an investigation carried out by David Ewart, a "colored" proprietor from St. Thomas in the East, revealed that the previous manager of Harbour Head Estate, a Mr. Kerr, had been discharged for mismanaging the plantation. During his tenure as estate manager, Kerr had been responsible for "order[ing] the estate's black ranger to whip two Africans for sitting down on the job, eating canes, refusing to return to work, resisting the ranger, and fleeing when he attempted to seize the canes."[74]

Schuler's example of the Harbour Head Estate reveals the complexities of power and punishment in post-emancipation Jamaica. The presence of the "colored" proprietor Ewart shows that although plantations themselves were generally spaces of white male hegemony, this was not always the case. Also, the example of the black "ranger" whipping laborers of African origin shows that even within the black community there was a "power order" that helped to sustain the plantation economy.[75] Thus, ethnic and racial boundaries could be manipulated at will as the likely Jamaican Creole Ewart was ascribed with power over the non-native African laborer.

Even as Ewart's presence at the apex of a plantation and the example of the black ranger disrupt standard notions of who typically held power within the plantation economy, the example of the African laborers "sitting down on the job, eating canes, refusing to return to work, resisting the ranger, and fleeing when he attempted to seize the canes" also illustrates the futility of attempts at total dominion over the bodies of the working classes. The multiple transgressions committed by the African laborers are displays of agentic behavior, particularly as it is apparent that they were aware of the controls that were in place to stem such displays. Also, the example of the insubordinate laborers invites comparison with the activities of individuals who, like Bruno Bettelheim, have found ways to express their subjectivity even in authoritarian environments. Bettelheim noted that his ability to survive imprisonment in Nazi concentration camps in 1938 and 1939 was because he "became convinced that these dreadful and degrading experiences were somehow not happening to 'me' as a subject, but only to 'me' as an object."[76] Although it is impossible to know whether the African indentured workers engaged in a similar rationalization, what is evident from their actions, as in Bettelheim's case, is that "the body itself [can be] involved in varying and shifting constructions of agency."[77]

Like those indentured workers of African origin, immigrants from the East Indies also found that their employers sought to dominate their bodies through coercive and punitive legislation and practices. Literally and figuratively their bodies were circumscribed as workers and inhabitants of their new home.[78] Rules within the workplace determined the extent of their mobility—both inside and outside of the plantation. The continuities here between slavery and apprenticeship are noteworthy. Like the black slaves and apprentices, East Indian laborers were valued primarily as workers, and when they were punished it was mostly in ways that attacked the very bodies with which their worth was judged. Venturing beyond the boundaries of the estate meant that a pass was required. An even more serious charge than that of leaving the estate without a pass was outright desertion. Those convicted as deserters could be made to pay a fine of five pounds sterling, or they could be imprisoned for thirty days. Other crimes that indentured immigrants could be convicted of included malingering or being indolent at work, governed by Jamaica's Law 23 of 1879.[79] Furthermore, East Indian laborers from Friendship and Spring Garden Plantations and others from estates in Hanover, Jamaica, were routinely subjected to corporal punishments for a variety of infractions—many of them work-related.[80] For instance, Harinder Sohal points out that Indian laborers from Hanover were sentenced to fourteen days' hard labor in the district prison for being absent from work.[81] By comparison, employers were seldom convicted of crimes committed against immigrants—a discrepancy many scholars have noted.[82]

The treatment of indentured immigrants in other parts of the British West Indies also helps to reinforce the assertion that even with the shift in the ethnicity of the laboring body, that punishing the body was one tactic that reinforced the position of laborers—particularly in relation to the elite classes—and solidified the power of the plantation economy. This theme about the meeting of the body and punishment comes out in the work of Madhavi Kale, where she examines the system of indenture in British Guiana. Writing about one incident of flogging on the Vreed-en-Hoop Estate, Kale delineates a system of punishment that was reminiscent of punishments of blacks during slavery. In one notable example,

Henry Jacobs, an interpreter for the Indians on the plantations, was alleged to have ordered a flogging of workers. It was said that the driver Monobud had severely conducted the flogging with a cat-o'-nine-tails, resulting in the workers' backs being severely cut. Although they had been taken to the "Sick House" after this beating, this space seemed to offer them little respite as their wounds were "washed with Salt and Water." Jacobs was prosecuted for his role in this assault, forced to pay a fine of twenty pounds sterling, and ordered to be confined for a month in the jail in Georgetown, "with provision for further imprisonment if the fine was not paid."[83] What is remarkable about Jacobs's punishment is the fact that he was white. Despite so evidently few prosecutions against whites for assaulting people of color, his conviction—and confinement—shows that white proprietors could actually be punished by corporal means for assaults against laborers.

This intersection of the work space and the criminal courts—particularly as experienced by indentured workers—was remarked upon by George William Des Voeux, who served as a magistrate in Demerara, British Guiana, between 1863 and 1869. Des Voeux contended that the majority of the complaints heard in the courts were for breaches of labor laws and that, not surprisingly, the majority of those against whom complaints were brought were immigrants and free laborers. In pointing out how widely and how deeply the tentacles of the law reached, Des Voeux wrote: "The law had been so framed and its net, covering all possible offences, was woven so closely that not even the smallest peccadilloes could escape its meshes; so that, in fact, the manager, whenever a labourer annoyed him, had almost always in reserve some trifling neglect or other legally defined offence on which he could bring a complaint involving fine or imprisonment with hard labour, or both."[84]

In spite of this, the immigration laws stipulated that a government officer was to be appointed "with a special duty of protecting the immigrants from ill-usage."[85] Moreover, the colonial governments were empowered to cancel any contract in cases of misconduct by master or servant. In addition, estates that employed East Indian immigrants were to be visited periodically by an immigration agent who was empowered to enquire into complaints, and this agent was required to report periodically to the governor of the colony.[86] One can see the similarities between the immigration agent and the stipendiary magistrate. What can also be gleaned from this is that administrators clearly saw the need to protect immigrants from abuse. Furthermore, they saw the need to appoint agents to act as arbitrators between two groups whose goals were diametrically opposed. In response, laws were passed to address all possible areas of friction between the immigrants and their employers. One notable example is the law that stipulated that employers "ill-using" their employees were liable to be fined up to forty-eight dollars, sentenced to imprisonment with or without hard labor for up to two months, or both.[87] Based on the punishments of indentured immigrants and the laws governing their lives, one can see that they occupied a liminal position between slavery and freedom, and as such they stood on a shaky precipice between criminality and lawfulness.[88]

It could be said, therefore, that the climate of draconian punishment that was pervasive during slavery was also present in the post-emancipation period. As a case in point, Trotman points out that "just as slavery was violent, so too its successor, indentureship, was a system that demanded physical violence and was replete with cases of cruel coercion. The whip was as commonly used as a mechanism for labor persuasion as it had been in the worst days of slavery. . . . Indentured laborers could be whipped and coerced with impunity, and all kinds of violence [were] used against the bodies of those who found themselves bound to labor on the plantations."[89] To support this argument, he cited cases where both male and female immigrants in Trinidad had been severely punished for wrongdoing. Trotman cites the example of Sahti, who died fourteen days after being beaten by the son of the estate proprietor to whom she was indentured in Trinidad. For his part in the beating, the estate proprietor's son got off scot-free, since the coroner determined that Sahti had died of natural causes.[90]

In spite of the legal and punitive strictures placed on East Indian indentured immigrants to reinforce their social status, they, like indentured workers of other ethnicities, did not refrain from engaging in agentic behavior within the spaces in which they were constrained. Sohal cites the case of immigrants on the Belvedere Estate in St. Thomas, Jamaica, who attacked the sub-agent, a Mr. Hoskins, for sentencing one of their fellow workers for breach of indenture. The immigrants involved in this fracas were sentenced to terms of imprisonment ranging from three to twelve months.[91]

Indenture and the discordant bodies of immigrants were not the only phenomena that tested Jamaican elites' ability to enforce their brand of law and order. Indeed, acute ruptures of the society itself provided a test for disciplinary and punitive ideologies. For instance, the ruling classes' response to the Morant Bay Rebellion in Jamaica provides one of the more extreme examples that highlight sharply the position of the black laboring body as a degraded object and efforts to maintain the socio-racial order. The Morant Bay Rebellion reveals how the black body symbolically and tangibly became a contested site for power—both in the grasp of a dissipating power by the plantocracy and as an assertion of working-class autonomy. The "swift and brutal" response to this rebellion demonstrated a convoluted mixture of contempt and fear held by the ruling classes for the Jamaican proletariat.[92] After the Morant Bay Rebellion, punishment was the machinery used to terrorize, exact retribution, serve as an example, punish, repress, and assert control over the black body, all at the same time.[93] The reprisals also demonstrated how racist and classist ideologies could find real expression in the execution of the law—legislation that was antagonistic toward the laboring classes and at odds with the spirit of the Abolition Act of 1833 and equality.

The rebellion started on October 11, 1865, when approximately four hundred blacks "marched into the town of Morant Bay."[94] These blacks, with Paul Bogle as their leader, represented only a small fraction of those who were unhappy with socio-economic conditions and the Jamaican judicial system, dissatisfaction that had been registered as early as the 1850s.[95] The sluice-gates that had kept this dissatisfaction in check had been opened earlier in 1865 with the Colonial Office's negative response to a petition of St. Ann's blacks for land to farm.[96] Upon reaching Morant Bay, the disgruntled protesters "plundered the local police station of its fire-arms and presented themselves at the Court House where the vestry were meeting."[97] In the mêlée that ensued, the school and adjoining courthouse were burned down, and Baron von Ketelhodt, the custos (principal magistrate of the parish), and other government officials were killed. Over the next three days, the rebellion spread to other parts of the island, including the Plantain Garden River district, Manchioneal, and Elmwood.[98]

Colonial governor Edward John Eyre responded to rioting in Morant Bay by declaring martial law, thereby suspending the ordinary law in eastern Jamaica. British troops and a Maroon organization were called on to deal with the outbreak. When the smoke cleared, approximately four hundred blacks had been killed, about six hundred had been flogged, at least one thousand houses owned by the peasantry had been destroyed, and entire villages had been razed.[99] The destruction and retaliation that had been sanctioned by the government entailed 20 percent of the parish's population being made homeless. Villages including Somerset, Fort, and Stony Gut "were burnt out of existence."[100] The annihilation of black villages—Stony Gut was described as that of Paul Bogle's—was intentional: Colonel J. Francis Hobbs had issued orders to have the "rebellious settlement [Stony Gut] . . . utterly destroyed."[101] Through the destruction of the houses owned by the peasantry and the villages in which they lived, one can see that not only had rebellious ideologies been attacked but so also had the body of a group of people: the villages were examples of black self-extension. In explaining how an attack on physical objects could be simultaneously an attack on a body of people—a civilization—Elaine Scarry writes, "When Berlin is bombed, when Dresden is burned, there is a deconstruction not only of a particular ideology but of the primary evidence of the capacity for self-extension it-self: one does not in bombing Berlin destroy only objects, gestures, and thoughts that are culturally stipulated but objects, gestures, and thoughts that are human, not Dresden buildings or German architecture but human shelter."[102] A similar ideological and corporal deracination occurred with the destruction of Stony Gut, Somerset, and Fort.

The government's response to the Morant Bay Rebellion did not only involve symbolic acts of annihilation. Blacks were executed for offenses like killing es-tate stock.[103] Bogle was summarily executed, and his alleged accomplice, George William Gordon, was arrested and taken to Morant Bay, where he was tried and hanged.[104] Certainly, the aims of elite officials during these reprisals were to hu-miliate the peasantry, annihilate potential and real disruptive forces, remind the working classes of "their place" in society, and assert plantocratic power. That this retaliation was colored by the dual factors of class and race was underscored by Jamaican journalist Henry Vendryes, who supported the government's re-prisals. Vendryes saw these actions as nothing more than the "pacification of the peasantry."[105] Evidently the law would viciously rebuff the black proletariat who demanded redress.

Themes of legitimacy, illegitimacy, and illegality, particularly with regard to punishment, also can be seen in the rebellion. The retaliation of the government was made all the more powerful because it was stamped with the power of legal-ity, whereas the actions of the peasantry were delineated as illegal, vicious, and "barbaric." There was also the notion that the working classes had betrayed the sovereign, as seen in Eyre's assertions:

> I believe that were condign punishment to fall only on the ignorant people who
> have been misled into rebellion, and the educated coloured man who led to that
> rebellion to escape, a very unfortunate impression would be produced upon the
> public mind, which in the present state of this colony might lead to very serious
> results. It is only by making it plain to the entire population that the guilty ag-
> itator and user of seditious language will meet the same punishment as the un-
> educated tools whom he misleads, that we can hope to check and put down the
> spirit of disloyalty and disaffection already so rife in the land, and which may
> at any moment occasion in other parishes outrages similar to those which have
> recently occurred in St. Thomas-in-the-East.[106]

Even after the Morant Bay Rebellion had ended, its terrors remained visible. Not only were the bodies of men and women marked, but the Jamaican land-scape also displayed evidence of the punishments of blacks during the reprisals. During their tour of Jamaica in 1866 Thomas Harvey and William Brewin noted that they had met "invalids"—persons whose bodies had been so assaulted by the punishments that they had been disabled. Harvey and Brewin pointed out that women and men had both been severely punished during the governmental reprisals, noting that at Bath about four hundred men and two hundred women had been flogged with cat-o'-nine-tails made of wire. Commenting on the physical landscape in the wake of the reprisals, Harvey and Brewin stated: "At [Coley] sixty or seventy houses were burnt; and at Somerset, which impressed its destroyers as the highest example of negro prosperity and luxury, every house was destroyed, except two standing together near the lower entrance to the village."[107] From a reading of this it is not an exaggeration to argue that the pockmarked landscape was akin to the marked bodies of the peasantry. Both the geographical terrain and the bodily terrain of the peasantry bore witness to their alleged crimes and the punishments enacted against them and their livelihood. Furthermore, these visual markers made an emphatic claim about the superior and final power of the colonial and imperial government.

What is also noteworthy about the governmental reprisals is the prominence they apparently gave to the black male body. There were allegations that black men had been shot and killed and their bodies left by the roadside. There were also reports of black men being hanged without trial.[108] In the nature of these reprisals comes a sense that a maligned white masculinity had needed to assert dominance over a recalcitrant black masculinity and that an embarrassed planter class had needed to vindicate and reclaim—however imperfectly and futilely— a compromised social status. This foregrounding of the black male body was visible in correspondence attributed to J. Elkington, Jamaican deputy adjutant-general, who in a letter to Colonel Hobbs wrote that Captain Lewis Hole was doing "splendid service with his men all about Manchioneal, and shooting every black man who cannot account for himself, (sixty on line of march)."[109] The insistence that every black man had to "account for himself" also signaled the infantilization of black males as they, unlike the white soldiers, did not have the authority to traverse Jamaica freely in times of war. Captain Hole not only confirmed the legitimacy of the draconian acts that his army committed against black men, he also evidences his soldiers' terrorism by noting that the rebels fled at the sight of them.[110] The phrase referring to black men who could not account for themselves also invokes laws against vagrancy, riotous assembly, and idleness that had been passed prior to 1865. These laws that set out to proscribe blacks' mobility and right to assemble highlighted white fears about black uprisings, and the actions of the workers participating in the Morant Bay Rebellion certainly qualified as vagrancy and riotous assembly.

Elkington's letter continued: "Nelson at Port Antonio hanging like fun, by

Court-martial. I hope you will not send in any prisoners, civil law can do nothing. . . . Do punish the blackguards well."[111] Although the air of legitimacy around the army's actions is unmistakable—as seen in the courts-martial—there is also a sense of recklessness and lawlessness about these actions. The idea of "hanging like fun" connotes a disregard for black life and a disdain toward the black male body. Further, that this was written down implies complicity, as Elkington did not appear to question Nelson's actions. And, having been written about, in a sense the hangings did not end but continued as Elkington's letter carried them beyond the temporal and spatial boundaries of when and where they occurred. Elkington's act of writing added to the permanency of the punishment. Etched on paper, the hangings became etched in the contemporary and twentieth-century discourses on the rebellion.

Black women also figured in the Morant Bay Rebellion and therefore represented some of the individuals punished in the reprisals. Out of the 354 persons executed after the rebellion, seven of them were women.[112] The presence of these women in the rebellion and the fact that some of them were executed, regardless of their numerical relative insignificance, helped to concretize the idea of the black virago—the violent black woman. In a dispatch sent out just after the outbreak, Governor Eyre noted that "[t]he women, as usual on such occasions, were even more brutal and barbarous than the men."[113] Eyre's attention to the black women who participated in the rebellion and his insistence on their brutality is telling, particularly when one considers that they made up a minority of those involved in the fighting. Essentially, on a textual level, the presence of these women in Eyre's dispatch hints at the discursive irruption that their presence caused in prose where men were the dominant subjects. On a macro level, Eyre's reference to these women signals a sense of unease caused by the image of women as violent agents. In this regard, Eyre shows that black women occupied a liminal space within colonial constructions of femininity. On the one hand, they were regarded as monstrous, as not quite women, but on the other hand, their sexed bodies shattered this notion. Furthermore, while these glimpses of the black women who participated in the rebellion lent credence to the supposed incorrigibility of black women, they also served as a convenient foil to those images disseminated of white women, who were often delineated as the victims or potential victims of prurient black men.[114]

Conclusion

Elites in post-emancipation Barbados and Jamaica used the law and punishment in an attempt to bring about the subjection of the black and brown laboring classes, while simultaneously reinforcing the inviolability of the white body and its hallowed position within the socio-racial order. The successful marriage between the legal system and the socio-racial order depended on a set of discursive and tangible practices that in many ways compromised the promises of emancipation. In making "performance utterances," the arm of the law was far-reaching. Not only did it define criminal bodies, but it also helped to legitimize how these bodies were to be punished and the position of these bodies in the social structure.

CHAPTER 4

Confined Spaces, Constrained Bodies

*Land, Labor, and Confinement
in Barbados after 1834*

Liberty, or freedom, signifieth, properly, the absence of opposition;
by opposition, I mean external impediments of motion; and may
be applied no less to irrational, and inanimate creatures, than
to rational. For whatsoever is so tied, or environed, as it cannot
move but within a certain space, which space is determined by the
opposition of some external body, we say it hath not liberty to go
further. And so of all living creatures, whilst they are imprisoned,
or restrained, with walls, or chains; and of the water whilst it is
kept in by banks, or vessels, that otherwise would spread itself into
a larger space, we use to say, they are not at liberty, to move in
such manner, as without those external impediments they would.

—THOMAS HOBBES, *Leviathan*

The development of a substantial prison system in a slave
society was full of contradictions. The prison as a form of
punishment worked through the principle of "less eligibility,"
which held that the conditions of penal institutions (and
other state institutions, such as workhouses for the poor)
had to be worse than the conditions of the poorest person
outside the institution; otherwise, poor people's rational
choice would be deliberately to get themselves incarcerated
to gain access to the better conditions inside. In a free-labor
society, the very denial of autonomy involved in incarceration
automatically introduced an element of "less eligibility."

—DIANA PATON, *No Bond but the Law*

Unlike relatively land-rich Jamaica with its labor scarcity, Barbados, with scarce land and an overabundance of workers, presented imperial and colonial legislators with an altogether different set of problems prompting different responses from them in the period after slavery. Jamaica was well known for its audacious and peripatetic peasantry. During testimony of William Carr to the commission that investigated the suppression of the Morant Bay Rebellion, when asked if he would be glad if he had a steady supply of Creole laborers, particularly for whom he would not have to provide provision grounds, Carr noted that they "would not do it" as the workers in Jamaica were "not like those in Barbadoes" and were "not dependent upon estates for their livelihood."[1] Space, Carr felt, clearly had an impact on the attitudes of Jamaicans as it emboldened them with the knowledge of what lay beyond the plantation. Moreover, whereas the introduction of indentured laborers was posited as the saving grace for the Jamaican plantation economy in the period under question, the exportation of labor was often floated as the answer to Barbados's overpopulation and seen as a guarantor of social stability. As this question of labor shaped Jamaica's approach to punishment, so too did it color Barbados's laws and responses to governing the bodies of its subaltern classes.

Bearing this in mind, this chapter takes on an ambitious project. Through an examination of Act 597, "An Act to Regulate the Emigration of Labourers from [Barbados]," the first section of the chapter uses the trope of a landlocked laboring class to show that confinement took on leviathan qualities in Barbados in the post-emancipation period. By applying Thomas Hobbes's ideas about liberty and natural laws, it argues that this act, passed during the apprenticeship period, compromised the promises of freedom that were made in the 1833 Abolition Act. Additionally, it applies a Foucauldian framework and borrows from Jeremy Bentham's Panopticon model to argue further that the act and similarly restrictive post-emancipation legislation may be seen as having a disciplinary function in that they fixed the notion of the black laborer while also reinforcing the socio-racial hierarchy. Although this act was prima facie an emigration act, this chapter argues that it also was a restrictive *labor* act that complemented similar labor legislation and socio-economic practices like the tenantry system that tied laborers—and black bodies—to the plantation.[2] This act and its enforcement, by placing restrictions on the emigration of Barbadian workers, helped to instantiate the notion of an immobile labor force while giving planters continued access to a highly vulnerable segment of Barbados's "redundant population"— its laborers—who were in a disadvantaged position vis-à-vis the planters and other workers who were competing with them in a labor market of apparently endless supply.[3]

In the second section of this chapter, this image of a landlocked laboring class is extended to show its relationship, metaphorically and literally, to a similarly spatially bound class of persons: those locked in jails and houses of correction. In looking at dimorphic categories of boundedness, this chapter argues that issues of land, labor, and confinement not only became discursively and legally tied to each other but also that they were the forces that together constrained the bodies of the Barbadian laboring classes.[4]

Inhabitation: Confinement and
the Politicization of Place

After 1834, owing to Barbados's high population density, plantation owners in Barbados enjoyed a command over the bodies of the laboring classes that was virtually unrivaled in other parts of the British Caribbean.[5] Hilary Beckles notes that on August 1, 1834, the Abolition Act of 1833 effectively gave the planters of Barbados 66,925 apprentices, 52,193 of whom were categorized as "praedials" and 14,732 of whom were categorized as "non-praedials." Beckles writes that because of this abundance of laborers, planters knew that "if they could maintain effective socio-political control of apprentices, the labor market would function in the interest of the plantation sector."[6] Whereas sugar production fell off in many of the British West Indian territories after emancipation, sugar production in Barbados—and in other high-density colonies like Antigua and St. Kitts—remained consistent with pre-emancipation levels and sometimes even exceeded it.[7] No doubt some of Barbados's economic success was due to the fact that it had 501 apprentices per square mile.[8]

This excessive ratio of inhabitants to land and laborers to the plantation economy continued well beyond the days of slavery. Robert Schomburgk in his expansive history of Barbados notes, for example, that in 1844 there were 734.8 individuals to each square mile.[9] Of this population, 56,004 were males and 66,194 were females.[10] This people-to-land ratio had grave social consequences as it made it difficult for the working classes to enjoy the kind of relative economic and social mobility enjoyed by subalterns in other parts of the Caribbean, most notably Jamaica. Whereas Jamaica's topography proved amenable to the development of peasant and Maroon communities like New Crawford Town, Accompong, Moore Town, and Scotts Hall—emphatic symbols of black corporal and socio-political autonomy—Barbados's landscape did not offer similar opportunities.[11] In fact, Barbadian laborers would have been hard-pressed to engage in the same type of audacious motility as Jamaican laborers since between 1841 and 1844 Barbados had the highest population density in the region. Jamaica's population density stood at just eighty-six persons per square mile (see tables 7 and 8 in the appendix).[12] These demographic realities had a significant impact on the lived experiences of inhabitants from both islands, and many Jamaican ex-slaves were able to develop into a successful autonomous peasantry.[13] On the other hand, after 1838 it would not have raised a colonialist's eyebrow to hear Governor John Pope Hennessy of Barbados utter statements like these:

> No doubt the planters and manufacturers in the other Islands want that which we can well spare, the enterprise of the labourers. Though almost within sight, and within 12 hours by steamer of these shores, where there exists a redundant and poverty oppressed multitude, the planters of the other islands have to import Coolies from Hindoostan, and the manifest facilities and encouragements which the State should secure for the passage to and fro of Barbados labourers have not yet been provided.[14]

Indeed, Barbadian planters had grown so accustomed to their stranglehold on land and labor that post-apprenticeship and emancipation legislation and punitive practices took on audacious extremes as planters disregarded the promises of emancipation and tried to control their laborers. The 1836 Emigration Act of Barbados represented one of the more notable instances where the law, land, and labor were manipulated to constrain the bodies of laborers in the post-slavery period. Faced with the prospect that the promise of high wages would lure their redundant pool of laborers to territories like British Guiana and Trinidad, Barbadian legislators, according to Claude Levy, "resolved that the anti-emigration act of 1836 would be strictly enforced, and [they] imposed a fine of £50 on any individual who attempted to 'decoy, or entice away . . . any child under sixteen years of age.'"[15] Act 597, "An Act to Regulate the Emigration of Labourers from This Island," passed on November 30, 1836, did not only target "any child under sixteen years of age." Essentially it had the effect of circumscribing the recruiting activities of potential employers from outside the region at the same time that it attempted to lock the bodies of Barbadian laborers into 166 square miles of land. The passage of this act also confirms that the plantocracy had been successful in transforming the physical landscape into a space that was politicized and restrictive.[16]

What was also noteworthy about Act 597, besides the image of the Barbadian state deciding when or if its working-class inhabitants could leave the country, were the paternalistic reasons advanced for its creation. In proposing the act to Lord Glenelg, Governor Smith saw his role and the role of the government as akin to the paterfamilias of ancient Rome. The ultimate sovereignty of the laboring population lay not within workers, the tone of the act suggested, but in the superior authority of the state, which not only knew better but could also protect the laborers from themselves and the "crimps" who were attempting to lure them away from the island. Smith saw the workers not as adults, some of whom desired to work outside of the island, but rather as the victims of a "complete system of kidnapping."[17] Of course, this is not to intimate that there were no laborers tricked into leaving the island, nor does it fail to recognize that some agents from British Guiana may have used dishonest recruitment methods to lure away unsuspecting men and women.[18] It is important to point out that this act targeted laborers and not professionals. The fact that Barbados's economy depended heavily on the work of laborers for its success suggests that this law was motivated more by elite self-interest—and the desire to keep a pool of easily exploitable labor that could be corralled for use in the plantation economy—than out of a concern for exploited individuals. The act specifically targeted "able bodied labourers" and "skilful artificers of all descriptions," apparently ignoring the fact that professionals also might be interested in leaving the island.[19]

Barbadian elites' obsessions with the role of the state, social welfare in the form of provisions for the poor, and individual responsibility also found expression in these efforts to restrict emigration. The debate on this issue did not center on whether it was an individual's right to move to places where it was felt that individual potential could be realized. Neither did the debate on emigration focus on whether there was a labor glut in Barbados and how best to deal with its ramifications. Instead, the migration debate was racist and classist in tenor as a major theme was that emigration provided the perfect avenue through which the working classes could amble into familial irresponsibility. As the argument went, it would lead to the creation of a class of "impotent families" and "helpless infants" who would become wards of the state.[20] To ensure that the island's poor laws would not suffer undue stress—particularly, according to Smith, on account of the nation's large white population—any laborer, artificer, or pauper seeking to emigrate first had to meet with the churchwarden of the parish in which he or she lived, to ascertain whether the intending émigré had any dependents.[21] Dependents could include any children belonging to the potential migrant—legitimate or illegitimate—grandparents, and parents, and if it was found that the intending émigré had any of these and had failed to show how they would be supported in his or her absence, then the application to migrate was denied. This law was not all one-sided, however. It also stipulated that if the churchwardens or anyone tried to unfairly obstruct the emigrant's departure, then they could be fined up to ten pounds sterling, one half of which was to be paid into the public treasury "for the uses of the Island," while the other half was to be awarded "to the person so obstructed."[22] Although this last section of the act appeared to ensure that the rights of laborers were upheld, the act's enforcement meant that control of the outflow of workers would be paramount.

The impact of emigration was debated in the Barbadian House of Assembly in the 1840s. In one speech, it was noted that by 1840 the laboring population had been depleted by at least 2,157, a number that supposedly demonstrated that "the practical effect of the local enactments did not in reality unduly impede the voluntary exercise of their locomotive privileges."[23] Ultimately the speaker, Governor MacGregor, cast freedom of movement as a privilege granted by the colonial and imperial governments rather than as a right to be exercised by free citizens—at least in the case of manual laborers.[24]

Even though in his address MacGregor opined that emigration had tapered off, his insouciance and optimism did not match the vigilance with which earlier government officials regarded laborers who expressed a desire to travel overseas. Prior to MacGregor's address to the House of Assembly, the government had banded together with the police magistrates to oversee attempts by the laboring population to migrate to other colonies. Consequently, a number of key questions that the members of the police magistracy were asked to answer in their quarterly reports entailed emigration. For example, from the quarterly reports between October 1 and December 31, 1839:

> Has emigration to any considerable extent occurred among the labourers of your parish[?]. If so, specify the number, and state to what cause you are disposed to attribute this novel propensity on their part.

> From your knowledge of the character and feelings of the Barbados peasantry, do you conclude that their emigration had been spontaneous or otherwise?

> What are the ages, generally speaking, of the emigrants from your parish; and of which of the three classes of males, females, and children, have the majority of emigrants consisted?

> Are you of opinion there is a surplus population in this island, and that a large proportion of labourers might be spared without disadvantage, for the benefit of Colonies where labour is comparatively scarce?[25]

Although many of the police magistrates answered these questions by noting that laborers either did not exhibit a desire to emigrate or that reports of emigrating laborers had not been recently heard—as was the case in the parishes of St. James and St. George, respectively, for instance—some of them reported that Barbadian laborers were still emigrating, even in the face of government efforts to restrict their mobility.[26]

Along with monitoring the comings and goings of its laborers by employing the police magistrates in a fact-finding mode, the Barbadian government
entrusted the magistrates also with the power to either allow or restrict laborers' free movement. Answering questions relating to the extent of migration and
the age and gender of migrants, the police magistrate of St. Philip, P. L. Applewhaite, noted that more than one hundred laborers had left his parish. Likewise,
Francis Thornhill, the police magistrate for St. James, noted that he had granted
three certificates to laborers so that they could leave the island. Thornhill noted
that all three were men between the ages of sixteen and twenty. A. H. Morris,
who had jurisdiction for St. Lucy, was not only able to give the age range and
gender of the twelve individuals who had left the island from his parish, he was
also able to give information as to where the blame for their departures should
lie. He attributed this exodus to "that mischievous publication, the *Liberal*, and
the machinations of a Mr. Thomas Day, of British Guiana."[27] Morris noted that
the seven males and five females to whom he had issued emigration certificates
were generally able-bodied adults.

The reports supplied by J. Carew (police magistrate for St. Thomas) and
the magistrates for the populous St. Michael—E. H. Moore, R. Hendy, and
C. Gill—echoed Morris's assertion that the majority who left the island were
able-bodied men and women in their prime. Carew's detailed report, for instance, revealed that thirty-eight-year-old Edward Miller, thirty-year-old John
Tony, thirteen-year-old Mary Ann Elizabeth, and eighteen-year-old Thomas
Gunnel were some of the individuals to whom he had issued emigration certificates.[28] Though it is not known whether these individuals actually left the
island, Carew's data reveal that those intending to leave were generally young
and able-bodied. Similarly, the three police magistrates for St. Michael noted that
from July 1 to September 30, 1840, emigration certificates had been issued for
fifty-six adult males and twenty-five females, three of whom each took an infant
with them. Magistrates Hendy, Gill, and Moore further broke down this data
and revealed that thirty-eight of these emigrants were artisans bound for Trinidad, St. Lucia, Demerara, and Dominica; thirty-five were classified as domestics going to Trinidad, St. Lucia, and Demerara; and the others included three
agricultural laborers and five porters.[29] Arguably, these detailed descriptions of
the intended émigrés—the attention paid to their bodily comportment and their
age and gender—provide evidence of the act's ability to codify the working
classes, to reduce them to a code that intimated whether they were potential as-
sets to the plantation economy. Thus, the act performed a disciplinary function;
in Foucauldian terms it was "concern[ed] with individualizing observation, with
characterization and classification, with the analytical arrangement of space."[30]

As emigration continued to provide fodder for debate, lawmakers and laity alike carefully manipulated the narrative to suit their aims. For instance, emigration was linked to the high infant mortality in the early 1840s and the decline in agricultural production that was said to have hit the island.[31] It was also linked to strained relations between the laborers and their employers.[32] In light of this, it is easy to see why it became the duty of the police magistracy to regulate the flow of migrants leaving Barbados. This politicization of the Barbadian landscape, according to scholars Laurence Brown and Tara Inniss, had been orchestrated by Major-General Henry Darling, who they categorize as "far more sympathetic than his predecessor [Governor MacGregor] to the attempts by the local planters to limit working-class emigration from Barbados to the canefields of Trinidad and British Guiana."[33] Fearing that there would be a labor shortage and an increase in child mortality, the House of Assembly responded by stipulating that individuals who wanted to migrate first had to prove that their family would be provided for while they were out of the island.

Schomburgk also put forward his views on the emigration of laborers from Barbados, although he attributed it more to what he saw as blacks' innate restlessness and not to socio-economic pressures. He concluded that "a thirst for novelty and change, which is a prominent trait in the negro character, induced a great number to leave the island, without providing for their offspring, or such of their aged relatives as were dependent on them for support."[34] Schomburgk blamed parental neglect for the deaths of 596 children in 1841, and although he noted that this neglect had occurred when lower-class mothers abandoned their offspring by migrating, he was also careful to see paternal absence as a major factor leading to these deaths. He contended that "much more numerous instances occurred where the father of the child emigrated and left the burden of the child to the mother, who, thus abandoned to her own resources, had not the means of providing for its sustenance or attending to its necessities."[35]

In spite of the disfavor with which the migrating intentions of laborers were viewed, neither plantocrats, police magistrates, churchwardens, nor edicts from the House of Assembly could completely stem the tide of their departure. Laborers voiced their displeasure to limitations on their movement, "accusing the legislature of tampering with their rights as free persons to travel and work where they so desired," according to Beckles. And they asserted their corporeal sovereignty by migrating to other colonies. Beckles writes that by 1870 approximately sixteen workers had left the island for other colonies.[36]

Attempts to control the mobility of the laboring classes were not limited to Barbados. For example, Bonham C. Richardson has shown that a similar situation obtained in the case of St. Kitts and Nevis, where attempts were made to discourage the migration of black laborers. He notes that just prior to full emancipation, on July 2, 1838, Lieutenant-Governor MacLeod of St. Kitts had "spoke[n] to many of the island's workers, warning them against emigration and suggesting that some who already had been lured away by labour recruiters had been 'sold as slaves into strange countries.'" Along with such verbal attempts to discourage emigration, Richardson points out that legislation was used to restrict the outward mobility of Leeward Islanders. Emigration acts were passed by the local assemblies "requiring arriving ship captains to post bonds and disallowing them from leaving seamen behind as recruiters."[37]

As Richardson notes, the strictures that were placed against Kittitians and Nevisians were not always to restrict their exodus from the island. In many cases, laws relating to vagrancy and trespassing prevented workers from going from estate to estate in search of higher wages within the colonies themselves. He notes also that the activities of various seaport workers, including stevedores and dockworkers, were "strictly monitored on both islands, and 'loiterers' were prohibited from dockside areas, lest crowds assemble and mass departure result."[38] Although Richardson does concede that these legal restrictions "had only temporary effect" because many of them were either disallowed or modified by the imperial government, he showed that planters were attempting to control laborers by attempting to impede their mobility.

Similarly to the Kittitian and Nevisian plantocrats, the Barbadian plantocracy attempted, through other legislative means, to maintain a labor force that was highly disciplined—that is to say, constrained to place by restrictive legislation—thus making it easily exploitable and readily available for use in the plantation economy. The fact that Barbados had a redundant pool of laborers meant that restrictive legislation could have had a disciplinary impact on them, as they were likely to be sober with the knowledge that they had few choices in a market where there was a labor glut. The 1840 Contract Law, with its restrictive clauses that bound laborers to plantations, may be seen as complementing this high population density. The original law, which was passed in 1838 but subsequently rejected by courts, stipulated that "any worker who provided five days of continuous labour to a planter was deemed as being hired for one year." Under this law, workers could reside on a plantation, in housing provided by the plantation owner, as long as they continued to provide continuous labor for the planter. If the workers prematurely terminated the contract, they were required to find alternative housing, and they were entitled also only to the "value of crops planted by [themselves] on plantation lands allotted for [their] use—the value of which was determined by a Justice of the Peace from the parish in which the estate was located."[39]

As Beckles points out, the workers who found their working lives being governed by the Contract Law would also have found that their personal lives were similarly policed. Workers could be made homeless if they were accused by their employer of being insubordinate, and they could even be imprisoned. Other so-called crimes for which workers could be imprisoned included "forming illegal combinations," gambling, and using foul language. The punitive ethos of this law was reinforced by the visible presence of a policeman whose duty was to ensure that aspects of the Contract Law were enforced.[40]

The 1840 law, according to Beckles, "transformed the free wage worker into a *'located'* plantation tenant [emphasis added]."[41] Instead of contracts being binding for one year, they bound the laborer to a plantation for one month. Moreover, laborers were required to pay rent to the plantation owner for any buildings and land that they used, which Beckles estimated amounted to one-sixth of their wages. The laborers lost much of their corporeal sovereignty under the new law as it stipulated that they had to provide labor "exclusively for the estate on which [they] resided, and in return, employers reduced the rent on cottages and ground provisions."[42] Laborers who did not perform satisfactorily could be given one month's eviction notice.

That the internal Barbadian landscape remained constrictive in the late nineteenth century can also be seen in the passage of the Apprentices Act of 1890.[43] The strong arm of the law was again exercised by the police magistrate as it was lawful for him "to bind any loose, idle, or unsettled persons under the age of twenty one years to apprenticeship, for any term, until he or she arrive at the age of twenty one years."[44] The language used in this act is consistent with the legal language of the period and with Barbadian social history. Yet the language itself is evocative as it shows that even after the abolition of slavery various shades of boundedness remained in place. The employment of terms like "loose," "idle," and "unsettled" in the Apprentices Act conveys the image of wandering bodies or at least bodies that were in a state of perpetual yet unproductive movement across the Barbadian landscape. The ability of *police* magistrates to "bind" these bodies to plantation labor, by extension a productive form of movement, not only emphasizes the disciplinary and punitive nature of the legislation but also illustrates that the central aim of this act was to nullify the unregulated mobility of these potential laboring bodies. Thus, if one were to employ Hobbes's argument that one of the characteristics of liberty is "the absence of external impediments" imposed against and upon the bodies of individuals, then laborers in post-emancipation Barbados did not possess the freedom that the Abolition Act had promised.[45]

Along with creating a virtual space of confinement out of the Barbadian landscape, the three acts under examination may be seen as having disciplinary aims similar to those of Jeremy Bentham's proposed Panopticon. Like Bentham's ideal disciplinary model, the "Act to Regulate the Emigration of Labourers from [Barbados]," the Contract Law, and the Apprentices Act may be seen as creating a type of constrictive architecture out of Barbados's social and topographical landscape. Metaphorically, these acts rendered the boundaries of the island—and the plantation more specifically—like the "circumference" of the Panopticon model in that they hemmed in the island's laboring classes. These boundaries were then regulated by the "polyvalent apparatus of surveillance" (Bentham's phrase) consisting of churchwardens, police magistrates, legislators, and justices of the peace. These officials certainly were "external impediments of motion," in Hobbesian terms, as they enacted a model of discipline whereby some of the most poorly paid laborers in the British West Indies were discouraged from seeking a livelihood elsewhere.[46] Moreover, the Emigration Act also invites comparisons with how townspeople were to be treated in the event of a plague in Europe in the seventeenth century.[47] Citing evidence from the Archives militaires de Vincennes, Foucault notes that the order published at the end of the seventeenth century discursively transformed towns into "enclosed, segmented space[s], observed at every point, in which the individuals are inserted in a fixed place, in which the slightest movements are supervised, in which all events are recorded, in which an uninterrupted work of writing links the center and periphery, in which power is exercised without division, according to a continuous hierarchical figure."[48] By being concerned only with regulating emigration of laborers and artisans, the Act to Regulate the Emigration of Labourers fixed the laboring classes into a specific place, the Barbadian plantation economy. Moreover, in recording the desires and movements of those who sought to leave the island, this act linked the Foucauldian "center" (the plantation—that site of employment for laborers and artificers) to the "periphery" (the plantation economy), the laborer to the land, and, by extension, the colony to the metropole. Indeed, this act made a personal choice a public concern, eliding individual choices with a narrative about what was best for the state. Bound up in this series of linkages, moreover, were hierarchies of power in which laborers and artisans were at the base of the socio-economic ladder and colonial and imperial authorities at the apex—a hierarchy that was crystallized, in part, by a simple idea in legislative architecture, the Act to Regulate the Emigration of Labourers.[49]

The Emigration Act's gestures toward Bentham's Panopticon did not end with its restrictive and disciplinary orientation. Indeed, the ideals and aims of this act also invite parallels with Bentham's proposed disciplinary model. Like Bentham's Panopticon, the act's aims were ambitious. It certainly sought to have, as Bentham wrote, "morals reformed—health preserved—industry invigorated—instruction diffused—public burthens lightened—Economy seated, as it were, upon a rock—the Gordian knot of the Poor-Laws not cut, but untied!"[50]

As has been demonstrated, the Emigration Act, the Contract Law, and the Apprentices Act sought to preserve the plantation industry. In the case of the Emigration Act, Governor Smith was concerned that "public burthens" would not be increased by the dependents who supposedly would be left as wards of the state if laborers migrated without making provisions for their welfare. Both the Emigration Act and Apprentices Act sought to ensure also that through the preservation of an apparently peaceful work climate the health of the plantation economy would be guaranteed. In the case of the Emigration Act, this was particularly visible in the persecution of the "crimps" whose presence and activities were thought to encourage animosity between laborers and their employers.

Restrictive legislation that tied laborers—as opposed to elites and white-collar workers—to the island had corporeal consequences besides the most obvious one of controlling the outflow of bodies from Barbados or binding them to plantations. For one thing, this kind of legislation increased the number of ways in which certain bodies could be penalized.[51] Moreover, by marking some bodies as more prone to deviance and socially and economically disruptive behavior than others, restrictive legislation like the Emigration, Contract, and Apprentices Acts effectively helped to rationalize a philosophy of confinement that was concerned primarily with rendering bodies useful.

Confinement and the Manipulation of Space

Although the Barbadian landscape continued to be a highly restrictive space throughout the nineteenth century, one may argue that the jail remained the space of confinement, discipline, and punishment par excellence. Not only did the wider Barbadian society directly contribute to the jails by providing them with their inhabitants, conditions within the society were also reflected in these spaces. For instance, the image of a population constrained by a lack of accessible, arable land may be likened to the confined populace who occupied overcrowded jail cells. Additionally, those sentenced to penal confinement would have found conditions in the jails at least as inhuman as the social conditions on the outside. In fact, Paton's argument that the notion of "less eligibility" (see chapter epigraph) guided prison administration in Jamaica is also true for Barbados to some degree.[52] Thus, the employment of punitive technologies like the treadmill and solitary confinement, along with overcrowded jails and the withholding of creature comforts to inmates, combined to make conditions within spaces of penal confinement worse than those in the wider Barbadian society. By using conditions in the wider society as a measuring stick, elites in Barbados and the metropole worked to establish a modus operandi for spaces of confinement that helped to cement the symbiotic relationship between the wider society and spaces of confinement.

In spite of this working relationship between the outside and the inside, the system of confinement in Barbados, as it had been in Jamaica, was in constant flux—sometimes in direct response to local societal pressures and at other times in response to wider pressures. As a result of these pressures, the system of "less eligibility" may not have operated as unadulterated as local jail personnel and other administrators may have liked. For instance, prior to Captain Pringle's visit to Barbados in 1837, improvements were made in the colony's penal landscape in an effort to "avert British interference in local affairs." The improvements had been precipitated in part by the reports of noted abolitionists James A. Thome, Horace Kimball, and John Scoble, who got Barbadian jail commissioners and other officials to concede that jail conditions were unsatisfactory.[53] The new prison regulations included the removal of the treadmill and the stipulation that female inmates were no longer subject to corporal punishment. They allowed still for the flogging of male inmates, though only by the governor's orders, and prison cells were to be cleaned daily.[54] Pringle's 1838 report would still be noteworthy for revealing continued deficiencies in the island prisons.

Barbados, like Jamaica, had several types of housing for those who flouted the island's laws. In the early nineteenth century these included a main jail that was located in Bridgetown, six houses of correction that were attached to the special magistrates' court, and cages or temporary lockups in Speightstown and Holetown. Each of these types drew their populations from different criminal constituencies. For instance, the houses of correction, which were constructed after emancipation under the direction of the Rural Police Commissioners, housed apprentices (committed by the special magistrates) and free men and women (committed by local magistrates during their petty sessions).[55] The temporary lockups housed prisoners who were waiting to be examined or tried at these petty sessions.[56]

Besides having a variety of spaces of confinement, what is also evident about Barbados during the early 1800s was how the administration of discipline and punishment fell under the purview of certain types of professions. For example, at the time of Pringle's visit to Barbados, the jail was managed by a board comprising the island's Church of England bishop, the president of the Council, the Speaker of the House of Assembly, and the three police magistrates of Bridgetown. The provost marshal was responsible for governance within the jail.[57] A glance at this coterie shows how religion and politics were melded to administer discipline and punishment.[58] From a reading of this one could even argue that spaces of confinement in nineteenth-century Barbados were encased in what must have seemed like an impermeable cloak of authority from God and the law.[59]

One of the obvious features of spaces of confinement in Barbados in the post-slavery period was the centrality of the strictly regulated and subdued body. This is reflected in rules and practices that stressed disciplining and punishing already confined bodies—rules that had an official and discursive seal of approval. These rules were not simply a catalog of dos and don'ts. Ensconced within them were ideas about gender, race, and class and what these meant in terms of punishment. The rules also revealed a hierarchy in prison relations, with the police magistrates possessing a superior authority to the prison superintendent. For example, the fourth rule of the regulations submitted in 1836 by the jail commissioners of Barbados for consideration by the governor stipulated that "for contumacious and disorderly conduct of any such male prisoner, the superintendent shall prefer a complaint before the police magistrates, who are hereby authorised to punish any such misconduct with corporal punishment, not exceeding 39 lashes, or by close or solitary confinement, or labour on the treadmill. . . . And for all disorderly and contumacious conduct in any female prisoner, the magistrates may direct her to be punished by close or solitary confinement, not exceeding 14 days for any one offence."[60]

In this stipulation, one can see a gendered application of punishment. The decision against one form of corporal punishment in favor of another for women can be seen elsewhere in nineteenth-century Barbados. The provost marshal Benjamin Walrond pointed out to Pringle that female inmates in Barbados were not supposed to be put on the treadmill—it was considered to be an "improper punishment for them." It had not always been thus, however, and he noted that the decision to abandon this form of punishment of women had been reached gradually. Walrond contended that when the treadmill was first established, the superintendent had been allowed to carry a "cat" (whip) made of twine that could be used on male or female prisoners whenever they refused to step. This practice had continued until November 1836, after which the governor made an application to the board of commissioners that stated that the cat should not be used on women and that it should be used only on those men whom police magistrates had sentenced to be so whipped. By May 1837 it was deemed illegal for women to be sentenced to the treadmill. In spite of these regulations, testimony provided by female inmates showed that women continued to be so punished. For example, at the time of his visit, Pringle obtained testimony from three female apprentices who contended that not only had they been made to dance the treadmill but that their feet had been severely cut when they were on it.[61] What the testimony from these women helps to illustrate is that although there had been a concerted effort to stop women from being sentenced to labor on the treadmill, and to mitigate other forms of punishment, legal rulings were not always followed by a new reality.

The importance ascribed to the body as a site of punishment is also evident in the types of punishments carried out within spaces of confinement. Punishment in the jails and houses of correction in Barbados, as was the case in Jamaica, was largely corporal in nature and could be very brutal. For example, the use of the cat-o'-nine-tails was not uncommon in Barbadian jails. In addition, although solitary confinement was noted to be a form of punishment that could be employed by prison officials, it was regarded as less effective than whipping, particularly for members of the working classes. This was expressed by prison officials in Barbados in an 1836 report:

> The solitary cell is a punishment most keenly felt by the active and, to a degree, enlightened mind, when shut out from all external objects, and forced upon reflection. The gross natures and obtruded intellects of our convicts will sleep away the time, and suffer comparatively little. We in like manner are deprived of the power which is possessed in an English gaol, of addressing exhortation to the prisoners by the means of letters; few or none of our prisoners (the greater part of whom are apprenticed labourers) can read; it is not only useless to give them little plain religious tracts, but they cannot read rules hung up in their cells, nor see, was it constantly placed before their eyes, as it would be, that they will benefit by and be treated more kindly for orderly behaviour. As a preventive to crime, we are deprived of the effect (most powerful in England) of the fear of loss of character, by having been imprisoned.[62]

The authors of this statement provide insight into the philosophy that buttressed penal confinement in Barbados during the apprenticeship period. Religious instruction, regimentation (as demonstrated by the image of rules hanging in the cell), orderly behavior, and shaming were seen as integral to the confinement experience. The quotation suggests also that solitary confinement was most suitably used against those who were educated, as this education would presumably allow the confined to reflect on confinement and so benefit. The notion that the only useful body was one at work comes out also in the image of convicts sleeping away their time, which reifies the dichotomy of the laboring body and the idle body. Additionally, the quotation reveals a mind-body split, whereby the ability to reflect on one's actions—and thereby perhaps turn from a criminal life—is cast as the preserve of those possessing "enlightened" minds, whereas the laboring classes are squarely aligned with the corporeal and, by extension, "obtruded intellects."

In spite of this vote of no confidence for solitary confinement as an effective punishment against certain criminal types, spaces of confinement were at least in theory regarded as the final resort in the entire legal system centered on discipline and punishment. Evidence from the second report from the Board of Superintendence on the state of the jail in Barbados, November 10, 1836, is used to support this assertion. The members of the board contended,

> With regard to the dependence which the public may place on this gaol as the means of suppressing crime, we think it an erroneous opinion that crime can be kept down, solely by the terrors of prison discipline, ever so skilfully and faithfully enforced. The gaol is only a necessary part of the system of government, an aid, and final resort; the most important part of this system is wise legislation, based on statistics, tending to the prevention of crime, the abstraction of temptation, and the wholesome and constitutional regulation of the actions of individuals. *To permit, by the omission or laxity of laws, the facility of committing crimes, and the ability of persons destitute of regular employment or estate to live in idleness, is the sure way to fill this prison with tenants, who will go hence rendered worse by contamination.* [emphasis added][63]

Penal confinement, the board suggests, was only to be used in those cases where other systems of behavior modification and deterrence had proved ineffective. These other systems included "wise legislation," which was to be based on evidence gleaned from statistical data, the removal of the temptations to which individuals might fall, and the regulation of the actions of individuals.

What these recommendations represent is the idea that crime and its prevention are based within individuals. In cases where causes of criminality were thought to be somewhat exogenous, Barbadian officials still assumed that individuals succumbed to criminal behavior, capitulating to desires of the flesh, desires that could not be tempered by mental capacities. It follows therefore, as suggested in the report quoted above, that if individuals on the brink of criminality could be policed successfully and their questionable behavior regulated effectively by sanctions, then the jails would not be used. The weakness in this argument, however, is that it does not address complex forms of criminal activity and appears instead only to be concerned with crimes that can be attributed to "persons destitute of regular employment or estate." This is particularly telling when one notes that the idea of binding bodies to the land as a solution to criminality is suggested in the quotation. In essence, one form of boundedness or confinement was to be substituted for another. A theme that emerges in this quotation, visible too in many other approaches to punishment and discipline put forward in nineteenth-century Barbados, is that the plantation was key to the maintenance of law and order. The plantation was the site where potentially troublesome bodies could be put to productive use.

This ethos of "productive motility" advanced as a solution to criminality formed a key part of prison policy and governance in nineteenth-century Barbados. This idea is particularly evident in expressions of the importance of labor and its ameliorative benefits, especially its supposed ability to transform criminals into hardworking, law-abiding citizens. Pringle's visit to Barbados in 1837 revealed the important role played by the penal gang and other forms of labor in the culture of confinement in that colony, a role that continued in the latter part of the nineteenth century. A second area where this ethos of corporeality was visible was in the punishments, supplementary and otherwise, that were often inflicted on already constrained inmates for infractions committed while in prison or that had been handed down as part of their original sentences. Corporal punishment of inmates in nineteenth-century Barbados included the use of the treadmill and the further constriction of the body by placing the imprisoned in chains and stocks.

Along with the multiply punished body in places of confinement in Barbados, and bodies being put to productive use, there were also the bodies of those committed to confined spaces for *work-related* offenses. The ubiquity of black laborers in Barbadian places of confinement, when examined in light of the reasons for their confinement, helps to substantiate the conclusion of scholars like Walton Look Lai that in the post-emancipation period, work infractions were dealt with by the criminal court system rather than within the work space.[64] As a case in point, in evidence from the District C House of Correction, three apprentice boys were given six stripes each with a birch rod for allowing cattle to stray into crops. Other apprentices were confined in this institution for insolence to their employers, idleness, and absence from work.[65] Thus, for their perceived poor performance on the plantation worksite, these apprentices were subjected to penal confinement. Their removal from the plantation to the District C House of Correction reiterates the links between the plantation economy and spaces of confinement. It illustrates also that the plantation was a vertical monopoly in Barbados. The ideologies that governed the plantation's existence often provided the rationales for individuals' confinement.

As tables 9 and 10 in the appendix suggest, Barbadian jails and district prisons continued to play a key role in the punitive landscape. They demonstrate also that the jailed and imprisoned were not only people who had committed work infractions on plantations but also debtors and those who had committed felonies and misdemeanors unrelated to plantation work. The data show that the confined population consisted both of individuals who had been tried for their crimes and those who were awaiting trial, and they offer a window through which one can peer into Barbados's socio-economic conditions. The jail population was predominantly black and male, with the numbers of black men and women confined significantly greater than the numbers of white men and white women confined. Black men often outnumbered white men by more than ten to one in categories of those imprisoned, whether tried or untried, felons, and those who had committed misdemeanors, with the debtor category the only one where the ratio was consistently lower. The gap between the numbers of white women tried and confined for misdemeanors vis-à-vis black women who fell under the same category was even more significant. In 1841, as a case in point, four white women were tried and confined for committing misdemeanors compared to 192 black women. In 1843 and 1844 black women were more than one hundred times more likely to have been convicted and confined for misdemeanors than white women.[66] The situation was just as alarming in the case of black and white women tried and convicted for felonies. In 1841 only one white woman was convicted and imprisoned for a felony, compared to 120 black women. Between 1842 and 1844, there were no white women imprisoned for committing felonies, whereas 156 black women were imprisoned for felonies. These statistics could be attributed to the greater numbers of black men and women in the general population.[67] But it must be pointed out that the overwhelming preponderance of black men and women speaks to the nature of the plantation society. With work infractions punishable by terms of imprisonment, with a superior morality ascribed to the white female body, and with the bodies of blacks marked as criminal in a manner that was not so marked on white bodies, there were thus more infractions for which blacks would be punished by imprisonment.

All persons confined in penal spaces, like the boys who were confined in the District C House of Correction at the time of Pringle's visit in the 1830s and those who were incarcerated in the jail and district prisons in the 1840s, were subject to a punitive and disciplinary ethos that stressed total control over their bodies. This mind-set was reflected in what can be considered the minutiae of prison life, like what types of sleeping conditions were provided for inmates and the daily schedule to which inmates were subjected. What is also noticeable about this ethos is how it was influenced by the race, social class, and criminal classification of the confined. For instance, although Pringle observed that the jail in Barbados held both black and white inmates, he revealed also that English soldiers who were confined had hammocks to sleep in, whereas other prisoners slept on boards without bedding or blankets.[68] Although Pringle did not explain the rationale for this discrepancy, it suggests that there was a hierarchy based on ideas about race that resulted in English soldiers being afforded levels of comfort not given to other criminals. This view is all the more compelling when one notes that in Jamaica, some thirty-six years after Pringle's visit to the Caribbean, calls were made by the commissioners of the British prison inquiry of 1873 to allot more cubic space in their cells to white prisoners than to black prisoners.

Differential treatment based on criminal "type" is illustrated by evidence supplied by a Mr. Nicolls, who was the jailer at the time of Pringle's visit to Barbados. Nicolls noted that only debtors could have visitors from the outside without having to obtain a certificate from the provost marshal, whereas other classes of prisoners would have to obtain this written permission.[69] The provost marshal was also required to be present when non-debtors had visitors, and he had to see or know what was in the letters prisoners received.[70] This surveillance, policing, and control remained in place in Barbados in the latter half of the nineteenth century, as they had been at the time of Pringle's visit, continuity that suggests that this control was an important part of the philosophy undergirding punitive praxis in Barbados. In 1870, for instance, prisoners in Barbados who were sentenced to hard labor were not allowed to have any visitors, nor were they allowed to send or receive letters. This latter stipulation could be rescinded only if the confined were given a certificate of good conduct from a visiting justice or inspector of prisons, "upon whose recommendation the Governor may grant such indulgences."[71] The other instance where this rule would be repealed was in those cases where prisoners who were under sentence of hard labor were seriously ill. This practice of attempting to seal off the confined from the outside world was not an unusual one. It was adopted in various guises in places of confinement in the metropole in the nineteenth century, including Brixton and Millbank Prisons. One former female matron of these prisons noted that inmates were allowed to receive letters only once a month. This aspect of the inmates' lives was so regulated that "if a letter arrive[d] for a prisoner before a month [had] expired from the receipt of the last epistle, it [was] detained for the full term, unless there [were] news of a death."[72]

Labor was another mechanism used to exact control over already constrained bodies. Penal labor—whether it was categorized as productive or purely punitive—tended to embrace, rather than undermine or reject, a mind-body dichotomy, as penal labor was perceived to have qualitative and quantitative benefits for the confined, for spaces of penal confinement, and even for the wider society. Diverse benefits that accrued from such labor were apparent at the Town

Hall Gaol, located in Bridgetown, where Pringle found prisoners working in the "ballast-yard," working the "shot-drill," and breaking stones that were used to repair the public roads. Still others were responsible for the upkeep of the grounds at Government House.[73] Barbadian female prisoners did laundering or broke stones that were used for burning lime.[74] The importance of this form of labor, particularly in pecuniary terms, can be gleaned from the following summary, in which "*l*" represents pounds sterling: "If we estimate the value of adult convict labor to be 8*d*. per diem, we find that the value of cooking, baking, and washing at Glendairy amounts to 138*l*. 13*s*. 4*d*. per annum; that of the convicts at the dredge and ballast-yard 346*l*. 16*s*; the Government House grounds 122*l*. 8*s*.; and the value of the stone broken for the highways is 66*l*. 13*s*. 4*d*., at the low rate of 4*d*. a-load: making the total-value of the work performed by the convicts to be 674*l*. 10*s*. 8*d*."[75]

What these monetary estimates reveal is that although spaces of penal confinement were, architecturally speaking, private enclosures unto themselves, they did not operate in isolation from the wider society. The boundaries between the spaces of confinement and the public world were a lot more porous than colonial officials would have had one believe. The evidence for Barbados shows that even as persons were removed from the wider society as punishment, their punishment often consisted of working in the very public space in which they were deemed unsuitable to live. In 1882, for instance, inmates from Glendairy Prison worked at places as diverse as the Central Police Station in Bridgetown, on the grounds at Government House, and on the public roads. Up to the end of February that year, some inmates had even worked at the island's "lunatic asylum" in Codrington Hill.[76] Thus, one can see that the labor performed outside the jail's walls proved not only beneficial to the public, it also generated ample profits for the jail.[77] It is also not an exaggeration to argue that the penal system in Barbados in the nineteenth century helped to prop up the plantation economy. This direct contribution to the viability of the plantation economy was demonstrated in the creation of a cooperage in 1879 where convicts in Glendairy made sugar hogsheads and puncheons.[78] At the "lesser" prisons too the nexus between the public and private, the plantation economy and the prison, is also evident. At District A, C, and D prisons some of the stones broken by inmates were sold, and their proceeds were paid into the colonial treasury.[79]

In 1900, labor continued to be seen as the saving grace not only for Barbadian inmates but also for the very existence of the prison. The *Annual Colonial Report* of 1900 for this island set out in detail the remunerative value of prison labor. Based on the figures from this report, in 1900 the estimated value of male convict labor totaled £2,327, while the monetary value of female labor totaled £165, for a total of £2,492, as compared with a total of £2,538 in 1899.[80] The monetary value of this labor hints at a gendered division of work within the prison. Within the main jail in Barbados men performed specialized and highly skilled tasks like carpentry, painting, and tailoring, whereas women did laundry, cooked food for the prisoners, cultivated arrowroot, and prepared coconut fiber for mattresses, among other things.[81] Male prisoners working on the outside reconstructed breakwaters and quarried stone. Interestingly enough, some male prisoners who worked inside of the main jail in Barbados also cooked, although they tended to specialize in baking. While evidence suggests that women cooked only for the prison population, male bakers prepared their goods for populations outside of the prison, which solidified their value within the public sphere at the same time that it emphasized women's peripheral status within it.

Although physical labor was important in maintaining the prison economy and the plantation society, other types of activities conducted within the confines of the prison were also related to sustaining Barbados's plantation economy. For instance, the Boys' Reformatory and Industrial School at Dodds provided the home for Barbados's botanical station. Though one may be tempted to dream of exotic flora to rival the varieties at Kew Gardens bred in this space, the principal aim of the station was "the carrying on of Sugar Cane Experiments." These experiments were "conducted with a view to ascertaining the best varieties of sugarcane, to raising new seedling sugarcane plants, and making comparative manorial tests of various combinations of chemical compounds."[82] Although it is not known whether the boys confined in the reformatory were allowed to conduct any of these experiments or what role they played, if any, in these scientific ventures, there is a central thesis being enacted here in the confluence of the body made useful, spaces of punishment, and the wider plantation economy. Namely, when confined, inmates had to be engaged in productive work.

Barbados's spaces of penal confinement were related to the wider society in another sense. Along with being promoted as spaces to deal with criminals, they were actively promoted as sites to deal with those who had failed to take advantage of what the land offered. The combination of low wages and the high cost of living that characterized this period so severely affected the quality of life for the laboring classes that in 1863 there was an increase in looting on estates.[83] Law enforcement authorities responded by arresting 3,727 workers for stealing. While in prison, this class of laborers became violent, and the governor, according to Levy, "reluctantly agreed to revive corporal punishment as part of prison discipline." The jailer seemed not to agree with the governor's new "get tough" policy, however, as he released 1,961 of these prisoners to prevent them from dying in their cells. So severe was the problem of impoverishment and hunger in Barbados during the 1860s, Levy writes, that "scores of starving workers perished in the roadways on their way home [from prison]."[84]

The tendency to use prison as a stopgap for poverty did not end in 1863. In 1869 Colonial Secretary Granville also saw the prison as the solution to control a potentially restive and already severely constrained populace.[85] Historian Bruce Hamilton notes that between 1870 and 1875, a total of 1,641 persons were imprisoned for up to four months for failing to pay what were often small debts. Of this total, 1,306 were male and 335 were female. Juveniles too were often confined in jails for petty offenses like stealing sugarcane, and while in jail they were sometimes punished for offenses including bedwetting and "laughing and playing."[86]

The link between poverty and confinement was played out further in the types of crimes committed by the laboring classes. Sir Thomas Graham Briggs, member of the Barbados Council, was said to attribute "most of the petty crime that prevailed, particularly cane stealing, to the instigation of hunger." Hamilton supported this assertion by noting that a return of magistrates' proceedings for March 1876 showed that 152 persons had been charged with food stealing in comparison to those who had committed other offenses, 75 in number. A similar situation prevailed at the District B prison in St. George where forty-seven persons had been committed for food stealing but only nine for other offenses.[87]

Besides being notorious for its failed Confederation scheme, John Pope Hennessy's tenure as governor was noteworthy for its decidedly progressive and compassionate tenor, particularly with regard to attempts at disciplinary and punitive reform.[88] From the time of his arrival in Barbados in 1875, Hennessy seemed to be a man with change on his mind. One of his first tasks on the island was to investigate conditions in the jails in Barbados. He did this by examining the defaulter's book of the jails (which contained information about prisoners' offenses and punishments) and visiting some of the jails in the island.[89] From this comprehensive examination, Hennessy made a number of discoveries that compelled him to categorize conditions and punishment in Barbados's jails as the worst in the British West Indies. For example, he found that the number of floggings of prisoners over a six-year period was far greater than that of Jamaican prisoners over a commensurate period.[90] In a memorandum to the Colonial Office in 1875, Hennessy also noted that between 1870 and 1874 a total of 239 floggings were administered at the six prisons in Barbados, in comparison to 26 floggings administered in the prisons in Jamaica.[91]

Attempting to elicit reform by shaming the Barbadian public, Hennessy argued that Barbados was alone in the British Caribbean with respect to the extent of its reprehensibility. Citing the examples of jails in St. Lucia, St. Vincent, and

Grenada, where there had been no cases of flogging in 1875, he asserted that in Barbados, "in the first months" of that year, fifty prisoners had been flogged for infractions while confined. Outside of flogging, in the male department of Glendairy Prison, Hennessy found that in 1875 a total of 555 punishments had been employed against inmates, an astonishing practice, in Hennessy's view, "the daily average number of prisoners in that prison being under 72." According to Hennessy, this deplorable situation had compelled a Mr. Watts, the inspector of prisons, to call for wholesale penal reform, a call that he endorsed wholeheartedly. He also noted in his minutes to the House of Assembly that he had not been able to gain help ameliorating conditions from those with the authority to make the changes. Hennessy asserted that "some of the Magistrates and Prison Officials upheld the practice of flogging on the ground that 'for this class of people, it was the only deterrent punishment.'" Still, he was persistent. Hennessy pointed out to Barbadian jail officials that the imperial government "had expressed the hope in the year 1873, that the practice of flogging would be discontinued in Barbados," and he even showed them the returns (official reports) from the metropole and other British colonies "that cruel and degrading punishments were not sanctioned by the most experienced authorities, and that such punishments did not diminish the number of prison offences, but tended to increase them." Barbadian prison officials remained as resistant to Hennessy's entreaties as he was persistent. They were alleged by Hennessy to have responded to his claim about the deleterious impact of flogging with the assertion that "neither Her Majesty's Government nor [Hennessy] understood the people here, and that anything like leniency would only lead to an increase of prison offences."[92]

Indeed, his outspokenness and the reformist and participatory attitude that he brought to the administration of the penal system in Barbados put Hennessy on a collision course with the country's elites. In correspondence to the Earl of Carnarvon, the colonial secretary, Hennessy referred to the onerous and unpopular position that he occupied as he tried to get Barbadian administrators to adopt changes in the jails. Writing about his disapproval of the conduct of the visiting justice of Glendairy, FitzHerbert Alleyne, Hennessy noted that he had tried to prohibit Alleyne from using flogging as a method of punishment against inmates. Hennessy pointed out to Lord Carnarvon that this attempt had proved to be very unpopular and that it had "aroused the indignation of [Alleyne] and his friends." In stressing how difficult it would be for him to ban the flogging of inmates, he added: "[Alleyne] is a son-in-law of Sir Bowcher Clarke, and he has many relations in the House of Assembly, and in the Legislative Council. So extraordinary is the state of Society in Barbados, that any veto on Mr FitzHerbert Alleyne's floggings, is regarded by many of the leading gentlemen of the Island as an unwarrantable interference with magisterial rights."[93] Not only was Hennessy showing that as a reformer he basically stood alone, he also revealed that attitudes regarding the use of draconian forms of punishment were far-reaching.

As the governor of Barbados, Hennessy also lobbied for the judicial systems in the Windward Islands and Barbados to be melded and for the establishment of a central prison.[94] He saw this centralization as important to the better governance and administration of these colonial territories.[95] Although this proposal did not come to fruition, Hennessy's efforts certainly helped to steer the debates on punishment in Barbados in the 1870s. And prior to his departure for Hong Kong in 1876 to assume that colony's governorship, he was able to close the Town Hall Gaol under the provisions of the 1839 West India Prisons Act.[96]

Outside of the closure of the Town Hall Gaol, Hennessy's influence on the penal landscape of the British West Indies in the late nineteenth century is unknown.[97] What is clear, however, is that between 1879 and 1898 there was a diminution in the numbers of individuals confined in Glendairy Prison who received corporal punishment. Figure 1 in the appendix, depicting the number of inmates receiving corporal punishment in the prison between 1879 and 1898, gives a visual image of the lessening of corporal punishment in Barbados even as it continued. The graph's trajectory in the later years, particularly from 1890 to 1898, showing sharp decline, coincides with the introduction of alternative sanctions. One can argue that the body-punishment relation that had undergirded penal discipline was being challenged through these sanctions. These alternative sanctions included the introduction of the metric of good conduct to determine whether inmates could be granted tickets of leave. This was instituted in January 1850 and was seen as a method that could lead to the transformation of criminals. These releases from imprisonment were granted to any convict who had "behaved himself well during two thirds of his imprisonment," although juveniles could not receive tickets of leave.[98] Individuals who were granted tickets of leave were required to meet with their district police magistrate each week "and give a satisfactory account of himself or herself, and of his or her place of abode, and of his or her mode of life."[99] Tickets of leave could be revoked and the offender remanded to jail to complete his or her original sentence of confinement for a variety of transgressions, including being idle, leading a "dishonest life," or for committing any "substantive offence."[100] The popularity of the ticket-of-leave system may be seen in its continuation to the end of the nineteenth century. Under the Convicts' License Act of 1883, these tickets of leave could be granted to any confined person during his or her confinement.[101]

Statistical data can be important in showing measurable data, but they can also be revealing in what they suggest qualitatively. For instance, tables 11 and 12 in the appendix show that over half of Barbados's imprisoned population was illiterate, which correlates with illiteracy in the wider society. From this one could surmise that male and female convicts in Barbados throughout the nineteenth century tended to be the poorer, uneducated members of society. Between 1896 and 1901, only in 1900 was the percentage of confined men who were illiterate under 50 percent. Predictably, a somewhat lesser percentage of male prisoners were illiterate than women.

Yet the tables also challenge a shibboleth about the characteristics of jail populations, the one that holds that prison populations are always predominantly male. As a comparison of tables 11 and 12 shows, Barbados's imprisoned population in 1896–1901 consistently comprised more females than males, unlike in other parts of the Caribbean, like British Guiana and Trinidad, which tended to be predominantly male.[102] This gender imbalance seems also to have been true of Barbados's juvenile convict population: at least in 1901 the numbers were two boys and seven girls.[103]

Why was Barbados's jail population majority female during this period, especially when one notes that in the 1840s this was not the case? It is impossible to fully interrogate the data, but the colonial reports from which they are taken hint at a gendered apprehension of crime and punishment. One reason why more Barbadian women were imprisoned than Barbadian men may have been because women could not be whipped as punishment, which Paton noted for the case of Jamaica.[104]

Perhaps also female criminals were regarded as particularly harmful to the moral fabric of society and imprisoned more regularly for crimes that for men would have been treated as misdemeanors. The case for this is compelling when it is noted that the principal offenses committed by women—acts that presumably led to their imprisonment—included disorderly conduct, using abusive language, assault, and fighting. Arguably these would have actually been more prevalent than other types of crimes and easier to prove and prosecute since they tended to occur in public spaces, in the presence of witnesses. Moreover, the presence of larger numbers of women in spaces of confinement is in keeping with the notion of the incorrigibility of the female criminal. Throughout the discourse on punishment, even as there were calls to mitigate punishments meted out to female convicts, there were just as many calls for them to be harshly punished since, a common argument went, conventional punishments were incapable of reforming them. These figures, showing an increase in both the male and female imprisoned population in 1896–1901, might also reflect the increased importance of the jail as a technology of punishment as Barbados moved farther away from its slave past and into an era where the jail was embraced as a symbol of modernity.

By the beginning of the twentieth century, there were changes in some aspects of Barbados's penal system. The association system, under which inmates were required to share prison cells, had been discontinued, and Glendairy Prison was operating entirely on the separate system, with each prisoner having his or her own cell "excepting when the numbers exceed[ed] 388."[105] In Glendairy there were 266 separate cells for male prisoners and 122 for female prisoners. Still, overcrowding continued to be a problem in the prison, particularly in the lower prison. Although in Glendairy's upper prison each inmate had a separate cell of 995 cubic feet, in the lower portion of the prison there were three prisoners to a cell, with each having just 258 cubic feet of space, and there were twelve prisoners in each associated ward who were left with just 260 cubic feet of space per person.[106]

Conclusion

As this chapter illustrates, confinement in nineteenth-century Barbados was wide-ranging. It was not just in enclosed, constructed spaces that bodies were constrained. Laws in Barbados like those that attempted to staunch the flow of emigrants from the island show that there were various categories of confinement and boundedness on the island in the post-slavery period. By illustrating the links between the plantation as a site of employment, the wider plantation economy, and spaces of confinement, this chapter has shown that there was a symbiotic relationship between spaces, physical bodies, and the social order. Whether for punishment or exercises in colonial and capitalistic might, place and space were used by elites to constrain the bodies of Barbadian laborers and reinforce their position within the plantation society.

CHAPTER 5

Enclosing Contagion

Aberrant Bodies and Penal
Confinement in Jamaica

Discipline sometimes requires *enclosure*, the specification of a place
heterogeneous to all others and closed in upon itself. . . . But the
principle of "enclosure" is neither constant, nor indispensable, nor
sufficient in disciplinary machinery. . . . One must eliminate the
effects of imprecise distributions, the uncontrolled disappearance of
individuals, their diffuse circulation, their unusable and dangerous
coagulation; it was a tactic of anti-desertion, anti-vagabondage,
anti-concentration. Its aim was to establish presences and absences,
to know where and how to locate individuals, to set up useful
communications, to interrupt others, to be able at each moment to
supervise the conduct of each individual, to assess it, to judge it,
to calculate its qualities or merits. It was a procedure, therefore,
aimed at knowing, mastering and using. Discipline organizes an
analytical space. [emphasis in original]

—MICHEL FOUCAULT, *Discipline and Punish*

Whereas the passage of an emigration act was one part of how geographical spaces were used to control the Barbadian masses in the nineteenth century,
the Jamaican laboring classes were largely spared this type of corporeal control,
especially as it related to restrictions on their migration to more promising socio-
economic environs.[1] What Jamaican legislators and colonial officials could not
do in terms of regulating and disciplining laboring bodies within geographical
spaces, however, they more than made up for in their regulation of the bodies
that inhabited penal spaces. Thus, in Jamaica, jails and houses of correction remained major sites wherein blacks experienced a form of corporeal control that
involved surveillance.

This chapter shows that jails and houses of correction in Jamaica not only partitioned the so-called criminal classes from the law-abiding, they also reinforced the socio-racial order by continuing the colonial project operative on the outside. Their goal was similar to that found by Florence Bernault in the case of colonial Africa in that spaces of penal confinement in Jamaica "encouraged the preservation of social antagonisms vital to white hegemony and contributed actively to the task of ascribing race as the major marker of difference between rulers and ruled."[2]

Drawing on the work of human geographers and scholars like Robert D. Wilton, David Sibley, and E. Jeffrey Popke, I situate the discourse and practice of penal confinement in nineteenth-century Jamaica in theories about space, race, and the reconstruction of personal identities.[3] Although the work of these scholars deals with macro aspects of space, like the geographical landscape, I look at space on a micro level. I argue that ideas about space and its ability to unmake and remake individuals were a major part of prisons' raison d'être. This reading, seeing the built environment through the lens of punishment and individual identity, reveals that penal spaces in nineteenth-century Jamaica were not "dead" spaces.[4] This selective borrowing from the work of humanistic geographers shows that in nineteenth-century Jamaica, penal space was experienced as an enclosure that was at once "real, imaginary, and symbolic."[5]

This chapter also considers the contributions of Amos Rapoport, who argues for a symbiotic relationship between the built environment and individual subjectivity. In this sense, spaces of penal confinement in nineteenth-century Jamaica represented "a system of non-verbal communication."[6] This is true not only in the sense that state officials "communicated" ideas of legality and illegality through the confinement of individuals but also through the fact that within the practice of penal confinement ideas about the black body and blacks' place in the society were also firmly established.

Penal Spaces as Sites for Unmaking Alterity and Reinforcing the Socio-racial Order

The enclosed quarters of jails and houses of correction in nineteenth-century Jamaica represented a system of regimentation and control that to some degree mimicked relations in the outside world in that they reproduced ideas about a pathological blackness and the debased black body.[7] Yet these penal spaces were also buttressed by a paradoxical ethos. Although they were fueled by the idea that corralling and housing members of the criminal classes together could simultaneously punish and reform them, they were also tempered by the notion that lurking within these individuals remained potential criminality. It was only with surveillance, redemptive labor, and strict control that this criminality could be managed.

Apart from the fact that spaces of confinement in Jamaica were fulfilling their role as the consummate total institutions, there were many punitive practices within the institutions that reinforced their corporeal bent. Moreover, the statutes that brought these spaces into being tended to emphasize the corporeality of these institutions by employing evocative and motive terms like "able-bodied," "labor," "idle," and "disorderly" to categorize the individuals who would be confined in them. The language that was used in these statutes, although consistent with the times, tended to evoke images of wild, uncontrolled bodies at the same time that it emphasized that these would not be tolerated.

This pall of corporeality was visible earlier in "An Act for Establishing Public Workhouses in the Several Parishes of This Island," passed December 16, 1791.[8] The importance of this act to defining a successful social order was reinforced by its continuation after the abolition of slavery. In 1836 the Marquis of Sligo gave an unambiguous nod to the corporeal orientation of spaces of confinement when he asserted that "simple confinement is not at all the same punishment to a negro that it is to an inhabitant of a colder climate; they do not feel so acutely the deprivation of society; even solitary confinement is here a very inferior mode of punishment; and confinement in the workhouses, unless accompanied by diminution of food or hard labour, possesses no horrors for them."[9]

The act for establishing public workhouses in Jamaica represented an early attempt to establish institutions to deal with persons who, although "able-bodied," were thought to be unwilling to earn a living. So as not to encourage these persons into a life of idleness, and recognizing that "there [were] a great number of white vagrants and other disorderly persons about [the] island, who ought to be confined and set to work," this act ensured that workhouses in Jamaica would discourage and punish the apparently inseparable vices of unemployment and criminality. Thus, the workhouses would "compel idle and disorderly persons, by their own labour, to contribute to their own subsistence, and [would serve as] proper receptacles for all idle and runaway slaves in the several parishes of this island." So as not to discriminate among idle persons by using race or color, this act also made it clear that

> all white persons and free negroes and mulattoes, able in body, who, not having wherewith otherwise to maintain themselves, use loitering, and refuse to work for the usual common wages, and all other idle white persons, free negroes and free mulattoes, wandering abroad and begging (except soldiers, mariners or seafaring men, licensed by some testimonial in writing, under the hand and

seal of some justice of the peace, setting down the time and place of his or their landing, and the place to which he or they are to pass, and limiting the time for such their passage, while they continue in the direct way to the place to which they are to pass, and during the time so limited), shall be deemed rogues and vagabonds.[10]

From a reading of this act, one can see how Jamaica's elites defined criminality and glimpse the ideological foundations on which penal confinement was built. The impression gained is that an orderly and law-abiding society was characterized by an always-working populace, unless they had the means to maintain themselves without having to rely on the largesse of the state.

In Jamaica, both during slavery and well after its end, houses of correction were used to confine those who did not have full sovereignty over their bodies. This assertion is borne out in records provided by Stipendiary Magistrate John Thomas Bell in 1836: "Please receive into the house of correction the within-mentioned runaway and have her in safe custody until duly claimed by her overseer."[11] Lionel Smith, during his tenure as governor of Jamaica, saw spaces of confinement as sites for punishment rather than for the reformation of the criminal. In a dispatch to Lord Glenelg, Smith asserted:

> I hope your Lordship did not infer from my Despatch of the 12th June last, that the state of our prisons and workhouses possessed my entire approbation; one of the many evils of slavery has been the neglect of all such buildings beyond the immediate object of personal security, for they were not resorted to as places for the punishment and reform of prisoners, because the individual power of masters over slaves gave them more prompt means of punishment without incurring the expense of prison maintenance, or the loss of labour.[12]

Admittedly, the intrinsic function of these spaces was not solely to confine potentially wayward bodies. They served also as spaces in which to punish individuals defined as criminals and, in the cases of parish prisons and houses of correction, by putting already constrained individuals to work. Evidence to support this may be gleaned from "An Act for the More Effectual Protection of Persons and Property, and to Appoint Constables, and for Other Purposes," which was passed in Jamaica on June 15, 1836. Clause 14 of this law stipulated that houses of correction and designated parish prisons were to be prisons for hard labor only.[13] This clause stipulated further that "no person shall be otherwise received therein except for the punishment of solitary confinement; and in such prisons there shall be no distinction in the good and wholesome food or diet given to prisoners able to work, but in cases of debility or sickness the attending surgeon or physician of any such institution shall order all prisoners who may be in a weak or sick or debilitated state, to be put into the parish asylum, which usually is and ought to be attached or near to the house of correction."[14]

At the time of John Pringle's visit in the late 1830s, Jamaica was divided into the counties of Surrey, Middlesex, and Cornwall, each of which had its own jail. Pringle noted that those awaiting trial before the chief justice or under sentence by the court made up the bulk of those confined in the county jails. Surrey, Middlesex, and Cornwall were further divided into twenty-one parishes, with petty and quarter sessions of court held in each parish. Each parish also had its own jail and house of correction, although in several of the parishes these two institutions would sometimes be under the same roof. During his investigation in Jamaica, Pringle noted that the majority of prisoners sentenced to confinement in the houses of correction, by contrast to those in the jails, were mostly apprentices. Those confined in houses of correction who had been committed there by local magistrates had been sentenced for crimes like theft, trespass, and assault, while those who had been sentenced by the stipendiary magistrates had been sent there for disputes between plantation owners and apprentices. Those in the jails—with the exception of those waiting to be transported or those sentenced to death—were usually free persons.[15]

In 1837 Jamaican jails were under the control of the provost marshal, who had the authority to appoint deputies to different districts of the island to serve as keepers of the jails, and the deputies in turn had the power to appoint subordinate officers. At this time also, regulations for the jails and their inspection were entrusted to a jail committee made up of local magistrates. Along with being responsible for appointing subordinate officers, the deputy provost marshal was responsible for serving summonses, writs, and warrants—duties that the deputy provost marshal, according to Pringle, frequently passed on to his underjailer. As a consequence, the jails were "often left for several days in charge of a boatswain, who in some places, as at St. Anns and Montego Bay, is a convict for life." To add to the idea of the insecurity that seemed endemic in the jails, Pringle noted that there was no night watch or patrol, a lapse to which he attributed the frequent escapes from the jails at Morant Bay, St. Elizabeth, and Buff Bay.[16]

Lapses did not end with the absence of night patrols. Pringle found that there was little systematization within the Jamaica jails and that there was no systematic classification and separation of prisoners. The only type of classification that existed was based on sex, and separation by sex occurred only at night. The exceptions to this problem of lax classification were seen in the jails in Spanish Town, where the debtors had a separate yard from other prisoners, and in Kingston, where both debtors and females had a separate yard.[17] Some distinction was also between apprentices and non-apprentices, as is seen in the jail books. These contain entries of the prisoners' names, specifying the dates convicted, committed, and discharged, and they list apprentices and non-apprentices separately.

Although reports of abuses had led to Pringle's assignment, his own report, published in 1838, contained numerous references to the ineffectiveness of jails and houses of correction as punishment. For instance, he noted that although Section 5 of the Jamaica Gaol Act of 1834 stipulated that the confined should be provided with work, he felt that such labor would be a more effective punishment if prisoners sentenced to short terms "were made to perform in silence" and under "strict supervision." Such an approach, he believed, "would be more severely felt than working on the roads, and in some degree tend to effect amendment by creating a dread of recommittal." Pringle asserted later in his report that the treadmill could be "considered as work within the walls, or at least a substitute; it does not, however, act as an equal punishment, being much less felt by those accustomed to it than by others who are not."[18]

This idea that hard labor potentially could unmake forms of alterity said to exist within certain individuals was prevalent in both the colony and the metropole in various periods. In eighteenth-century Britain, for example, the Penitentiary Act, or Hard Labour Bill, stipulated that all offenders were "to be kept to labour of the hardest and most servile kind."[19] Edward Cardwell, principal secretary of state for the colonies, also held the view that penal labor had rehabilitative and transformative benefits. In a dispatch sent to the colonies on January 16, 1865, he opined that "labour enforced by the tread-wheel or the crank for a minimum term of imprisonment or portion of the sentence, is considered by the Lords' Committee to be essential in the case of every prisoner condemned to imprisonment with hard labour." He added:

> It is, indeed, by severe suffering in the earlier portion of a sentence, rather than by sufferings prolonged through a series of years, that a deterrent effect is produced; for the class of persons by whom offences are generally committed do not look far forward, and they are governed by what is presently and not by what is distantly within their view. Rigorously penal labour, therefore, which is generally of necessity wholly or more or less unproductive, should be enforced at first; and afterwards, in long sentences, it may be possible to combine industrial employment with some relaxation of penal rigour.[20]

The acute attention that was paid to ensuring that the confined were inconvenienced also formed a part of the ideology of unmaking. This, too, was a way of ensuring that the alterity that was assumed to be present in certain individuals would be extinguished. The successful obliteration of alterity was seen as making the difference between a changed individual and a recidivist. To this end, confinement in nineteenth-century Jamaica rested on the principle of "less eligibility," a philosophy steeped in ideas about racialized bodies and reforming the criminal body.[21] What this philosophy meant in practice, according to contemporary historian Diana Paton, was that conditions inside of spaces of penal confinement in Jamaica had to be qualitatively and psychically worse than conditions on the outside. Jamaican prisoners were therefore provided with the bare minimum that was necessary for their comfortable existence inside of these spaces. Prisoners in Jamaica wore no uniforms, nor were they provided with any bedding—instead they slept either on a raised bench or on the floor. Moreover, cleanliness was neither strictly enforced nor encouraged, as the confined were not provided with soap.

This philosophy of "less eligibility" contrasted with conditions that obtained in metropole corrections. Heather Tomlinson, writing on English prisons in the nineteenth century, notes that the maintenance of good health in the prison system was thought to be related to cleanliness and hygiene, an idea that was supported by the requirements that prisoners be bathed on entering the prison "and at monthly intervals thereafter." Providing even more of a contrast to spaces of penal confinement in Jamaica, architectural changes in English institutions included the fitting of baths in the basement of the prison at Pentonville. It was stipulated also that the prisoners were to be bathed in tepid water, and the number of prisoners who were to be bathed in the same bath water was outlined. The prisoners were issued brooms each morning at Pentonville, with which cells were to be kept clean.[22]

The idea of "less eligibility" was also expressed in the food allotted to those confined in the prisons and workhouses of Jamaica. Although specifically referring to the 1840s, John Daughtrey, the inspector of prisons in Jamaica at that time, pointed out in his report that although prison diet was important to the overall health of the prisoner, the quality of the food should be "plain and coarse" and basically "less palatable than the prisoner has been accustomed to when at large."[23]

The racialized expression of the concept of "less eligibility" is unmistakable. An investigation into the operation of the prison system in Jamaica in the 1870s revealed, for instance, that beds were not used in any of the prisons. Instead, inclined planes of wood called "guard-beds" were used in the associated wards, while those who were housed in cells slept on the floor. This was explained away with the statement that "very few of the class of people from which the prisoners are drawn here have, or wish to have, any better accommodation at home."[24]

Space and how it could be used as a part of discipline and punishment are seen not only in its qualitative manifestations but also in its quantitative, measurable manifestations. The authors of the 1870s report acknowledged that the number of cubic feet allowed for each prisoner was indeed "very small." They went on to add that based on "the opinion of most of the medical men who were examined by us that no such ill-results as might have been expected have followed from the confined space in which the prisoners are locked up. This may be accounted for partly by the habits of the population when in their own homes, and partly by the constant perflation of air through the wards and cells."[25]

This concept of space and what was sufficient or insufficient without diminishing the severity of punishment seemed only relevant, however, in terms of skin color. The authors of the report felt that "in the case of white prisoners a much larger number of cubic feet [was] necessary, and this, we gather from the opinion of the medical witnesses, should not be less than 600 cubic feet [per person]." However, the amount of space given to individual prisoners varied. The fourteen male prisoners who were locked up in the Hanover District Prison in Lucea had only 192 cubic feet of space per person.[26]

In 1885, debates about space and its relation to condign punishment were still prevalent. In a report on crimes and prisons in Jamaica, it was noted that "the cubic space in the cells of the General Penitentiary is very small—330 and 375 feet, when 800 is considered the minimum."[27] In an acerbic comment on this practice, historian Patrick Bryan writes that this discrepancy in the sizes of prison cells was not, however, proof "that Jamaican prisoners at the time were half the size of Englishmen."[28]

Although offering comfort to the constrained body was not a paramount aim of penal discipline, the spiritual and intellectual welfare of the prisoners generated some interest in Jamaica. In fact, religion was seen by colonial officials as one of the key ingredients in the reformation of criminals—even though this assertion comes with some caveats, as the spiritual reformation of the criminal tended to be driven largely by the same self-interest that governed penal administration. Even though it was seen as necessary, instruction, whether secular or religious, was not to "interfere or conflict with the hours of labour."[29] In this sense, it appeared that Jamaican elites had put a colonial stamp on the various metropole-based theses that sought to explain criminal behavior. Consequently the Jamaican brand of the "evangelical thesis" was given less weight than the "associative thesis" (that the human mind seeks to repeat that which gives pleasure and avoid that which gives pain) —unsurprising in an economy where labor was king. Like proponents of the evangelical thesis in the metropole, Jamaican elites knew that they had to reform the "moral defectiveness of each prisoner" through the "sanctifying influence of the Holy Spirit." But the evidence suggests that they knew that ultimately their criminals had to be reformed through "a measured quantity of pain over a period of time sufficient to reverse the attitude to criminal action and the vices believed to be associated with it."[30]

The Jamaican Act to Amend the Prisons Consolidation Act in 1856 reflected aspects of this evangelical thesis by giving the governor the power to appoint a chaplain for the General Penitentiary and for each prison with a population of one hundred or more. Highlighting the elitism and divisions within Christianity, this chaplain could only be a member of the Church of England "duly licensed by the Bishop." In the thirtieth section of the act, island curates were required to visit the prisons in their parish to which a chaplain had not been appointed and "perform Divine Service and afford religious instruction to the prisoners confined therein at such time and in such manner as the Governor should direct, so as not to neglect their parochial duties." This appointment of clergy was to have transformative qualities on the minds of the inmates, yet it was felt that this could happen only if the clergy were a daily fixture in the prison. Thus, it was revealed in the report from the prison inquiry of the 1870s that a clergyman should be appointed who could "devote his whole time to the prisoners placed under his spiritual care." The authors of the report concluded: "We cannot see how a body of ministers, who merely perform a single service in rotation on Sundays, and attend at rare and uncertain intervals for a single hour during the week, can exercise the same influence for good over the minds of the prisoners as a chaplain." Using statements from a Father Hathaway to further support their argument, the commissioners were keen to show how moral osmosis might work. Hathaway, who had been a minister to Roman Catholic prisoners in Millbank and Tothill Fields in England, is reported to have said:

> I think a man who goes about the prisoners and obtains moral influence over them would do more good than all the preaching in the world; I say so from my own experience, because at Millbank, when I was merely allowed to preach twice a week, very little was done; but when I was allowed to go and speak to the people in private, a great deal of good was done, and the Government Inspector reported that there was an immense improvement in the very first year; for permanent reformation, nothing can supply the moral influence of a man whom the prisoners know and feel to be their friend.[31]

At the other prisons in Jamaica, including those at Lucea, Montego Bay, Falmouth, and the short-term prison at St. Ann, the committee members reported that services were conducted on Sundays. However, religious services were not held in the Middlesex and Surrey County Gaol, and ministers did not visit the jail "except when prisoners [were] confined there under sentence of death."

These examples led the committee members to conclude that "the religious instruction of the prisoners is left to chance, and in most cases is very much neglected."[32]

This casualness in providing religious instruction to the confined at the Middlesex and Surrey County Gaol seems at odds with a later communication, in 1886, in which it was intimated that religious instruction formed an integral component of penal policy. In fact, this 1886 dispatch delineated a contemporary form of ecumenicalism. Its author noted that the religious services at the penitentiary were by clergy from several denominations, including Baptists, Roman Catholics, Wesleyans, and ministers from the Church of England. Provisions were even made for cases where the number of prisoners from one denomination was said to be too small, and in this case the said prisoners would be "placed under the charge of the Chaplain of one of the larger denominations."[33] In addition to this attention to the moral instruction of the confined, attention was also paid to their secular instruction, and by 1885 a school had been opened in Jamaica's General Penitentiary.[34]

The reform of the spirit was a key component of penal ideology in the rest of the British West Indies too. For instance, the prison in Antigua also included a chaplain in its roster of personnel. He too had a key role to play in the lives of the confined as he was primarily responsible for their spiritual and moral reformation. In Antigua he came in the person of the Reverend Robert Holberton, who visited the prison every Sunday morning from seven to eight to "read prayers and deliver a religious discourse to the inmates." A more macabre role included accompanying those who were to be executed to the "last sad scene of their mortal career."[35]

In constructing and designating the spaces of jails and houses of correction as sites to unmake the criminal and transform him or her into an upstanding citizen, prison administrators and colonial and imperial authorities relied also on a variety of disciplinary and punitive techniques, each of which required that some degree of force be applied to the body. For instance, in the houses of correction, prisoners' hair was shaved off, male and female prisoners were chained and worked on public roads, and corporal punishment was often awarded by the local magistrates for breaches of prison protocol. In addition, convicts were often sentenced to labor on the treadmill. The treadmill was employed, for example, at the house of correction and jail at Spanish Town, with prisoners being worked on it for periods of five, eight, and ten minutes. Similarly, at the house of correction and jail at Halfway Tree in St. Andrew, the treadmill was used to punish convicts. The men were kept on for fifteen minutes, the women for ten, with a half hour for rest in between stints. Convicts went on eight times a day, though Pringle was careful to point out that the treadmill was seldom used. Flogging was also resorted to, although it was only done for "general crimes" and was carried on outside on the public road.[36] The use of the treadmill at the house of correction in St. Andrew was also confirmed by Thome and Kimball. Although, like Sturge and Harvey, they were members of an anti-slavery society and thus used their trip to the British West Indies to highlight the abuses in the apprenticeship system, their findings are noteworthy. They noted that both male youths and women with young children were forced to dance on the treadmill.[37] Both male and female prisoners were also punished on treadmills in houses of correction and jails in other parishes during the apprenticeship period. Also, in St. John, both men and women were chained with fetters six feet long, and with the combined weight of the chain and collar being three and a quarter pounds. All told, out of the thirty-two jails and houses of correction visited by Pringle, twenty-four of them relied on methods of punishment that targeted the body.[38]

Direct attacks against the bodies of black prisoners occurred in other ways besides via the treadmill and ever-present whip, although one of their principal aims—to transform—remained identical. At the house of correction and jail at Spanish Town, male and female prisoners were chained, with a collar around their necks. These chains were six feet long and weighed five pounds. By comparison, women who were confined in the house of correction and jail at Port Antonio in Portland were not chained. That practice had been discontinued after 1834, according to Mr. Redmond, the supervisor of the jail.[39]

The politics and potency of difference that characterized the wider society also found expression in places of confinement, in spite of George Grey's admonition that all inmates were to be treated equally. This meant also that somatic differences became a way of distinguishing between the confined (the criminal) and those who were not. Also, these differences provided a visual marker in the process of unmaking and remaking individuals. In essence, Pringle found that in the Jamaican jails the apprentices were generally treated more harshly than the "free-convicts," thus giving lie to Glenelg's assertion that the apprenticeship system brought with it the full trappings of freedom. Pringle showed, for instance, that whereas the free-convicts were not locked up until eight in the evening, the apprentices were locked up two hours earlier, at six. However, he also pointed out that in the houses of correction some English sailors were subjected to the same hours of confinement as the apprentices.[40] Another difference was in the use of restraints. Whereas apprentice convicts in the Kingston jail were fettered with leg irons weighing between nine and fifteen pounds, other convicts, mostly soldiers, were not fettered.[41] Essentially, it was noted that chains were used when it was felt that the situation warranted it—in the case of those who had tried to escape, for instance. Other examples that illustrate that a pall of corporal punishment hung over prisons in Jamaica were seen in the Surrey County Gaol at Kingston, where it was discovered that prisoners had been whipped, including one by the name of Thomas Gordon, for refusing to work. At this same institution, other prisoners had been flogged with various instruments, including a "cowskin" whip and sticks. The European soldiers who had been confined in this jail confirmed this selective use of corporal punishment when they told Pringle that black convicts had been hit, "but only when they deserved it, from their insolent and disrespectful language to the officers."[42]

Like the jails, the houses of correction in Jamaica were driven by the philosophy that penal discipline that was largely physical was the key to good penal administration and necessary for the reformation of the criminal. This may not be too surprising considering that the regulations in the houses of correction were based on the Jamaica Gaol Act. Consequently, there were many similarities in how these two places of confinement were administered. For example, as in the jails, the "boatswains" of the yard and the penal gang in the houses of correction were prisoners themselves, some serving a life sentence. Betraying an almost insidious continuity, the supervisors in the houses of correction were usually ex-planters or former businessmen. Their wives also played a role in these institutions, normally serving as matrons (overseers of female prisoners), but, in Pringle's words, usually "above the duties of such a situation."[43]

It should be pointed out, however, that at the same time that the bodies of the laboring classes were being debased within places of confinement, prior to Pringle's visit there had been a slight mitigation in some of the punishments carried out in them. This was exemplified in Pringle's findings that corporal punishment was resorted to infrequently, that at some jails female convicts were not flogged, and that pregnant women were never placed on the treadmill.[44] Paton's findings, however, reveal paradoxes in this exercise in compassion that were absent from Pringle's report. She showed that even though apprentice women could not be whipped outside of the prison walls, they were often whipped while imprisoned. In addition, the stipulation that female apprentices could not be whipped also made them more likely to be imprisoned as a form of punishment.[45]

Indeed, at the time of Pringle's visit, places of confinement in Jamaica functioned by exerting an almost total control over the bodies of the confined. This was manifested in the forms of regimentation that presumably were intended to inculcate habits of obedience and discipline into individuals. There were strict regulations over all aspects of the inmates' time. As a case in point, Pringle found that all prisoners sentenced to hard labor could be worked for up to ten hours a day. Strict observance of time was also to be maintained by those who worked in the penal gang. Prisoners working in these gangs were required to be locked up in their cells by seven in the evening, except in the case of debtors. This strict regulation of the life of the criminal is demonstrated further in Pringle's assertion that "the utmost order and strictest silence was to be observed by all prisoners when at work on the treadmill."[46] This regulation of the tempo of the prisoners' lives and even their speaking reinforced that spaces of confinement were punitive.[47] In this sense, the daily rhythm characteristic of spaces of confinement would have helped to differentiate the confined from the jail personnel as they would have been subject to different temporal spheres.[48]

Punishment for inmates contravening prison regulations was corporeal in nature. It could range from being placed in solitary confinement to being put on a diet of bread and water for up to six days. Jailers and other prison officials were also liable to be punished for breaches in jail regulations. Those officials who flouted the rules of these institutions were liable to pay a fine or penalty of up to twenty pounds, and if they defaulted on this payment they could be imprisoned in the jail or house of correction for a maximum of sixty days.[49]

After Pringle's visit in 1837, although spaces of confinement continued to function as sites whose managers sought complete control over the bodies of the proletariat, his findings precipitated changes in the penal system. In a dispatch of 1838, Lord Glenelg noted that when Pringle had visited the British West Indies over the previous year, he had discovered a class of prisoners who were still defined as runaways and confined for this now defunct crime. Those languishing in jail under anachronistic laws and mores were ordered by Glenelg to be granted a "free pardon" since "the continued punishment of these offenders must be an unprofitable suffering now that there are no longer any persons who could be deterred by it from the repetition of similar offences."[50] This issue was also taken up by Lionel Smith during his governorship in Jamaica, prompting him to pardon several prisoners who had been confined under the slave laws. Thus, on July 13, 1838, he pardoned prisoners like Samuel Mills, who had been committed in February 1831 for running away; Thomas Watt of St. Mary's, who had been imprisoned since 1824 for robbing his master; and Neil from St. Thomas in the East, who had been imprisoned in 1831 for "practising obeah." All told, Smith pardoned 173 men and women who had been confined in houses of correction and jails.[51]

The discovery of this class of prisoners and other penal anachronisms prompted the British government to pass the Act for the Better Government of

Prisons in the West Indies, also known as the West India Prisons Act, in 1839. The provisions of this act were framed partly on Pringle's report on prisons in Jamaica and "partly on the precedent of provisions relating to the same subject as it respects prisons in [Britain]."[52] This act would also eventually be evidence for twentieth-century scholars like Philip D. Curtin who would argue that the laws and institutions of the British West Indies, Jamaica in particular, drew their inspiration from Britain.[53] Curtin would assert that Jamaican legislators "found it convenient to neglect what the home government neglected" while they reformed "what the home government reformed."[54] This view is supported by a call in 1836 from Barbadian governor Lionel Smith for the jail system there to be assimilated, "as far as local circumstances may allow," with that of the mother country.[55]

The West India Prisons Act transferred the regulation and management of the prisons from the colonial legislatures to the West Indian governors. Glenelg saw this as "the only effectual mode" of accomplishing a uniform system of prison superintendence in the British West Indies. In spite of Glenelg's endorsement of this act, it was met with great resistance by the members of the Jamaican House of Assembly, who went as far as to declare it unconstitutional and even "refused to do any business until it was repealed."[56] In spite of the rabid disapproval of the Jamaican government to this act, at a very basic level it demonstrated the Crown's concern for prisoners in the colonies and a realization that they had to be treated with some degree of humanity and equanimity.

Other changes were also made in Jamaican prison administration. For instance, the keeper of all places of confinement, whether county or parochial jails or houses of correction or other prisons, was to reside at the place of confinement. As was the case in England, the keeper was not to be engaged in any other profession. There was also to be more systematic surveillance, and as far as was "practicable" the keeper was required to visit all the wards, see all the prisoners, and inspect all the cells, at least once every twenty-four hours. A matron was to be appointed to oversee the female prisoners and was also expected to reside at the place of confinement. During surveillance, the matron was to accompany the keeper of the jail when he visited the female prisoners.

The changes in Jamaican penal administration also addressed the opacity and lack of systematization that had previously characterized it, particularly in regard to punishment. An act to regulate all of the jails, houses of correction, and other spaces of confinement, passed in Jamaica on December 21, 1839, stipulated that all punishments, whether administered by resident officers or visiting justices, were to be recorded in a journal. Also, the issue of classifying different categories of prisoners is evident in the act: it stipulated that male and female prisoners were to be housed in separate buildings or parts of the prison or house of correction "so as to prevent them from seeing, conversing, or holding any intercourse with each other."[57]

Surveillance and the Controlling of "Moral Mischief"

Captain J. W. Pringle, mineralogist and fellow of the Royal Engineers, had embarked on a new odyssey when he spearheaded the investigation of prison conditions in the Caribbean.[58] When he set out for the British West Indies in 1837 bearing the mandate of the British government, his task seemed simple enough: to investigate colonial prison discipline and administration.[59] After the publication of James Williams's narrative earlier that year, along with other reports of abuses in the jails and houses of correction in Jamaica, Pringle's appointment saw the imperial government taking a more aggressive stance in the administration of institutions that had till then been left primarily in the hands of the colonial governments.

Pringle was only one individual in a long line of persons like Henry Coleridge (1825) and Joseph Sturge and Thomas Harvey (1837), who had investigated and written about conditions in spaces of confinement in the British West Indies. Though Pringle's predecessors did not have the stamp of approval from the British government like he did, their contributions were nonetheless valuable.

Although working within an environment with established mores about punishment, spaces of penal confinement, and the punished, Pringle contributed substantively to the discourse about how to control wayward bodies in the colonies. Beyond that, his findings and report led ultimately to changes in the administration of jails and houses of correction in the British West Indies, Jamaica in particular. However, the underlying assumption remained that these spaces were either to contain or unmake forms of alterity. This unmaking, it was presumed, rested on the application of corporal punishment, the adoption of "habits" like industriousness and servile obedience, the inculcation of religious values, and a realization, particularly on the part of the laboring classes, that one's social status was always already determined. Pringle, in spite of his revelations about major architectural and cultural defects in Jamaican penal spaces, like the colonial and imperial officials with whom he interacted, concurred with this ethos of social and cultural determinism, and so his suggestions for improvements and his overall prison report were in keeping with these ideas. What was missing from his report was an analysis of how the prison could potentially breed forms of alterity. His report failed to answer some critical questions that officials in Jamaica and other parts of the West Indies continued to grapple with. What happens when the space set aside for reform, discipline, and punishment begins to produce its own alterity? Can managers of a diseased institution reform it and make it well while renewing its reason for being?

Although jails and houses of correction functioned as spaces to deconstruct alterity and construct acceptable morality, their setup, particularly the association system (shared cells), was thought to engender sexual immorality and other behaviors that fit under the alterity rubric. The commission appointed by Jamaican governor John Grant in March 1873 is one of the most notable instances of a colonial attempt to investigate what MP Kimberley saw as a "still defective" penal system. The commission was created to "investigate the internal condition of the Jamaica prisons with special reference to the question [of] whether the associated system engenders depravity and tends to the permanent degradation of youthful and casual offenders."[60]

Lord Kimberley was not alone in his concerns about the depravity that the association system was said to engender. In fact, Governor Grey, like Kimberley, saw the association system as an evil that needed to be stamped out. For both of these men the concern was not only that different classes of criminals were not separated from each other but also that prisoners shared quarters *at night*. It was this spatial closeness and physical proximity, which, in Grey's mind, could lead to sexual perversion. Although upon investigation the committee concluded that "there is no reason to believe that unnatural offences are at all prevalent," Governor Grey remained unconvinced and felt it was "impossible to feel satisfied that the evil [did] not exist." He was also adamant that "the only sure and perfectly effectual means of preventing it is to put a stop to all association of prisoners during the night."[61]

Grey's concerns about prisoners' nighttime activities echoed words from the past. In 1849 Jamaican prison inspector Daughtrey had opined that it was not wise to "crowd bad men together at night." Not only did Daughtrey regard this as counterproductive to the enforcement of "good order" and effective discipline, he also saw it as capable of engendering a kind of "moral mischief" harder to staunch than the disorderly behavior of inmates.[62]

Lighting and regular surveillance were seen as countering the wickedness that darkness was thought to engender in spaces of penal confinement, although the absence of light had previously been part of punishment in some instances— as when apprentices were confined in plantation dungeons as James Williams was.[63] The employment of Argus-eyed tactics like surveillance, it was felt, was necessary to control the unsanctioned conduct of prisoners' bodies. In Barbados, for instance, at the District A prison, the prisoners' dormitories were lit with gas lamps, while coconut oil lamps were used at Districts C and D. In addition, at

District A and C prisons, patrols and inspections of the dormitories were conducted every half-hour, while at District D the policeman on guard patrolled several times during the night.[64] This process of policing and surveillance, with its regimentation, was carried out with the aid of "telltale clocks," invented in the eighteenth century and intended to ensure that "night watchmen" were doing their duty.[65] This rhythm of surveillance and presence of lights, clocks, and half-hourly patrols not only betrays anxiety about potential loss of control over the bodies of the prisoners, it also hearkens back to the master-planter anxiety over the leisure activities of slaves. In both cases the object was control. In Foucauldian terms, "inspection function[ed] ceaselessly. The gaze [was] alert everywhere."[66] Managers of places of confinement in the British West Indies after 1834 sought total control over inmates' bodies, regulating and monitoring every aspect of their lives.

In other parts of the Caribbean too, the association system was seen as exerting a pernicious hold over the bodies of inmates and diluting the efficacy of places of confinement. As in Jamaica, the discourse regarding this also entailed dualism: darkness versus light, good versus evil, debauchery versus morality. In Trinidad, the association system and the female working-class criminal were deprecated in an 1883 newspaper piece. After noting the harmful impact of the don't-care-a-damns on Trinidadian society and expressing pessimism about society's inability to improve matters in this case, the author contended that prison seemed to increase rather than decrease depravity.

> With respect to isolation when in prison, any one who has heard of, or in any way has learnt of, the association which this class of women carry on among themselves, must readily conceive what a hotbed of vice must be the prison cell in which two or three women are allowed to sleep together. Apart from the natural tendency of their conversation, which is always that of encouragement to each other in the course for which they have become amenable to a short term of imprisonment, there are other indulgences which decency and propriety forbid the public journalist to mention publicly, but it may be well to say that the want of isolation in prison to a female offender of the classes we speak, is a want which plunges her daily in the depths of a far greater degradation than, perhaps, the misdemeanour which exposed her to a sentence of a few weeks imprisonment.[67]

Not only did the "public journalist" condemn female criminals, his reference to them as part of a particular class again shows how by casting the criminal as the Other, boundaries were created to distinguish them from "respectable" members of society. The author portrayed these women as licentious or having too much freedom, particularly with their bodies. This is implied through his attention to their visible presence on thoroughfares and public walks and evident in his view that their conduct in jails was audacious. After all, they were supposed to be reformed there and their bodies subordinated to the laws, the jailer, and punishment. Finally, these women challenged the very mold in which they had been cast, that of their gender and the lot that this entailed. Essentially, to this writer's dismay, these "loose women" did not uphold the "welfare [of their] community" as their gender dictated.[68]

Conclusion

In the final analysis, spaces of penal confinement in Jamaica, as in Barbados and the rest of the British West Indies, functioned as spaces to enclose perceived contagion from the rest of society. They functioned also to preserve the social order by reinforcing the raced, gendered, and classed inequalities that existed on the outside.

CHAPTER 6

The Punished Black Body and the Public's Gaze

Demarcating Socio-racial Structures through the Theatrics of Punishment

> But, in this scene of terror, the role of the people was an ambiguous one. . . . Not only must people know, they must see with their own eyes. Because they must be made to be afraid; but also because they must be the witnesses, the guarantors, of the punishment, and because they must to a certain extent take part in it.
>
> —MICHEL FOUCAULT, *Discipline and Punish*

> Some women managed to retrieve their locks, and when they were released from the factory, these locks made "a nice litle [*sic*] plait for the front, which gives [them] all the fascinating appearance of having long hair, and of course not having been punished."
>
> —JOY DAMOUSI, *Depraved and Disorderly*

Chapters 4 and 5 of this book show that spaces of confinement were a core part of the punitive and disciplinary landscape in colonial Barbados and Jamaica, and additional punishment, such as flogging, was equally embedded in these societies. This chapter shows that some of these punishments, including hair-cropping and prison labor in view of the public, depended upon the public gaze to be effective.

In addition, the public gaze that was called upon to help effect these punishments was also called upon to aid in the construction of a social narrative that marked blackness and the black body as problematic. In this regard, individuals who observed the punishments of others, through their ostensibly passive participation as onlookers, were part of a verification process. Their presence was used to cement the "fact" of a pathological blackness. In addition, the acts of punishment they witnessed were to be evidence of the alleged fundamental differences between blacks and whites and between black bodies and white bodies.

In Barbados and Jamaica, public punishments were enacted in a setting where race, color, class, and the plantation economy coalesced. As a result, although these punishments performed the same functions there that they did the world over—namely, shaming those defined as criminal by inviting the public to remark upon the punishment and the bodies of the punished—in Jamaica and Barbados public punishments were made responsible for producing and reproducing the social and spatial ordering inherent in the plantation economy. To be more precise, in nineteenth-century Barbados and Jamaica public punishments were used to reinforce the hegemony of colonial and imperial authorities and to reinforce the idea of the superiority of the plantocracy vis-à-vis the inferiority of the laboring classes. Perhaps most importantly, public punishments used the bodies of black men and black women to help craft a narrative about blackness and to further demarcate the socio-racial boundaries that gave the plantation society its local color.

To accomplish their administrators' ambitious aims, therefore, public punishments like hair-cropping, public flogging, public works, and hanging were geared to the continuation of the plantation economy.[1] The first sprocket in this gear was the use of bodies as broadsheets to publish the punishment, publication that was to simultaneously annihilate the crime (and its potency) and restore hegemony and a supposedly superior morality to the aggrieved party or parties.

A second sprocket in the gear comprised spectators, whose role was to express disapproval of the criminals—disapproval that would be read as condemnation of crimes and acknowledgment of the unshakeable authority of the aggrieved. A third and final sprocket was the staged and multifaceted performance of punishment. Not only was the punishment to be memorable, its execution was also to be visually arresting. Thus, for example, in the wake of the Morant Bay Rebellion in Jamaica, suspected rebels were not just shot, their lifeless, bullet-riddled bodies were then hung from trees for all to see—and to learn from. The staged element of public punishment was dependent upon a rapacious appropriation of space. In this regard, public punishments in nineteenth-century Jamaica and Barbados were often carried out in marketplaces and in front of courthouses—a calculated appropriation of spaces with dramatic and provocative potential. The marketplace, for example, known for its mélange of working-class optimism and black enterprise, was inverted and used for the spectacle of humiliation and terror.

In examining hair-cropping, public flogging, public works, and hanging and in ascribing potency to the spaces in which they were carried out, I draw on the work of Australian criminologist John Braithwaite, who in a 1989 study designates punishments inviting humiliation as "participatory form[s] of social control."[2] As participatory forms of social control, public punishments in Barbados and Jamaica in the nineteenth century begged for the crowd's involvement. Their success—in deterring potential criminals and cementing the social order—depended on a spectacle of contrite and shamed individuals. The viewing public was expected to respond to the state's punishment with awe and fear, while the punished individuals were to be a mirror of sorts in which the public would see themselves and recoil.

Because the bodies of the punished served as didactic devices, it was necessary also for them to be deployed strategically to target competing publics. These diametrically opposed publics consisted of the "criminal classes" and "law-abiding citizens," "loyal" and "disloyal" subjects, and elites and those from the working classes. Additionally, addressing these different publics, the punished body was used as a visual marker that helped to create and solidify the multiple boundaries defining each group. Moreover, by examining public punishments that were used in Barbados and Jamaica, this chapter notes the complicity of the state in defining and redefining the boundaries of what constituted legitimate and illegitimate punishments through the bodies of individuals.

As Michel Foucault and Joy Damousi intimate in the epigraphs to this chapter, this relationship between the public and punishment could be quite complex and even ambiguous. This complexity and ambiguity was evident also in the technologies of public punishment used in Barbados and Jamaica after 1834.[3] Therefore, even as it gives a nod to the ability of the public to contribute to the impact of punishment and to reinforce the racist ideologies upon which the plantation economy was structured, this chapter recognizes also that it was this very dependence on public participation that compromised the efficacy of public punishments. Even though the public gaze could be quite powerful (it could censure, render guilt, bear witness, punish, and transform), paradoxically, the public gaze could also nullify its seeming omnipotence. In this respect, and following the theories of contemporary scholars of punishment like Michael Ignatieff, it must be said that the real potency of the public gaze lay in the meanings ascribed to it.[4] A gaze could not render guilt if it was not delivered and received in this spirit; it could not condemn without the collusion of condemner and condemned. It had transformative and punitive powers only when the recipient accepted it as such. It was this need for reciprocity that brought the efficacy of public punishments into question and revealed their inherent ambiguity. This chapter acknowledges also that the idea of an amorphous monolithic public is erroneous and that the public's heterogeneity could compromise the potency of its gaze, thus reducing the potentially shaming and transformative impact of public punishments.

Finally, in writing about public punishments in the West Indies it has been useful to classify them into two types. First is the "shaming" type, wherein the threat of violence tended to be obscure and where the political aims of those administering the punishments were subtle.[5] The second type, spectacular public punishments like hanging, entailed violence and unmistakable political intent by those administering them.[6]

Shaming and Public Punishment

In the British West Indies, there were a number of punishments in which the public was courted, actively and passively, to participate in their successful execution. A successfully executed public punishment was one that implicated not only the individual or individuals being punished but also those who were witnesses to the punishment or its impact. Thus, in each of these punishments there was the verifiable character of the punishment, and at the same time these punishments inscribed the gaze of the public onto the bodies of the men and women they had marked.

Yet not all types of public punishments marked bodies in the same way, nor did they ask that the public look at the punished in the same manner. That is to say, not all types of public punishments were carried out in a horrifically violent manner like those inflicted upon the historical Robert-François Damiens, as described in the opening paragraphs of Foucault's *Discipline and Punish*.[7] Other types of public punishments sought to reform criminals and deter would-be criminals not by using the force of violence but through peer and communal stigmatization. Included in this category of stigmatizing or shaming punishments were hair-cropping and public works—penal labor while visible in public. Arguably, these types of punishment rested on the ethos that those who were so punished "remain[ed] strongly attached in relationships of interdependency and affection," in Braithwaite's words, and thus would "accrue greater interpersonal costs from shame."[8] Public punishments therefore rested on the assumption that the punished were individuals who were most likely to care about their peers' impressions of them and how they were viewed in society. A loss of face with either their peers or their community was thus thought to have a transformative impact on them. Moreover, their punishments would serve as cautionary reminders to observers that if they flouted societal mores they too would be recipients of similar sanctions.

Shaming types of punishments implicated not just the bodies of the punished. They were often also the punishments used to broadcast ideologies that buttressed the wider society. For instance, ideas held by colonial officials about black women and their supposed attachment to their hair found their way into discussions about the efficacy of punishments like hair-cropping, particularly in contrast to the supposed inability of whipping to reform black women. Yet it must be pointed out that even though hair-cropping was used extensively throughout the nineteenth-century British Caribbean, it was not always used explicitly for punitive reasons. It was often contended by various officials—including stipendiary magistrates, legislators, and even colonial governors—that this action was taken because of concerns about the health and cleanliness of the confined. In Governor Lionel Smith's rules for the conduct of houses of correction in Barbados issued to stipendiary magistrates in July 1835, for example, it was stipulated that all male apprentices sentenced by a special magistrate to corporal punishment with imprisonment, and all female apprentices sentenced to imprisonment with hard labor for at least two weeks, "shall have their hair cut off, and their heads washed, for the better promotion of cleanliness."[9] Additionally, the rules and regulations for spaces of penal confinement in Barbados for 1870 stated: "For the purposes of health and cleanliness, every convicted prisoner's hair [was] to be kept close cut, except in the case of prisoners confined for debt, damages, contempt, on remand for trial, or those committed for want of sureties."[10]

Still, throughout the nineteenth century, hair-cropping as a punitive tactic continued to find adherents in the British West Indies, particularly as a method to punish confined women. This was true in Barbados and Jamaica where the post-emancipation laws legitimated its use against all women, at least in theory. In Barbados, for instance, under section nineteen of an act of February 17, 1868, to "Consolidate and amend the law of this Island relating to offences against the Person," it was stipulated that males convicted under its precepts, who while committing their crimes had been carrying any instrument that could cause bodily harm, were to whipped. By comparison, women found guilty of the same offense were to have their hair "cut close on being committed to prison and kept close while undergoing imprisonment and until discharged from prison."[11]

Hair-cropping was also evidently popular in Jamaica. E. C. Wines, in his report from the 1872 International Penitentiary Congress, stated that H. B. Shaw, the inspector-general of prisons in Jamaica, noted that there had been a steep decline in the incidence of crimes committed by women, which Shaw attributed to the 1864 stipulation that women sentenced to hard labor were to have their hair "cut close." Wines reported the shibboleth, also articulated by such individuals as Des Voeux, that "a negro woman prizes nothing so highly as her hair."[12] Wines alleged further that some Jamaican women would have their shorn hair kept for them until they were released from jail, while those who were "less provident" would "sedulously seclude themselves until their hair [had] grown back."[13] This claim calls to mind the Australian female convicts who upon their release from prison would retrieve their shorn hair and use it to make "a nice . . . plait for the front."[14] Although Wines did not mention explicitly the public's role in these cases, its influence is nonetheless apparent. The idea of Jamaican women secluding themselves *after* their release from jail speaks to the ability of the public gaze to amplify the punitive qualities of hair-cropping. Their fear of exposure, self-perception, and the imagined responses of their peers to the sight of their shaved heads led the women to continue regulating, disciplining, and punishing themselves by continuing their seclusion, even after they had served their legislated period of confinement.

The supposed punitive benefits of hair-cropping were well known in other colonies, including St. Lucia, St. Vincent, and Trinidad, and its use was a core part of legislation and penal praxis in each of these territories. In an article in the *St. Lucian* of August 12, 1865, it was noted that legislators proposed cutting off the hair of female prisoners in the Royal Gaol in Castries.[15] Also, the third regulation for the internal discipline of the houses of correction for apprentices in St. Vincent specified, "Immediately on a prisoner being received, strict observation to be made that he is not laboring under any disease, after which the head should be shaved, or hair cut as close as possible, according to the directions of the Special Magistrate, and to be kept in that state whilst confined to prison."[16] John Anderson, the stipendiary magistrate for St. Vincent, saw hair-cropping as a very effective form of punishment. Noting that it could be employed successfully against "both blacks and coloureds of either sex," he found it to be particularly effective when applied to women.[17] So potent was hair-cropping thought to be that Des Voeux, who served as a colonial officer in several British colonies, including Newfoundland, Trinidad, British Guiana, and Fiji, noted that the mere threat of this punishment was enough to elicit compliance, particularly among women. Although admitting that this type of punishment was prohibited by Trinidad's secretary of the state, Des Voeux noted that the returns of 1877 for institutions of confinement in Trinidad showed that sentences of hair-cropping against women had been ordered. He opined that such sentences had been passed merely "*in terrorem*" and had not actually been carried out. He saw this as a necessary tactic since "there was a certain class of prisoners who were so hardened and irreclaimable that something more deterrent than the ordinary jail punishments—such as hard labor, short rations, and solitary confinement—was necessary in order to preserve discipline. The fear of being flogged operated as a wholesome restraint upon the men; but the women, knowing that this in their case was illegal, could only be kept quiet by the threat of having their hair cut off." Although Des Voeux hinted at the fact that female prisoners' insubordination was the result of them knowing that they could not be legally flogged, his following sentence suggests that hair-cropping had the potential to intimidate and regulate. In explaining the notorious efficacy of hair-cropping, he asserted further: "Negro women dread the loss of their hair even more than do Europeans, and I am inclined to think, from what I have observed, that many of the abandoned class referred to would, if they were offered the choice, even prefer to be flogged."[18]

Although there was an alternative argument that hair-cropping had health benefits, data from the *Barbados Blue Book* of 1882 raise questions about that argument by prison administrators and governors and instead point to a gendered and punitive deployment of the practice. An examination of the types of punishments of those in various spaces of confinement in Barbados reveals that hair-cropping was carried out only in the District A and C prisons, the two spaces that housed female prisoners. There was no entry for hair-cropping in either Glendairy or the juvenile prison. Also, in 1886, some forty-eight years after apprenticeship, six cases of hair-cropping for infringements of prison discipline had been carried out under Rule 260 at the District A prison. In the District C prison during the same year there had been two cases of hair-cropping.[19]

Yet the evidence suggests that the supposed "benefits" that accrued from hair-cropping were debatable at best in both Barbados and Jamaica, and in the final analysis its use was based predominantly on conceptions about the black female generally and specifically the notion of the incorrigible black female criminal. However, the deterrent effect that hair-cropping was said to produce in Jamaica was apparently not the case in Barbados. Evidence from the "Report on Gaols and Prisoners" from the *Barbados Blue Book* of 1882 shows that hair-cropping used as a punishment against recalcitrant female inmates had proved ineffective. In one example from the district prisons, it was shown that of the eight cases where women had had theirs cut as punishment, five of the women so punished were subsequently ordered to be worked in ankle straps, while another one was worked in irons, because hair-cropping "had been tried as a punishment without effect."[20]

Despite evidence provided to the contrary, why was hair-cropping viewed as such an effective form of punishment, particularly against black women? The answer is based primarily in the notion of reception—that is, how the punishment was thought to be received—both by the person upon whom it was applied and the persons who would see that it had been carried out. Even though hair-cropping, from a reading of the various prison rules, was floated as a genderless form of punishment, the evidence is clear that this method of punishment was not applied in a gender-neutral fashion. The lack of direct references to the deterrent impact of hair-cropping on male misbehavior shows that this form of punishment was gendered. In the West Indies, at least, forcing men to have their hair cut did not compromise their gendered identities, as a man with a bald or shaved head was not out of the ordinary.[21] By comparison, hair-cropping could compromise the gendered presentation of women—the loss of their hair could have been read as the loss of a physical trait essential to their identities as women. Thus, in proposing hair-cropping as one of the most effective forms of punishment against women, male colonial legislators and other elites were acknowledging that they were aware that hair, for many women, served as a symbol of their gendered identity. It could be said that colonial officials believed that recalcitrant women were more likely to obey if they thought that a symbol of their gender was threatened.

On another level, one that went beyond gendered identification, a woman with cropped hair was also an emphatic symbol of one who was punished, one who had done something wrong and had been chastised for this wrongdoing. A woman with a shaved head would probably have invited stares, remarks, and possibly gossip about her condition, thereby amplifying the punishment. An example of the ability of hair-cropping to mark both through its physical imprint on the body and psychologically through shame is illustrated in evidence provided by Stipendiary Magistrate Colthurst of Barbados. An entry in his journal of September 1836 noted that this tactic had been used against a "young quadroon woman."[22] His diary reads:

> Speaking of the practice of shaving the heads of the apprentices, a young quadroon woman, who had conducted herself very improperly to her mistress, was brought up about a fortnight before my arrival in the island, and convicted by my predecessor of insubordination, and sentenced to hard labour on the tread mill for fourteen days, and her head (as a matter of course) to be shaved. This was accordingly done, and on the expiration of her punishment, she was sent home to her mistress, in all respects tamed and amenable, until she found she was laughed at by her fellow servants for the loss of her hair.[23]

To hide that she had been punished, the "young quadroon" was said to have "purchased false curls" and thus been able to "exhibit a beautiful front."[24] From this example, using Foucault's formulation, justice and punishment had triumphed as the young quadroon's personal and public humiliation showed that the crime had been nullified and her wronged employer vindicated.

A reading of the corporal punishments of the young quadroon shows too that they were multilayered. Not only was her body used to fulfill the punishment of hard labor while in confinement, but her body also became the broadsheet that publicized her punishment. Even after she had served her fourteen-day period of confinement, her shaved head continued to mark her as having been punished and thus reinforced her criminal difference as compared to her law-abiding and unpunished fellow servants, who were then able to laugh at her appearance. In Foucauldian terms, through this legible marker "the condemned [woman] published [her] crime and the justice that had been meted out to [her] by bearing them physically on [her] body."[25] The punishment of the young quadroon had been completed because she had been laughed at by her peers.

Finally, hair-cropping, along with being a sanction leveled against individuals who had committed crimes, may be viewed as an assertion of colonial power and an attempted erasure of the power of alterity—the power of the crime and the criminal. Public punishment represented a draconian assertion of power by the white plantocracy. Hair-cropping, then, may be likened to the impact of Samson's betrayal by Delilah, an attempt to assert one form of power and nullify another: "And she made him sleep upon her knees; and she called for a man, and she caused him to shave off the seven locks of his head; and she began to afflict him, and his strength went from him."[26]

Yet, in spite of its ability to mark bodies as criminal, the punishment of hair-cropping, like other examples of public punishment generally, was inherently ambiguous and multilayered. For instance, in post-emancipation Barbados and Jamaica, hair-cropping was often carried out within the walls of the jail and only became a public symbol of punishment when those who had lost their hair left the jail for the outside world. One could even argue that hair that had been shorn and was growing back emphasized the ephemeral nature of punishment. At the same time hair-cropping reinforced the notion that the jail remained an important locus of punishment, as the hair would continue to grow back outside of the prison walls. Thus, in this sense, it could be asserted that the outside world represented rejuvenation and a break with punishment at the same time that it worked in tandem to complete the impact of the punishment.

In spite of their employment in Barbados and Jamaica in the post-emancipation period, public punishments generally occupied an ambiguous position within the realm of punishment. This ambiguity was manifested in the fact that the power of public punishments was never wholly in the hands of those executing them. For instance, sentences of public works, like hair-cropping, could not be fully enacted unless they were consumed by the public. Yet for these punishments to be effective they were not to be viewed by a public knowledgeable about the workings of the law; rather, in the minds of colonial and imperial legislators, they were to be consumed by an impressionistic, pliable, and terrorized populace. In addition, this viewing, and the interaction of the punished with the public, had to be strictly controlled and monitored if the punishments were to be effective. In nineteenth-century Barbados public work by prisoners formed a key part of prison discipline, and convicts were routinely employed in places like the ballast yard or at the grounds at Government House and even at other institutions, like Central Police Station in Bridgetown or the "lunatic asylum."[27] In 1892, public labor continued to be performed by those housed in Barbadian jails. Male prisoners were employed pumping water at the quarry in Codrington, repairing the yard at Central Police Station, and pumping water at District A Police Station.[28] Prison warders were usually employed to prevent convicts from running away during these stints outside of the prison walls—an appointment that could be said to have emphasized the tensions inherent in the encroachment of the private life of the prison into the outside world. The private world of spaces of confinement was meant to be the antithesis of the public world. The public world represented freedom and the potential approval of peers and the community, and because of this, it could be argued, there were liable to be acute tensions when these two worlds met.

The idea that contact between the public and the prisoner had to be regulated was a subject taken up in diverse quarters—by officials and citizens alike, both foreign-born and native to the islands. As a case in point, Henry Coleridge, in his travelogue documenting social conditions in the British West Indies in 1825, saw the effective manipulation of space as central to the successful application of public punishment. In his view, the spaces occupied by prisoners and the public had to be strictly demarcated, with the public having limited access to the criminal. He condemned the construction of the jail in Antigua because its design did not, in his view, accomplish these ends. The fact that some of the windows in the jail in Antigua faced the street and some were on the ground floor made it a less than ideal space for punishment.[29]

Concerns about being able to strictly control the interactions between the public and the punished continued to be expressed during the nineteenth century. For example, the commissioners appointed by the imperial government to spearhead the enquiry into prisons in Jamaica in 1872 concluded that the system of letting prisoners engage in public works should be abolished. The perceived inability of jail officials in these cases to delimit the boundaries between the criminals and the law-abiding citizens led the commissioners to denounce this as an ineffective form of punishment. They contended that Jamaican prisoners engaged in public labor were poorly supervised, and they argued that the prisoners could escape or communicate with and even receive presents from their friends. To drive the nail further into the coffin of prisoners' public works, the commissioners asserted that "the average negro cares so little for the mere degradation of imprisonment, that the exposure to the public gaze does not counterbalance these disadvantages; in fact, we think that the sight of a gang of men, supposed to be undergoing punishment, idling away their time in the roads, tends very much to diminish the dread of imprisonment, which it is so desirable to impress upon the population."[30] It is evident from these words that the commissioners had noted the breakdown between the public gaze and effectual punishment. In essence, the effect of the public gaze had been lost on both the punished and those who were witnesses to the punishment, nullified by what Ignatieff calls the transformation of punishment from "a solemn act of the state to a popular bacchanal."[31] What was sensed was that prison life was characterized by frivolity and idleness, that the "average negro" had made a mockery of the state apparatus, and that public punishment neither punished nor summoned feelings of dread from those who had observed it.

Coleridge's concerns about the lack of control over the convicts in Antigua in the early nineteenth century and the trope of the "average negro" of 1870s Jamaica showed, moreover, that colonial governments were not always successful in transforming neutral spaces into punitive milieus. Neither were they always able to control the bodies of the punished or the stories that these punished bodies told. In both cases, the punitive space had been reappropriated by the convicts. Instead of serving as sites that gave rise to shame and emphasized their status as punished individuals, they instead became sites of sociability, a quality that was associated with freedom, not punishment and confinement. The punished had blurred the boundaries between the free and the unfree, and, perhaps more significantly, the "blackness" that emanated from the idle and frolicking was not the debased and contrite blackness that the authorities hoped to produce. Instead, it was a blackness that was an affront to authority.

The fact that the dependence of public punishments upon the spectacle could render them impotent was not peculiar to the British Caribbean. Ignatieff also identified this dependence upon a ritualized spectacle of punishment as a major flaw in punitive practice in Britain in the eighteenth and nineteenth centuries. He saw public hangings, the use of the pillory, and public whippings as key instances where the crowd, the condemned, and punishment met—a macabre meeting that was imbued with symbolism. Painting a vivid picture of punishment that equally integrated elements of communal condemnation and state violence, Ignatieff noted that offenders who were pilloried were usually those who "aroused a high degree of public indignation; these included shopkeepers found using false weights, persons convicted of hoarding or speculating in the grain trade, or persons convicted of homosexual assault." According to him, these offenders would be "locked in head stocks in a marketplace or in front of a jail and sentenced to endure an hour of the crowd's abuse." Ignatieff noted cautiously, however, that

> such a punishment relied for its enforcement on the feeling of the populace. It could be a horror if the crowd pelted them with stones and offal, but if it sympathized with them there was little the magistrate could do to prevent the hour in the pillory from becoming a public triumph. Such was the case when Daniel Isaac Eaton, the aged and distinguished radical printer, was sentenced to an hour's pillory in Newgate in 1813. Much to the government's chagrin, Eaton's head was garlanded with flowers and he was brought refreshment during his ordeal, while the police and magistrates in attendance were reviled and abused.[32]

Ignatieff expounded on this point further by stating that "all such ritual punishments depended for their effectiveness as a ceremonial of deterrence on the crowd's tacit support of the authorities' sentence. Hence, the magistrate's control of the ritual was limited."[33]

Shame, that "feeling of distress or humiliation caused by consciousness of the guilt or folly of oneself or an associate," it may be argued, was the underlying sentiment that made punishments like hair-cropping and public works favored sanctions among colonial and imperial officials.[34] By relying on perceptions about black women's psychic fears and their ideas about their appearance and about how the condemned regarded their peers and the public's opinions of them, colonial and imperial officials attempted to manipulate individual and group behavior. Additionally, they used the bodies of individuals to illustrate the reach of their power. Yet, as the evidence makes clear, the reliance on the participation of the public to complete the impact of punishments like hair-cropping and public works could potentially compromise or even nullify the power of the state to punish. "Spectacular" types of public punishments, it may be argued, relied less upon this unstated public collusion and state persuasion and rested more upon the state's ability to act unilaterally and call upon a combination of punitive tactics that relied upon force, terror, and might.

Spectacular Terrors, Black Bodies, and the Public Gaze

Outside of shaming punishments like public works and hair-cropping, there were other instances where the public gaze and punishment met, albeit in a more volatile fashion. This was particularly evident in those public punishments like hanging and flogging that violently marked the bodies of those they targeted. Elaine Scarry's categorization of torture has been particularly helpful in delineating this subset of public punishments.[35] Like torture, the "spectacular"

forms of public punishments that were used in Barbados and Jamaica were constituted of three major elements that Scarry identifies as torturous: "pain [was]
inflicted on a person in ever-intensifying ways"; "pain, continually amplified
within the person's body, [was] also amplified in the sense that it [was] objecti-
fied, made visible to those outside the person's body"; and finally, "the objec-
tified pain [was] denied as pain and read as power, a translation made possible by
the obsessive mediation of agency."[36]

The violence against those who had challenged colonial authorities in the
British West Indies—both in the pre- and post-emancipation periods—and the
pain that accompanied this violence was always read as power, with the bodies
upon which the violence was inflicted and the pain experienced serving merely
as the means to that end. In writing about forms of punishment that relied heavily on applications of pain and violence, Vincent Brown sees the employment
of "ritual execution" of slaves by the Jamaican colonial state as a major way in
which it was able to reinforce its hegemony. He maintains that these executions
that were steeped in melodrama and infused with violence—often involving the
mutilation of slaves who had committed suicide—gave the "governing authority
a sacred, even supernatural dimension." Rebellious slaves were executed just as
dramatically. The ultimate aim of these tactics, Brown argues, was social control.
Citing evidence from contemporary observers like Colonel Humphrey Walrond, Matthew Gregory Lewis, Thomas Thistlewood, and C. G. A. Oldendorp,
Brown notes that the severed heads and limbs of slaves, often affixed to prominent locations like poles by the roadside and "well travelled paths," "served to
haunt those places with memories and narratives of crime and punishment."[37]

Whereas Brown looked at the bodies of dead slaves to show how the state appropriated bodies to demonstrate that its power was infinite, Diana Paton illustrates how bodies in a different state of being—that is, mutilated bodies—could
be used to transmit the same message.[38] For instance, from 1746–82 records of
slave trials in the parish of St. Andrew, Jamaica, Paton provides detailed descriptions of how slaves routinely had an ear, leg, or arm chopped off as punishment
for "status offenses"—crimes that she says "could by definition be committed
only by slaves," with running away being the most prevalent crime for which
they were prosecuted.[39] One of the more memorable individuals to whom she
refers is the runaway slave Ben, who, as punishment for this offense, was to have
"half his right foot removed."[40] In Ben's case, like those of many who were subjected to spectacular public punishments, the punishment appeared to turn on the
argument that he had betrayed the state. By running away, one might argue, Ben
had attempted to appropriate state property and deliberately tried to harm the
social, economic, and political ordering of the state. For this betrayal, therefore,

the loss of half of a foot, as opposed to an entire foot, was more effective dramatically. To lose half of a foot might have required more explanation because of its aberrancy—resulting in a question-and-answer session that might amplify the fact that the crime of running away had been vindicated.

These types of punishments that involved mutilating the living and displaying the bodies of the dead were used by state officials primarily for their macabre qualities. It was not sufficient for the officials to demonstrate that they held power over life and death. What they also had to show, through the staging of the punishments, was the vastness of this power—in that they also controlled the *quality* of their subject's life and death. Moreover, by carrying out macabre punishments, the punitive apparatus was legitimated, and, perhaps more importantly, the state's power was reinvigorated and reestablished after it had been compromised by the actions of those who had stepped outside the boundaries of established socio-political mores. Additionally, these punishments served to reinforce the socio-racial boundaries as the literal bodies of blacks were used to mark out the boundaries of what constituted acceptable behavior.

The executions of rebels carried out in the wake of the Christmas Rebellion in Jamaica (December 25, 1831, to January 4, 1832) lend credence to this argument. In recounting the details of the executions, nineteenth-century missionary Henry Bleby noted that one common characteristic of this particular punishment was that the insurrectionists were hanged in the marketplace of one town. He contended that these executions had been so commonplace that the public was satiated. Bleby painted an image of people in the marketplace going about their buying and selling with insouciance, "scarcely turning round their heads to look at the awful scene that was being enacted in their presence; so entirely had they become familiarized with the slaughter of their fellow-creatures!" He noted also that the bodies of the insurrectionists would hang from the gibbet "stiffening in the breeze" until the gibbet was replenished with "fresh" bodies. Based on this, one could argue that the act of hanging, and the gibbet on which Jamaican insurrectionists were hanged, provided onlookers with tangible evidence of what could happen if they challenged an omnipotent sovereign and its laws and representatives. According to Bleby, when the hangman cut down those who had been hanged, the "whole heap of bodies" would have to remain where they fell "until the workhouse negroes came in the evening with carts, and took them away, to cast them into a pit dug for the purpose."[41]

In these descriptions the black body, particularly that of the black man, is visible. The visibility is, however, strictly controlled: men are hanging from the gibbet, acting as executioner, or carrying away the bodies of their fellow citizens.[42] This image of the ubiquitous black male performing the unsavory, repetitive, factory-like tasks associated with hanging stands in stark contrast to the white male overseeing the proceedings while remaining unseen. Bleby effectively reproduced the "spectacular terror" that this ceremony of punishment was meant to evoke and illustrated that the ruling classes were able to divorce themselves from the enactment of this macabre punishment. He showed that their power to entrust the more polluting tasks to less powerful beings was not only true within the plantation but also within the larger society.

The examples from Paton, Brown, and Bleby suggest that spectacular forms of punishments tended to be reserved mostly for the enslaved—a practice that Paton attributed to the "expansion and racialization of the concept [of] petit treason" and "to the slaves' status as non-persons."[43] It may be argued, however, that this rationalization helps also to explain why in the post-emancipation period freed men and women were also punished in such a dramatic fashion after they flouted societal laws. When one examines the ways in which floggings and hangings were used by the government in the wake of uprisings by the subaltern classes in the post-emancipation period, it can be seen that debasement of blacks' bodies continued to be used to mark the socio-racial divide that existed in the plantation economy. An example of this can be seen in the punishments of those individuals who were alleged to have participated in the 1865 Morant Bay Rebellion.

Besides the venom with which the state reprisals were carried out after the Morant Bay Rebellion, what was significant about the reprisals is their being cast as didactic devices. This was evident in the ubiquity of the public displays of punishment—bodies displayed for visual consumption—and in official discourse about the rebellion that was circulated rapidly and widely for the public's consumption. Essentially, those who may have had designs on rebelling were to see and hear what could happen to them. They were thus to become the unwitting and ideally docile accomplices in the full and effectual execution of punishment.

In another example of the inscription of bodies immediately after the rebellion, people were shot with impunity by soldiers appointed by the state. For example, Colonel J. Francis Hobbs said that on October 15, 1865, his troops had killed between fifteen and twenty rebels on the hillsides and in trees. On October 19 he had ordered eleven prisoners from the rebel camp to be shot. After the executions, special constables then hung these men from trees.[44] According to Hobbs, the act of suspending the bullet-riddled bodies was deliberate and had clear aims. He thought that it would be "a good example to give to some of those in the neighbourhood who would see it."[45]

Hanging to death was also a common punishment carried out against those alleged to have participated in the Morant Bay Rebellion. Not only was hanging a decidedly emphatic symbol of the vengeance of the law and the state, it was also visually arresting to those who witnessed it. That hanging was to have all of the aforementioned aims is not in question. Captain Lewis Hole noted in an enclosure to Brigadier General Alexander Abercromby Nelson, for instance, that two insurrectionists, Andrew Worgs and William Jones, were hanged in the middle of Manchioneal during a court-martial that he had assembled.[46]

Additionally, in one of his dispatches to member of Parliament Edward Cardwell, Governor Eyre noted that four of the prisoners who had been captured and held on board the man-of-war *Wolverine* were hanged on an archway in Morant Bay. The evidence suggests that the executioners deliberately chose this site, as it was attached to the partially burned courthouse near where those involved in the rebellion were said to have committed massacres on October 11.[47] Although Eyre did not mention whether the hanging formed part of a larger spectacle of public punishment, its provocative location suggests that it did. And while damage to the courthouse superficially connotes that a crucial symbol of justice and punishment had been brought down, the hanging seems to have nullified that. Its site reinforced the power of the state, as the body of the building was still standing and could be a tool for punishment, even in its structurally compromised condition. Enacting the hanging there was to send the message to the peasantry and any who might have had thoughts of rebelling against the imperial and colonial authorities that in the end the power of the state would triumph.

One of the notable public executions in Jamaica during this time was that of George Marshall. The circumstances of Marshall's summary execution came to light during the Crown's inquiry into the government reprisals in the wake of the rebellion. Gordon Duberry Ramsay, the provost marshal and inspector general of police for St. Catherine during the declaration of martial law, was implicated in Marshall's execution and tried for murder. The evidence surrounding this case involves space, race, and the gaze. Several witnesses were called to testify, including James Beckett, captain of the cutter *Friendship*. Beckett testified that Marshall, whom he described as a "brown man," had been sentenced to receive fifty lashes for his participation in the rebellion. Marshall, according to Beckett's deposition, never received the full fifty lashes. Instead, with Marshall groaning in pain, Ramsay was said to have shouted "Sedition!" and ordered that Marshall be taken down and hanged.[48] Beckett described this:

> He was taken down from the gun carriage to the place of execution; he was tripped up, thrown on the ground, he was tied on the ground, he was raised up, the rope was thrown round his neck and the end thrown over the rail of the

steps of the Court House, and a man who was standing on the steps of the Court House haul'd the rope and drew up the man until he was high enough hoisted off the ground, and the man who was on the steps hauling up the man Marshall said "High enough," and some one said "Make fast." It was a soldier. I do not know him. Mr Ramsay was present. The man who put the rope round Marshall's neck gave him a stretch by the legs, and that not being satisfactory the same man took a large stone and put it between the arms and back of Marshall to give him weight. A little while after there was a little rain, and I and Mr Marshalleck went into the camp. I saw the man Marshall dead; his body remained there till next morning, when it was cut down and the body buried at the fort, and Mr Ramsay was present all the time.[49]

Although there were some inconsistencies in Beckett's testimony—for example, in one part of his testimony he said that these events occurred on October 18 but in cross-examination he stated that the execution was carried out on October 16—the main facts were corroborated by other witnesses. In the cross-examination Beckett elucidated on points that are critical to this chapter, namely, the use of space and the role of the public and the gaze—all of which played critical roles in Marshall's punishment. Beckett made mention of the "large open space in front of the Court House" that was referred to as the "market square." He noted that there had been other black people there, along with soldiers.[50] He also described Marshall as a "meagre little bit of fellow," a description that at first glance seems insignificant, but the fact that Marshall's small size was also commented on by a number of other witnesses calls for some analysis. Henry Ford, another deponent, a captain of the "irregular volunteers," also made a critical contribution. Like Beckett he noted Marshall's complexion: he was a "faircoloured man," "a Quadroon." Ford also pointed out that Marshall had been flogged by more than one sailor, with each one relieving the other after twelve lashes had been inflicted. Corroborating Beckett's testimony, Ford stated that Marshall had not received the stipulated number of lashes because the Provost Marshal Ramsay had ordered Marshall taken down from the wheel of the gun and hanged. What prompted this, according to Ford's testimony, was Ramsay's ire at a perceived scowl from Marshall. According to Ford's testimony Ramsay had said: "You scowl at me, you damn'd villain. . . . Take him down and hang him."[51] The irony in this exchange rests upon the gaze, this time Marshall's apparent scowl. This gaze, to Ramsay, represented insubordination; it appeared to nullify his presumed omnipotence. To Ramsay, Marshall's gaze signaled refusal to accept his authority, a slight to which Ramsay responded by ordering Marshall's execution. From this we can see that the gaze could be appropriated by those presumed to be powerless and used to challenge the authority of those assuming control.

Ford showed also how the public became complicit in Marshall's punishment. Describing himself as having been a "mere spectator," Ford noted that not only had he seen Marshall's execution, he had been "just without the range of the swing of the cat" when Marshall was being whipped. Moreover, he pointed out that Marshall's execution had been carried out in the open, and he suggested that there had been other executions, ones that were shielded from the public, and he described these ones as being carried out in a "formal manner."[52] Yet from Ford's testimony it is evident that he was not a "mere spectator" but was complicit in the execution. Ford's witnessing of the punishment, his remembering, and his retelling of its details helped to immortalize the punishment. Perhaps the presence of spectators like Ford also provided the rationale that Ramsay needed to sell his punishment. Without the presence of spectators there might have been no need for Ramsay to make a statement about his authority or that of the state. Neither would there have been a need to demarcate emphatically the boundaries—discursive and real—between the criminal and the law-abiding.

As in the earlier testimony delivered by Beckett, Ford's testimony implicitly invoked the dichotomous spaces of the condemned criminal and those occupied by the noncriminal—spaces that were as much discursive as they were discernible to the eye. Beckett and Ford both noted that the execution had been carried out in an open space. They also intimated that the onlookers had occupied the more neutral, safe spaces away from the scene of the punishment, whereas the space occupied by Marshall was marked first by his flogged and then by his dead body, along with the figure of Ramsay as the punisher. The periphery, meanwhile, had been occupied by other blacks (as noted by Beckett), members of "the lower orders," "[s]everal gentlemen, as well as a mixed crowd" (according to Ford), and some sailors.[53]

The ramifications and lessons of Marshall's execution were not to be immediate, but his public execution reinforced the ambiguous nature of public punishment. Essentially, Marshall's punishment seemed to be enacted for consumption by two main types of publics, the first of which comprised soldiers, sailors, and other aggrieved people. These were the members of a "legitimate" audience—representatives of the state, so to speak—who, in viewing Marshall's execution witnessed the supposed vindication of the wrongs that had been inflicted on Jamaican and imperial elites during the Morant Bay Rebellion. The second set of witnesses comprised the peasantry, who were to view Marshall's punishment with fear and fealty in recognition of the superiority of colony and empire. The testimony of Edwin Gentle, a bricklayer who was at Morant Bay during the period of martial law, lends credence to this argument. Gentle witnessed Marshall's flogging and execution as he stood approximately forty feet away from the scene. He also recalled seeing Marshall's body hanging from the courthouse the day after the execution.[54] That Marshall's flogging and execution were to have a deterrent impact on those witnessing their occurrence was noted by Ramsay himself, who, in a letter to Mr. Jordan—at the time of the rebellion, the governor's secretary—asserted that Marshall had become recalcitrant when earlier in custody with the other rebels. They had had to flog Marshall "to keep the *others* quiet" [emphasis added]. Ramsay also justified the hanging that he imposed, stating, "I did not know how many lashes he had received at the time, but, as the other prisoners were muttering and expressing sympathy, I ordered him to be taken down; he then shook his fist, and growled at me again, saying words to the effect he would do for me [*sic*]. There was no court-martial likely to sit for some days; and, considering that his remaining in the yard with other prisoners would be dangerous, I ordered him to be hanged."[55]

Ramsay's trial also engendered some ironies. It transposed the discourse that had surrounded the Morant Bay Rebellion, in that Ramsay, the white man who represented the law, was now cast as impulsive, emotional, and vindictive. Marshall, by contrast, was recast as a victim. In the minutes of Ramsay's trial, for example, Marshall was described as a "poor creature," a "flogged and writhing man."[56]

Public punishments did not all fall into neat categories of either shaming or spectacle. Arguably, punishments like public floggings consisted of a stigmatizing and shaming element along with an emphatically violent core. Public whipping was not as common in the post-emancipation period as during slavery, when it was ubiquitous.

Sometimes public punishments were ad hoc affairs, occurring in the heat of the moment, whereas others tended to be more premeditated. Of the former kind, as stipendiary magistrate of Barbados, John Bowen Colthurst recorded the example of a sentence of public whipping on an estate owned by a Mr. King. The thief, caught stealing sugarcane, was sentenced by Colthurst to fifteen stripes on the estate "in the presence of the gangs on the following morning."[57] In a dispatch from Governor McGregor to Lord Glenelg in 1837, it was noted that at the sessions in Barbados some criminals had been sentenced to be publicly flogged.[58]

Although public floggings in the post-1834 period could be "in the heat of the moment" responses, the example recorded by Colthurst and McGregor's dispatch to Glenelg illustrate that they were also a quotidian part of society. As with public hangings, particular value was ascribed to the places where the floggings were to be carried out and to the competing publics who would witness them.

This point has also been made by Jonathan Dalby, who provides data to show that public floggings had been the norm until the 1830s. Dalby notes, for example, that public floggings were carried out in the marketplace in Montego Bay. In Kingston they were carried out at the "lower pumps" of Church, Duke, and King Streets, and in St. Jago "on the parade." Citing evidence from the Surrey Assizes register, Dalby notes the case of Salvador Demoyes, who in 1811 was sentenced to be whipped outside the door of his accuser's home.[59]

James Williams's revelations lend credence to Dalby's claims about the widespread nature of public floggings in the early nineteenth century. In his narrative, Williams contended that Stipendiary Magistrate Rawlinson sentenced him and Adam Brown to be flogged by the police, in front of the courthouse. Not only were the condemned to receive twenty lashes on their bodies, a punitive act in itself, they were also to be subjected to the gaze of the public.[60]

In the post-emancipation period, public floggings, though rare, tended also to reflect the aforementioned "heat of the moment" tendency, even though one might argue that their occurrence was born out of socio-political conditions that supported the degradation of specific bodies of individuals. Still, when they did occur, they were received ambiguously, with opinion varying between whether they should be de rigueur during rebellions, under what conditions these punishments should be applied, or if they did occur, what these floggings should look like.[61]

Some of the most notorious examples of public floggings in the post-emancipation period came to light during the investigations in the wake of the Morant Bay Rebellion. For example, in investigations conducted by Stipendiary Magistrate David Ewart and S. D. Lindo (a Jamaican solicitor) in October 1866, it was revealed that women like Elizabeth Collins, Charlotte Scott, Margaret Minott, Ann Galloway, Mary Ann Tom, and Fanny Taylor had all been flogged during the governmental reprisals.[62] Although the data gathered do not state whether all were flogged in front of a crowd of onlookers, some of the punishments were carried out in public spaces. In his deposition to the Royal Commission of Enquiry into the Morant Bay Rebellion, James McComock Reid described the punishment that he personally had inflicted on Elizabeth Collins: "During martial law I flogged Elizabeth Collins with a cat on her naked shoulders, at Long Bay. She was tied hands and feet to a cocoa nut tree. I gave her more than twenty blows. The cat was made of black fishing lines. I did this by Mr Christopher Codrington's orders. He was present and saw me do it. The woman's back bled. Mr David Mein was on the left hand, with a sword."[63]

There was also the example of the laborer Charlotte Scott from St. Thomas in the East; she said she had been also whipped severely during martial law. Not only did Scott mention that her shoulders had been bared to receive the lashes, but she described how Constable Michael Pearcey and McComock had tied her to a coconut tree, "stripped [her] clothes to [her] waist . . . and [given her] 21 lashes on [her] bare back with a cat."[64] In both of these depositions the body of the punished woman is obtrusive. In fact, every aspect of Collins's and Scott's punishment, the lashes that they were ordered to receive, the partial removal of their clothing, and the tethering of their bodies to a tree, signaled that the corporeal quality of their punishment was to be emphatic.

Margaret Minott, a domestic servant from St. Thomas in the East, also testified to the assaults on her body during the government's reprisals following the rebellion: "Dick and John Bignall tied me to a cart wheel. Mr. James Codrington told them to tear off my clothes and make me naked to my waist. Defendant then ordered Alick Cooper to flog me, to give me 20 lashes. Alick Cooper then gave me 20 lashes on my bare back with a long guava stick. Defendant stood by and counted the licks. The first stick broke and they took another. My back bled, and defendant threw a mug of pickle over it. It burned me." Black women's bodies were not the only ones that were exposed during the floggings that occurred after the Morant Bay Rebellion. James Turner, a laborer from St. Thomas in the East, stated that his shirt had been removed for his punishment and that he had been tied to a cart and flogged with a "cat" that had wire in it.[65]

The floggings carried out after the Morant Bay Rebellion possessed characteristics that separate them from the floggings meted out to apprentices who had been accused of shirking their responsibilities or being insolent to their employers. Although they do possess an element of shaming, the ferocity with which the Morant Bay floggings were carried out, the fact that they were widespread, the charged ambience in which they were executed, and the calculated intent on conducting the punishment in public, tend to push these particular instances of flogging into the realm of terrorism.

Conclusion

From the evidence presented, it can be seen that public punishments were entrusted with a diverse range of tasks in Barbados and Jamaica. Not only were they negative sanctions that were applied to those presumed guilty, they were seen also as mechanisms to deter potential criminals and rebels. Punishments like hair-cropping and public works, like all types of public punishments generally, were participatory forms of control. State officials, condemned criminals, and observers, although occupying different vantage points in the drama of public punishment, were all essential to its successful execution. Finally, by targeting competing audiences, public punishments, like the bodies on which they were imprinted, were conduits through which diverse messages about class, race, gender, and power could be transmitted.

Moreover, punitive measures like hair-cropping, public works, public executions, and even public floggings all came to represent corporal markers that separated the condemned from the innocent and the elites from the laboring classes, while at the same time reinforcing the power and superiority of the imperial and colonial states. Additionally, through the act of punishment, the bodies of black men and women were harnessed to reinforce the socio-racial organization of the plantation society. Black bodies were debased through whippings, by being stripped naked, by being shamed, and by being put on display in their punished states. This debasement through punishment was part of a larger social discourse about blackness and how the bodies of blacks were to be used.

CHAPTER 7

The Difference That Gender Makes

Punishment and the Gendered Body in
Post-emancipation Jamaica and Barbados

On reaching the hall where Jackson was, Mr Fleming said
angrily: "I told you before, Mr Jackson, that you were not to lay
the brown girls down and whip them in the public yard. If the
house girls are to be punished it must be in some other way."

"Nothing, sir," replied Jackson, "will take the impertinence out
of that girl but the whip. I have put her frequently into the stocks,
and kept her there for a week at a time, but she comes out as saucy
and impertinent as she went in."

"And pray, sir," asked Mr Fleming, "what crime had the
girl been guilty of to render it necessary to subject her to the
punishment of the whip?"

"Impertinence and disobedience of order in leaving the
property at night," replied Jackson.

—CYRIL FRANCIS PERKINS, *Busha's Mistress*

The above epigraph to this chapter, although taken from a work of fiction,
is rich with details that give us a glimpse into nineteenth-century Jamaica, particularly about the nature of punishment there. It reflects the strength of patriarchal
institutions, and it shows punishment's place in one of these institutions. It does
this in the sense that men are seen as holding supreme power over plantation
women, as Jackson and Fleming are presented as the sole arbitrators in deciding
which form of punishment the "brown girl" is to receive for her crime. This
patriarchal dominance is reflected even through the fact that the conversation
is dominated by the male voice—a dialogic dominance that is paralleled in the
factual primary sources of the period.

This nineteenth-century account also supports the nonfictional data of the
same period in other ways. Just as punitive tools like the whip and stocks are

ubiquitous in the primary documents of the period, so too is there reference to these instruments here. The dialogue highlights also the importance of color in the British West Indies and how it, like other social determinants like race and ethnicity, shaped the experiences of individuals. That the *brown* girl was not to be whipped *publicly* suggests that this method of punishment might have been appropriate had she been darker. Moreover, the fact that Fleming asserted that house slaves were not be punished in that way suggests that notions about what were appropriate types of punishments were also determined by a slave's spatial and occupational position as much as by ideas about their position in the color hierarchy.

The dialogue between Jackson and Fleming also substantiates the findings in the primary sources that delineate women, particularly in their iteration as female criminals or deviants, as possessing a nature unlike that of men. Women were often thought of and cast as more recalcitrant, more impertinent, "saucy" even, whereas the men were often cast as volatile. These so-called emotional differences between men and women not only impinged on discourses and practices of punishment but also paradoxically were shored up by what British social sciences scholar Barbara Bush refers to as a "corporeal equality of the sexes."[1] It is this contradictory application of a gendered lens to punitive praxes that also helps to explain why even if black men and black women received the same types of physical punishment—whipping, for instance—it could at the same time be mandated that the women were to be punished with a less severe implement.

This corporeal equalization of black men and black women accomplished a number of things. It legitimated the use of black men and women as drudge labor and the concomitant punishments that came with any unsatisfactory execution of this labor. And in the "gender order" it separated black men from white men and, perhaps even more importantly, black women from white women and secured the hallowed position of the white female body.[2] This act of social, racial, and gender demarcation also helps to explain why the literature is replete with examples of black men and women being flogged or sentenced to labor in penal gangs or on the treadmill even after 1834, while examples of white men and women being made to undergo similar types of punishment are virtually absent.

The dialogue between Jackson and Fleming also shows the important role played by the physical body in reinforcing the hierarchical structure of the plantation economy. Indeed, its recurring motif is the subdued and docile body. This is seen in words like "lay . . . down" and the fact that the public was invited to look at the chastised body of the brown girl through mention of the "public yard."

The employment of a gendered lens to examine forms of punishment further complicates the phenomenon of punishment by inextricably linking it to sexuality. Not only were punishments leveled against crimes that were sexual or reproductive in nature, but also punished women were almost always defined as sexual beings, an action that tied female bodies to a trope of sexuality. By comparison, the deployment of black men as sexual beings tended to be more strategic, with black men being cast as sexual predators, primarily during times of social or national crisis. In this latter instance, the nation was designated as being under siege, and, whether deliberately or not, there was often slippage in the discourse whereby the attacked nation was also delineated as a geographical entity and represented through the bodies and supposed moral superiority of the white woman.

It is these competing and often contradictory images of men and women with which this chapter is concerned. By showing how the body in both punished and unpunished states was a gendered body, it investigates how law and punishment were used to reinscribe notions of femininity and masculinity onto the bodies of Jamaicans and Barbadians in the nineteenth century. It shows also how this marking was racialized, with the result that discourses and practices of punishment often juxtaposed a black or brown femininity against a white femininity, and a black masculinity was often cast in opposition to a white masculinity.

Appropriating Foucault for Feminism

Although Michel Foucault's work has proved indispensable, his *Discipline and Punish* is overwhelmingly masculinist and Eurocentric.[3] Although delineating the activities of female criminals like Marie Françoise Salmon and Madame Lescombat (Marie Catherine Taperet) in that work, Foucault tends not to problematize the gendered nature of punishment, an oversight that effectively elides women and their experiences as disciplined and punished subjects from his discourse.[4] Thus, not only are those who consult his work left with a one-sided analysis, they also read an incomplete examination of discipline and punishment in Western Europe. However, by taking up Joan Scott's challenge to engage gender as a tool of historical analysis, this chapter illustrates that in Barbados and Jamaica, gender—in particular, nineteenth- and early twentieth-century understandings of what it meant to be male and female—informed the philosophies and practices of discipline and punishment.[5] In addition, I argue for a more nuanced understanding of gendered practices in Barbados and Jamaica in the nineteenth century and note that ideas about male and female bodies were always mediated through the lenses of class, color, race, and ethnicity.

One of the first things that Scott does in advancing claims for gender to be used as a "category of historical analysis" is to outline in detail the difficulties in defining "gender."[6] Although Scott ultimately argues for gender to be used as an analytical tool, one equal to the intellectually established and widely embraced class, she notes that the case for gender to attain a similar status is often thwarted by confusion within the academy over what it means. This, according to Scott, has led to confusion over how and when the term "gender" should be used. Caribbean feminists have also intimated that the misuse of the term "gender," if not checked, can have serious consequences for its effective use in the academy and in society. V. Eudine Barriteau noted in 2003 that in the Anglophone Caribbean the term "has come to stand erroneously as a trendier synonym for the biological differences and signifiers implied by the word 'sex.'"[7]

Thus, even as it uses gender as the tool to show how the sexed body became the alibi to explain away the differing punitive treatments of men and women, this chapter also argues that in many cases colonial and imperial understandings about bodies, particularly female bodies, were as inconstant and sometimes as murky as the modern-day meanings of the term "gender." In many cases, what resulted from this sometimes strategic and often confused application of what it meant to be male or female in the nineteenth-century colonial Caribbean was a tug-of-war between those who took a more humanistic stance toward punishment and laborers in the British colonies and those who believed that the only effective application of the law was a corporeal and draconian one. Consequently, what we see in the literature is that calls for infusions of mercy and mitigation of punishments were often pitted against declarations of the incorrigibility of the typically black or brown female criminal and the volatility and emotionality of the black or brown male criminal.

In spite of this tug-of-war, however, there was also the tacit acknowledgment between the two camps that female bodies were intrinsically different from male bodies and that these biological, somatic differences should be manifested in disciplinary and punitive practices. Thus, for example, amelioration policies, particularly those of the nineteenth century and often intended to mitigate the draconian nature of enslavement, took on what scholar David Lambert refers to as a "pro-natalist" tenor that linked successful reproduction to reductions in physical punishment.[8] This pro-natalist ideology that guided mitigation of punishments in the early nineteenth century continued to influence the discourses and practices of punishment in Barbados and Jamaica well into the century. This may be illustrated through the actions of those magistrates in Falmouth, Jamaica, for example, who had ordered that pregnant women and nursing mothers were not to be punished by being placed in solitary confinement, even though, as Sturge and Harvey noted, this command was later rescinded by William Frater, the custos (principal magistrate) of the parish.[9]

For the most part, however, and in spite of the pro-natalist policies of the early nineteenth century, the punished black female body continued to dominate the discourse on punishment as compared with the virtual absence of a similarly punished white female body. An examination of the list of prisoners committed to the common jail in Barbados between 1835 and 1837 illustrates this contention. Out of a total of thirty-two women committed to the jail during this period, only one was white. Peggy Abbott, the woman in question, had been committed to the jail on April 1, 1835, for murder, but the only thing that we learn about her sentence—at least in this document—is that she was remanded on December 10, 1835. By way of comparison, black and colored women who had committed less serious offenses were dealt with immediately. For example, Ancilla, an apprenticed laborer who had been committed on September 5, 1836, for burglary, was sentenced to eleven months of hard labor and one month of solitary confinement. For receiving stolen goods, Susan Ames, a free black woman, was sentenced to seven years' transportation, which was later remitted to two years of hard labor.[10]

The evocative image of the punished black female body may also be illustrated through the example of Louisa Beveridge from Leith Hall Plantation in Jamaica, who was punished for insolence by Stipendiary Magistrate Thomas Baines. As punishment, Beveridge was sentenced to the treadmill for two days and was later reported to have died from apoplexy after being tied to the wheel by cords around her arms for refusing to "step the wheel."[11] An inquest was subsequently held to investigate the cause of Beveridge's death and to prevent a recurrence of this incident. A further investigation was called for, which not only sought to investigate Beveridge's death but also the general system of management of the workhouse in Morant Bay. The investigation revealed that women who refused to work on the treadmill were fastened to it by ligatures around their arms for as long as twenty-four hours in succession.[12] The insouciance of those testifying during the inquest, including the supervisor at the prison in St. Thomas in the East where Beveridge was confined, reiterated how the debasement of the black body had permeated the very confines of spaces of confinement. Gibson, the supervisor of the prison, testified that when Beveridge had arrived at the prison she had been "violent" and "obstinate." He also took pains to dissociate himself from Beveridge's death by arguing that "no deaths have ever occurred on the treadmill but those occasioned by the violence and obstinacy of the parties themselves." Continuing to absolve himself from blame, Gibson recalled: "After the great number of convicts that were pardoned by

Lord Mulgrave and his Excellency the present Governor, those that remain in the house of correction are of the worst and most dangerous and desperate characters."[13] Yet this insouciance may be read as ironic, especially when one considers those instances where a carefully considered empathy was expressed toward punished women.

In spite of the obvious fact that black women outnumbered white women in both Barbados and Jamaica, this demographic superiority does not account totally for the predominance of black female inmates in jails or houses of correction, nor does it categorically explain why they were punished more frequently than white women. In fact, the differential punishments meted out to black and white women, and to black and white men, were arguably the corporeal and punitive manifestations of the racist and sexist philosophies that buttressed the plantation economy.[14] These philosophies, according to Bush's estimation, had developed by the mid-eighteenth century during the period when "sugar monoculture was consolidated." They included ascribing diametrically opposed economic and gender roles to black and white women, with the result that white women "became the embodiment of modesty and respectability." Moreover, "Black concubinage became de rigueur and white women were artificially elevated as black women were unfairly debased. Such invidious distinctions emphasized the inferiority of black women, providing a convenient rationale for their economic and sexual exploitation."[15] This elevation of white women and the related debasement of black women, it is argued, helps to account for the corporeal and draconian types of punishments of black women, even in the face of cries about the delicacy of the fairer sex. Whereas white women were often seen as the embodiment of modesty and morality, black lower-class women in particular were often cast as always on the verge of criminal activity. Thus, it comes as no surprise that the Trinidadian "don't-care-a-damns" were seen as being as immoral as they were criminal. Indeed, these were the women who "flaunt[ed] their criminal indifference to every decency and moral feeling before the face of all, and poison[ed], as it were, the very atmosphere of the young and unguarded."[16]

Even in the face of the corporeal equalization of black men and black women and the particularly pejorative categorization of black women, however, the notion that these same bodies were somehow different from each other and should be treated accordingly impinged on penal practices. For example, a boy who was apprenticed to a coffee plantation at Craig-Hill in Jamaica was reputed to have told Sturge and Harvey that although both men and women who were sentenced to the treadmill at the Halfway Tree house of correction in St. Andrew were whipped, men were whipped with the cat-o'-nine-tails and women with a strap.[17]

At the same institution, Sturge and Harvey found that men and women worked "alternate spells of fifteen minutes each" on the treadmill, but what seemed particularly galling for them was that "no regard was paid to decency in providing [women] with a suitable dress to work on the mill."[18] At the jail in St. Ann too, Sturge and Harvey found that women sentenced to the treadmill were not suitably dressed and so were "liable to be indecently exposed."[19]

This image of the unsuitably dressed, almost naked black woman dancing the mill was a recurring motif in discourses of punishment. It was an image that was often deployed to criticize the punishment of women—a tactic that had the impact of erasing punished men from the discourses on punishment even as it brought notions of female delicacy, shame, and morality to the fore of abolitionist debates. For instance, James Williams, in his narrative that was deliberately produced for readers in Britain, described how black femininity was assaulted and compromised through the punished, exposed bodies of women who were confined in workhouses in Jamaica:

> The women was obliged to tie up their clothes, to keep them from tread upon them, while they dance the mill; them have to tie them up so as only to reach down to the knee, and half expose themselves; and the man have to roll up their trowsers above the knee, then the driver can flog their legs with the cat, if them don't dance good; and when they flog the legs till they all cut up, them turn to the back and flog away; but if the person not able to dance yet, them stop the mill, and make him drop his shirt from one shoulder, so as to get at his bare back with the Cat. The boatswain flog the people as hard as he can lay it on—man and woman all alike.[20]

Obviously attempting to elicit pathos from abolitionists, particularly the white women in Britain who were identifying with black women as fellow daughters, wives, and sisters, Williams continued:

> One day while I was in, two young woman was sent in from Moneague side, to dance the mill, and put in dungeon, but not to work in penal gang; them don't know how to dance the mill, and driver flog them very bad; they didn't tie up their clothes high enough, so their foot catch upon the clothes when them tread the mill and tear them;—And then between the Cat and the Mill—them flog them so severe,—they cut away most of their clothes, and left them in a manner naked; and the driver was bragging afterwards that he see all their nakedness.[21]

Williams's assertions that women who were being punished were often unsuitably dressed were substantiated by J. W. Pringle. Pringle, during his visit to Jamaica to investigate prison conditions in the British West Indies, observed at the house of correction at Morant Bay in St. Thomas in the East that the women who worked on the treadmill did not wear "drawers."[22] He found a similar situation at the house of correction in Kingston, as women who labored on the treadmill "had not drawers," though he was quick to point out that they "seemed sufficiently covered by their dress."[23]

The fact that confined men and women were regarded and treated differently was also confirmed by the deputy of the prison in St. Ann who noted that prisoners sentenced to the treadmill were usually flogged, although the men were struck on the back and the women on their feet.[24] Men and women were chained in pairs when working out in public in the penal gang in Montego Bay in St. James, and in Falmouth both men and women were worked in chains and iron collars in the gangs.[25] But Sturge and Harvey found at the jail at Lucea in Hanover that all the men who worked in the penal gang wore iron collars but not all of the women did.[26]

In the main, however, even though black men and black women were both recipients of corporal punishment, punished women tended to elicit more empathy than men who were punished. For example, Sturge and Harvey showed more concern for the female prisoners in Barbados who had their hair cut off or were sentenced to labor on the treadmill than they did for men who were similarly punished. They denounced these punishments by invoking notions of female delicacy, implying that women and men were intrinsically different, with the former to be guaranteed a form of protection that was not to be extended to the latter: "These barbarous punishments appear to be based upon the theory, that the negro female does not possess the deep feelings and delicate sensibilities of her sex; or if she does possess them, that they are incompatible with her servile condition, and ought to be obliterated."[27] In spite of Sturge and Harvey's denunciation of hair-cropping, it remained one of the methods of punishment used in the mid- and late nineteenth century. For instance, Trotman notes that there was a two-day island-wide riot in Trinidad in 1849 after there were attempts to make the shaving off of female inmates' hair a part of the prison regulations.[28] Also, in an 1885 dispatch on crime and prison discipline in Jamaica, hair-cropping was given full governmental endorsement when the author of the dispatch wrote that hair-cropping for females had been approved.[29]

This contradictory reception of hair-cropping as a punishment for women may be demonstrated further through the case of two non-predial apprentices from Jamaica, Maria Dacres and Cecilia Palmer. Dacres and Palmer had been sentenced by Stipendiary Magistrate Marlton to six days' solitary confinement in the workhouse for neglecting their duties. Though Marlton had ordered that their hair should not be cut off, his orders were disobeyed. For this act of disobedience, the supervisor of the workhouse was ordered to attend the next grand court. Sligo upheld the illegality of the punishment by dismissing the claim that Dacres's and Palmer's hair had been cut "merely for the sake of cleanliness." Instead, he showed that he was aware of the provocative and punitive uses of hair-cropping when he argued that it was "done on purpose to annoy the apprentices, whose punishments are generally considered here to be very much too lenient." Unwittingly, and in spite of his ruling, Sligo also seemed to reinforce the efficacy of hair-cutting when he added—obviously echoing the sentiments that had been put forward by observers like Des Voeux—that "as far as the happiness of the apprentices is concerned, . . . I am assured that they would rather submit to corporal punishment than the deprivation of the diligently-nursed locks."[30]

Official and unofficial condemnation of punishments of women were supported with legislative acts. By the Slavery Abolition Act of 1833 (Section 21), female apprentices were to be exempted from being whipped or beaten. Reports of this law being flouted led to the appointment of a select committee by the House of Commons in 1837 to investigate the truth of these allegations. As a result of the findings, measures were taken "to prevent the recurrence of the violation of that most important enactment." In addition, Sligo prosecuted those persons who were found guilty of subjecting female apprentices to corporal punishment in houses of correction. The select committee also objected to female apprentices being worked in chains while laboring in penal gangs as it was felt that "the labour and degradation involved in that punishment, would be a sufficient object of terror, without the addition of chains." In another show of gendered compassion, the committee added that "in the infliction of punishment, care ought to be taken to avoid anything which needlessly tends to lessen that self-respect, which, in the female character especially, it is of the highest importance to maintain, or, when it does not exist, to create."[31]

The Morant Bay Rebellion also illustrated how ideas about male and female bodies impinged on discourses about punishment. In addition, because wars and rebellions are coded traditionally as masculine, the women who were alleged to have participated in this uprising were particularly vilified, a vilification that stemmed partly from perceptions of them as having stepped outside the bounds of respectable femininity. Additionally, the negative delineation of the women who were identified as rebels was mediated by their racial and social locations as their actions, read as a challenge to established socio-political boundaries, signaled unwillingness to accept the strictures under which they had been placed.[32] Consequently, the black women who had participated in the rebellion were not only portrayed as active agents in the genesis of the disturbances but also, consonant with the portrayal of female deviants in general, as a disturbing and problematic irruption into masculine space. Thus, it should come as no surprise that they were described in terms that were particularly caustic, with Eyre asserting that they were "even more brutal and barbarous than the men."[33] This sentiment that disaffected black women were worse than similarly disposed black men was also expressed by white women. In her testimony to the commission appointed to investigate the Morant Bay Rebellion, Eleanor Shortridge made mention of the "fiendish expressions" uttered during the rebellion, and she also asserted that the women "seemed to be much worse than the men."[34] Thus, again it should come as no surprise that the "black woman as violent actor" trope gained currency during the rebellion. Black women like Caroline Grant, Sarah Johnson, Elizabeth Faulkner, and Nancy Murray were all presented as evidence of a compromised black femininity and womanhood. Grant, for example, was alleged to have attacked James Bonner Barratt "and to have gone to his shop door to kill him, and to have commanded the men to kill him."[35]

This "violent black woman" motif was also aligned with the trope of the black woman as bad mother, the latter idea being deployed after the rebellion to concretize the notion of the pathological and dangerous black woman. Using the figure of Johnson—who in four sentences was portrayed as a mother, rebel, and black—Governor John Peter Grant delineated her as holding a compromised position in all of these spheres. Johnson was alleged to have said that all mulattos and whites should be killed, and that if any of her daughters joined the whites that they "must be killed like the whites." This latter statement, according to Grant's dispatch, was evidence of Johnson's "disposition."[36] Thus, the fact of Johnson's motherhood was mentioned here not to reinforce her femininity, but rather used to paint her as a bad *woman*—thus calling into question her status as both woman and mother—because she was allegedly willing to harm her children.

Black women were also portrayed as having played a key role in the genesis of the rebellion, serving to further damage their already compromised femininity. In a dispatch of October 1866, Elizabeth Faulkner was accused of not only encouraging the rebels to kill the "buckra," she was also said to be one of the women who filled her lap with stones that were used to assault the volunteer white fighters at the courthouse in Morant Bay. Not only were their actions used as evidence to highlight suspect femininity, black women's alleged speech was also presented as evidence of their sanguinary nature. As a case in point, both through her actions and her words Nancy Murray seemed to be the embodiment of the rebellious black woman. Murray's speech appeared to betray her debased and compromised femininity, and her attire also hinted at her dangerous inclinations. Murray was seen wearing a "volunteer's cap," a provocative gesture that, when read along with the fact that her clothes were covered in blood, suggests that the cap was a sartorial display to boast that she, or at least the rebels, had been successful in killing one of the volunteers. Upon being asked how many white people had been killed, Murray was reputed to have said: "We killed the Baron and rolled him down. The brains is dashed out. We kill Parson Herschell, we cut his neck; and we killed Inspector Alberga, Mr. McCormack, and Mr. Hitchins, a captain of volunteers, and Mr. Cooke's sons, and Mr. Walton; and Parson Cooke got away; and Stephen Cooke escape, but if we could catch him, we would cut off his head."[37]

White women, in contrast to black women like Faulkner and Murray, were "rendered visible" in a very different way. Unlike the bodies, words, and actions of black women that seemed to litter the discourses of violence and bloodshed, white women were virtually invisible from those discourses. White women, for instance, were not portrayed as having played any major role in the rebellion. If anything, they were cast as objects of desire and objects in need of protection. When references were made to white women in the literature on the rebellion, they were often specifically referred to as "ladies," or with a "Mrs." attached to their surnames—which signaled that they were in need of white men's protection. Indeed, Governor Eyre intimated that one of the principal aims of the governmental reprisals was to "save the lives of the ladies, children, and other isolated and unprotected persons in the districts where the rebellion existed."[38] Sarah Knowles is one example of a white woman who seemed to fit the prototype of the consummate white damsel in distress. Knowles, like many other white women during the rebellion, was said to have been threatened by a black man. In Knowles's case, the black man was Peter O'Hagan, who was alleged to have threatened to cut off her head if she carried any gunpowder to the white volunteer fighters.[39]

Another subtext running through the discourse on the Morant Bay Rebellion and inextricably linked to the idea of protecting women was that white women were the objects of black men's marauding passions, which historian David Lambert also sees in his analysis of the 1816 Bussa Rebellion in nineteenth-century Barbados. Lambert notes that a "recurrent theme in white descriptions of the [Bussa] revolt was fear about black male sexual attacks."[40] When one notes the vitriol and repugnance with which interracial sex between white women and black men was regarded in the colonies, therefore, it is unsurprising that this notion of "black peril" (Lambert's term) was also an idée fixe during the Morant Bay Rebellion in Jamaica.[41] In his 1879 autobiography *Stirring Incidents in the Life of a British Soldier*, Thomas Faughnan noted that one of the rumors that circulated in Morant Bay was that at the outset of the rebellion George

William Gordon, Paul and William Bogle, and James and William Burie were going to attack the white population on Christmas night, kill the men, and "take their wives."[42]

According to other rumors that circulated during and after the rebellion, these five black men were not the only ones who saw white women as part of the plunder. "Hurra! Buckra country for us. Never mind the Buckra women; we can get them when we want": thus was said to be a rallying cry uttered by black male rebels.[43] If this proclamation were true, then the black men who participated in the rebellion were intent on reconfiguring the national landscape as much as they were intent on reversing the hue of patriarchy. The theme of the sexually intemperate rebel is obtrusive also when one examines some of the testimony from those who witnessed the rebellion. For instance, during her examination, according to the report of the Jamaica Royal Commission, Maria Hitchins noted that while some of the black male rebels shouted "Save women!" others thought that they should be killed, while still others thought that the white women should be saved because the black rebels wanted wives.[44]

The official report on the Morant Bay Rebellion also helped to uphold the notion about the desirability of white women even as it consolidated the sanctification of white female bodies—the latter illustrated by the assertion that even black women attempted to shield white women from the marauding black men: "We want the Buckra men to kill, but we don't want the women now; we will have them afterwards," was apparently heard by "a faithful woman . . . who succeeded in hiding her mistress and all the members of her family."[45] Of course, in the final analysis, the ultimate protection came from white men, as the evidence by Captain Henry Francis Luke shows:

1092. What force had you when you reached the Rhine estate, when you got up to these persons who claimed protection?
One hundred and twenty men.

1093. Altogether?
Yes.

1094. Who did you find there claiming protection?
Mrs. Shortridge, Mrs. Major, and several ladies whose names I do not remember, and several children. . . .

1098. What did you do in consequence of the claims for protection; what steps did you take?
I brought them away with my force.[46]

In any case, whether or not black men wanted to take white women for their wives, the punishments meted out to them in the wake of the rebellion suggest that punishment was used as a tool to reclaim a seemingly compromised and attacked white masculinity and to punish black masculinity that had stepped outside of its bounds. This assertion is borne out when one considers that 95 percent of those executed by the colonial military and paramilitary forces in the wake of the governmental reprisals were males. Lieutenant Colonel Elkington, Jamaican deputy adjutant-general, wrote: "Hole is doing splendid service with his men all about Manchioneal, and shooting every black man who cannot account for himself."[47] By shooting every black man who could not "account for himself," Hole and his men were reinforcing the social and racial order and showing that all black men belonged to a space and place that was determined ultimately by white men.

Ruptures in the social fabric were not the only context for gendered manifestations of punishment. In fact, the gendered application of punishment held a prosaic place in Barbadian and Jamaican society, as the laws of these two islands show. Although on the surface many of the laws appeared to be gender neutral, there were many instances where implicit differentiation was made between the sexes, particularly as it related to what types of punishment they could receive and what kinds of crimes they would commit. In other instances, laws that punished antisocial behavior unequivocally targeted one gender. Under Barbados's Larceny Act of February 17, 1868, for instance, a distinction was made in the types of punishments to be given to young males vis-à-vis those that could be meted out to females. Under the 1868 Larceny Act of Barbados, males under the age of sixteen could be whipped.[48]

This singling out of males under sixteen to be whipped for offenses was typical of the period. For instance, in Barbados's Malicious Injury to Property Act of 1868, males under sixteen who were convicted of "unlawfully and maliciously" destroying or damaging "with intent to destroy, any plant, root, fruit, or vegetable production" could be imprisoned with or without hard labor, sentenced to solitary confinement, or whipped.[49] Again one can see a central thesis at work: that the intent of punishment that attacked the body could at the same time be corrective (for those who were particularly young and still pliable) and vengeful (for the wronged party and the state).

Like the Larceny Act, the 1868 "Act to Consolidate and Amend the Law of This Island Relating to Offences against the Person" can also be used to investigate how a gendered philosophy could direct punitive practices.[50] This act made a clear differentiation between men's bodies and women's bodies—both as punished subjects and potential victims of the criminal classes. In making claims about male and female bodies, this act reinforced notions about female frailty— even in a society where black women were debased as a matter of course—and the de facto right of males, this time in the form of the state through the legal machinery, to protect the bodies of women and girls. Thus, in the section of this law that claimed to seek to do just that—"protect women and girls"—those convicted of rape were deemed guilty of a felony and were liable "at the discretion of the court . . . [to] be kept in penal servitude for life, or for any term not less than three years, or . . . be imprisoned for any term not exceeding two years, with or without hard labour."[51] From this one can see the sacredness of the female body in play, with any violation of it being punishable by harsh measures.

These attempts to protect the female body and thereby entrench the gender ideologies that were held by authorities in the metropole, Jamaica, and Barbados were also discernible in the 1877 "Draft of a Criminal Code and a Code of Criminal Procedure for the Island of Jamaica." This code made it clear that although "a person sixteen years of age" could be sentenced to any number of whippings that the courts saw fit, women "of any age" could not be flogged at all. In lieu of whippings, the court could "sentence a female to solitary confinement or any other such additional punishment as the law for the time being permits to be inflicted on a female for an offence against the rules of a prison." What is noteworthy about this apparent clemency toward females is that there was never such expression of clemency toward males. The unspoken assumption seemed to be that the bodies of men were better equipped to bear whippings. The question of compassion and leniency never seemed to extend toward males, far less the male body. Thus, it should not be surprising that within the draft criminal code, in descriptions of punishments for crimes that were sexual in nature, the perpetrator was always the nebulous "he" and the victim (the assaulted) was "her." One of the few exceptions to this rule was in the instance of "Unnatural Crime" where "whoever [was] convicted of unnatural carnal knowledge of any person, with force or without the consent of such person, shall be liable to penal servitude for life, and to flogging." For the most part, however, the language of this code erases the shared condition of human vulnerability, as it does not acknowledge that men can also be victims of violence, at the same time that it solely casts women as victims.[52]

State control of the body is also apparent in legislation regulating other sexual behavior. For instance, the 1868 Offences against the Persons Act of Barbados established heteronormativity in criminalizing same-sex relations. As Levy points out, sodomy was thought to be such a serious crime that in 1834 in Barbados it was punishable by death.[53] One can see that this section of the Offences against the Persons Act clearly blurred the lines between the public and private as it punished sexual activity between men whether committed in public spaces or the private confines of their homes. Moreover, it glossed over issues of consent as it did not consider whether the individuals involved were acting on their own volition.

There were also forms of sexual regulation that were specifically geared toward constraining the female body. In these cases, female bodies were used by the state as discursive and material tableaux for the inscription of ideas about morality, respectability, and women's proper place in society. It was in the prosecution of sexual crimes under the Act for the Better Prevention of Contagious Diseases that the state machinery tended to be most intrusive—both literally and figuratively—and in the process marked women's bodies in a real and ideological sense.[54] These acts ensured that the Jamaican and Barbadian states, however much they might be inclined to "leave for settlement to the individual conscience all questions of morals and religion, [could not] abandon to the care of the improvident and profligate the restraining of contagious maladies."[55] Thus, what was obtrusive about the Act for the Better Prevention of Contagious Diseases was not its targeting of alleged sex crimes—prostitution's policing is as old as the profession itself—instead, it was the way the colonial state manipulated the legal machinery to criminalize women's bodies. One could argue that although this act appeared to concern itself with stamping out venereal diseases like gonorrhea, it was really women's bodies that were treated as diseased—both from a moral and physical standpoint.

As a case in point, under the Barbadian version of the Contagious Diseases Act, women believed to be prostitutes could be summoned to appear before the police and made to undergo medical examination by a surgeon to ascertain if they were infected with a venereal disease. If a woman was found to be infected, the visiting surgeon would sign three copies of a certificate stating that she was infected with a contagious disease. Copies would be given to the woman in question and the police, with the understanding that the diseased woman would go, of her own volition, to the hospital for detainment and treatment. Under the Contagious Diseases Act any rights that an infected woman had over her body were suspended. Refusing to comply with the stipulations of this act could result in the woman being charged with an offense for which she could be imprisoned, with or without hard labor.[56]

Not only were women who were found to be diseased subject to confinement, their bodies and activities were also strictly regulated, even upon their discharge. For instance, women would be issued with a variety of certificates, including certificates of discharge from imprisonment, notices that stated that they were still "affected with a contagious disease" or that they were "free from contagious disease," or a certificate that relieved them from medical examination.[57] As Patrick Bryan has pointed out, the Contagious Diseases Act operated with great success in the case of Jamaica. He noted that between 1886 and 1887 "information had been laid against 174 women of ill-fame in Kingston."[58] Of these women fifty-five were sent to the Lock Hospital, twenty-eight left Kingston without medical examination after being served with magistrates' orders, eight left the city after medical examination, and ten were sent to prison for noncompliance with the law.[59] This punitive approach to what were considered disruptive forms of sexuality also continued in Jamaica in the 1890s. In 1891 364 women from Kingston and Port Royal were corralled under the Contagious Diseases Act. One hundred thirty-three of these women were sent to the Lock Hospital for treatment, while fifteen of them were sent to prison for noncompliance with the law.[60]

The use of the contagious diseases acts as tools of social and sexual control in Barbados and Jamaica reflected their imperial borrowings. They were used in similarly oppressive, class- and gender-biased ways as the acts in Britain from which they were birthed.[61] The British acts, according to historian Judith R. Walkowitz, not only were "specifically directed to women" but also "consistent with a set of attitudes and 'habits of mind' toward women, sexuality, and class that permeated official Victorian culture"—an ethos that was reflected in their colonial apparition.[62] Like their colonial offspring, the enforcement of the British contagious diseases acts also rested on cooperation between doctors, legislators, and the police. In addition, the specific designation of buildings as sites of containment formed a crucial piece of the puzzle in the drive to staunch this perceived moral contagion—in both the colonies and the metropole.

The notion that the female body had to be regulated by the omniscient state was delineated also in those post-emancipation laws that sought to "protect the person," a notable example being the "Attempts to Procure Abortion" section of the Offences against the Person Act of Barbados. In this regulatory sense, the female subject discursively metamorphosed from an object (the body) into a sentient, culpable individual (the criminal woman who had procured abortion). Under this act the fetus was sacrosanct. In cases of abortion, not only could a pregnant woman be prosecuted under this law, but also "whosoever shall unlawfully supply or procure any poison or noxious thing, or any instrument or thing whatsoever, knowing that the same is intended to be unlawfully used or employed with intent to procure the miscarriage of any woman, whether she be or be not with child."[63] Those found assisting any pregnant woman in obtaining an abortion received a relatively lighter sentence. At the "discretion of the court," these persons could be kept in penal servitude for three years or imprisoned for not more than two years, with or without hard labor. The importance of the fetus and the sexed body is also evident in the 1877 draft of the Jamaican criminal code that stipulated that pregnant women who were sentenced to death would have a stay of execution until after the baby was born.[64]

These philosophical understandings of gender and punishment, which were visible in practical and legislative terms, were also crystallized in a structural sense. In fact, the Female Penitentiary in Jamaica may be seen as the architectural and tangible embodiment of the attempts to enact gender differences. Although the Female Penitentiary was located within the General Penitentiary, it "was cut off by a high wall from all communication with the male side of the Prison."[65] Even this containment within the general penitentiary can be read as significant. One could argue that there was a bifurcated understanding of the female convict: female convicts were not only seen as different from male convicts, thereby requiring a different space for enclosure, but they were still somehow seen as possessing a character similar enough to that of the male convicts that they could inhabit the same general space.

The need to mark the female criminal as different from the male criminal was not only reflected in a structural sense, it also found expression in the types of punishments meted out to confined men and women.[66] The stereotypical image of the uncontrollable, hard to rein in black woman, as to be expected, had a significant impact on the types of punishments given to those confined in the female penitentiary. In Jamaica, H. B. Shaw described confined women under short sentences as a "most unruly lot," and although noting the efficacy of the "Dumb Cells," was quick to add that "the real deterrent a Negro woman dreads is to have her hair cut, and after long experience it is my opinion if enforced it would be a most valuable aid to the discipline of the Prison."[67] This form of punishment—and its uncritical and enthusiastic endorsement—was not peculiar to Jamaica or even the British West Indies. In the "Guide for the Religious Called Sisters of Mercy" of 1866, the benefits of head-shaving for women in the Magdalene asylums in Ireland were put forward as a sort of preemptive punishment:

> As Magdalen [sic] began the evidence of her conversion by consecrating her hair to her Redeemer, so do they, and thus give reason to hope that they really intend to imitate her in her penance as they have done in her sins. As a check to the wild sallies of passion and temptation; under these violent impulses, some, who would not yield to better motives, have been known to defer leaving the Asylum until their hair should be sufficiently grown, in whom in the mean time grace grew and passion subsided, and they became good penitents.[68]

These examples of Irish women in the Magdalene asylums who had their hair shaved off, along with the earlier examples of hair-cutting as punishment of Australian, Jamaican, and Barbadian women, illustrate that there was an approach to women and punishment that was at once British as much as it was colonial and transnational at the same time. Recalcitrant, unbending female bodies, this punishment suggests, were more pliable when put under the regulatory lens of shame. Moreover, the endorsement of this punishment as particularly effective against women was also tied to notions about the incorrigibility of the female criminal, and it followed from a trial-and-error search for a form of punishment that was as much regulative as it was corrective for the female criminal.

This idea that there was a particular brand of criminal, the incorrigible female, was also discernible in Barbados. The comments of H. B. Shaw about the "unruly lot" under his charge may be compared to similar comments made by a Mr. Price, who, while serving as the governor of the District A prison in Barbados in 1882, noted that good discipline was "not a fact" in that site of confinement. This was attributed to the presence of "girls of abandoned character." By contrast, the women at the District C prison, because they were not "such abandoned characters" as the women who populated the District A prison, were described as "more easily controlled."[69] This idea that women who were being punished were unruly, that their "characters" had somehow "abandoned" them, was a common theme running through much of the conversations about the female criminal. Underlying this theme, of course, was the idea that these women were often guilty of using their bodies in a way that was either morally unacceptable or that seemed inconsistent with the proscriptions of an ideal (white) femininity.

The idea of the female body, most notably its biological realities, also had an impact on the nature of confinement. For instance, although the evidence found thus far does not indicate that widespread attention was paid to figuring out how to deal with the presence of confined pregnant women or women who had children who were born in prison, the data do show that infants made up a segment of the population living within places of penal confinement. In one entry in the *Barbados Blue Book* for 1882, an infant was said to have died of diarrhea in the District C prison, while in the District A prison three infants had died. In the latter case, inquests had ruled that they had died of natural causes. Although an inquest appears to carry some measure of scientific objectivity, one wonders why the deaths of these infants were not questioned beyond the inquest, especially in light of the fact that no prisoners had died during that year.[70] Although the inquests may have given the deaths of these infants a kind of finality, they also tend to gloss over larger issues, most notably how to attend to the reality and the exigencies of the female body within spaces of confinement. Moreover, the inquests also gloss over an equally important issue, which is whether spaces of confinement were suitable for infants in the first place and how to deal with their presence once they were inside of them. In many ways, this evidence subverts the ideology of corporeal equalization of black men and black women that buttressed the plantation economy. At the same time it illustrates that prison officials in Barbados and Jamaica adopted and jettisoned at will the reality of the biological differences between men and women when these differences did not correspond to their vision of an effective punitive system.

Conclusion

By showing how ideas about men and women shaped nineteenth-century practices and ideologies of discipline and punishment in Jamaica and Barbados, this chapter shows that the punished body was also a gendered body. Thus, it makes the case that to understand the lived experiences of Jamaicans and Barbadians in the post-slavery period one must view them as persons whose gender was etched onto their bodies by discourses and practices relating to punishment. It also shows that one cannot speak about gender in the Caribbean without also talking about race. The gendered body was also the racialized body. This racialized and gendered body, therefore, became an important site for the marking of socio-racial boundaries.

Final Thoughts on What It Means to Punish Black Bodies

One of the enduring legacies of colonialism has been the attribution of inferiority to people of color. This has been manifested in many ways, most notably in delineating the bodies of people of color as aesthetically inferior to and less valuable than those of European descent, and by affixing people of color with stains of alterity from which they have been unable to escape. The power of this attribution could come from its being tied to institutions in society that are deemed to be objective and free from the taint of prejudice, among the more notable examples being legal and punitive systems.

As this work has shown, the attribution of inferiority, criminality, and alterity to people of color had a specific role in colonial societies. It justified the draconian punishments meted out to them and by extension helped to shore up the socio-racial order. More pointedly, this examination of practices and discourses of punishment in Barbados and Jamaica has demonstrated that in the nineteenth century, raced, gendered, and classed bodies were as essential to punishment in these islands as was the execution of punishment itself. In the British Caribbean, punishment gained increasing potency and remained a tool of social divisiveness because of the intangible values that were attached to it. This assertion may be substantiated further when one considers the thought-provoking questions posed by Gwendolyn Midlo Hall in *Social Control in Slave Plantation Societies*: "How was order maintained on a sustained enough basis for these slave societies to function? How were hundreds of slaves, who were being worked to death on isolated, rural estates and who were armed with machetes, convinced, for at least a significant length of time, not to murder their masters and overseers?" Hall posed these questions after asserting that the various security measures like pass laws and laws prohibiting the assembly of slaves were only enforced sporadically. For social order to be maintained, argued Hall, "the person of the white had been made inviolate."[1]

As this book has shown, it was this ethos of the inviolability of the white body and the subsequent debasement of the black body that underwrote disciplinary and punitive discourses and practices in nineteenth-century Barbados and Jamaica. Hair-cropping, the 1836 Emigration Act of Barbados and other punitive legislation, the state reprisals following the Morant Bay Rebellion, the use of the whip and the treadmill in jails and houses of correction in both Barbados and Jamaica—all were used, consciously and unconsciously, to reinforce ideas about bodies and their places in the plantation society.

In showing how punishment was apprehended and articulated in a dual context, local idiosyncrasies between Barbados and Jamaica have also been brought into sharp relief. For instance, by using Barbados's land and labor issues as a counterpoint to Jamaica's, I have shown that punishment is not an issue that can or should be investigated in and of itself but needs to be read and understood through wider societal forces as they also impinge on ideologies and manifestations of punishment. Thus, the trope of the punished body also raised questions about Barbados's and Jamaica's reference to themselves as free societies and reinforced the notion that the plantation economy continued to exert a strong grip on these colonies even as they made promises to make clean breaks with their history.

Yet this focus on disciplinary and punitive practices in Barbados and Jamaica has also revealed similarities between the two islands. For instance, I have shown that in spite of the relative sizes of their laboring populations and the islands themselves, the subaltern populations often received the same types of punishments for societal infractions. I have showed also that power, although guarded selfishly by the elites, was not theirs alone, and that individuals like James Williams, Nancy Murray, Rosey Sample, and Elizabeth Faulkner could appropriate power and use it for themselves. The examples of Williams, Murray, Sample, and Faulkner challenged the idea that punishment was something done to inert bodies. In fact, even as they took their punishments—with their bodies providing the tableau upon which the act of punishment was realized—these individuals also resisted and rewrote the narratives that attempted to define their place in the plantation economy.

In the final analysis, this book has been about more than just flesh and bones. By focusing on meanings ascribed to the disciplined and punished body, it has investigated the internal workings of apprenticeship and emancipation in Barbados and Jamaica. Moreover, it has shown that apprenticeship and emancipation were also experienced *on* the body and were not just abstract phenomena that signaled changing social, political, and economic climates.

APPENDIX

TABLE I

Punishments of Apprenticed Laborers in Jamaica, by Order of
Special Justices, from August, 1, 1834, to August 1, 1835

	Number Punished
Gender	
Males	16,221
Females	9,174
TOTAL	25,395
Nature of Punishment	
Flogging	7,125
Imprisonment	1,249
Treadmill	1,176
Penal gang	2,941
Repayment of time	9,433
Solitary confinement	2,886
Switching	585
TOTAL	25,395
Nature of Offense	
Theft	2,837
Running away	1,805
Neglect of duty	11,855
Disobedience	6,024
Cutting & etc. on cattle	322
Insolence	2,552
TOTAL	25,395

Source: Negro Apprenticeship in the Colonies, 36.

TABLE 2
Punishments in Jamaica, from August 1, 1835, to March 31, 1836

	Number Punished
Gender	
Males	15,996
Females	10,998
TOTAL	26,994
Nature of Punishment	
Whipping*	3,218
Otherwise	23,776
TOTAL	26,994

Source: Negro Apprenticeship in the Colonies, 36.
*Average number of stripes per punishment was 22.5.

TABLE 3
Punishments of Apprentices in Barbados from August 1, 1837, to September 30, 1837

Offense	Number of Convictions	Number of Acquittals, etc.	Punishment for Conviction
Indolence	1,549	95	Imprisonment for max. of 4 weeks and min. of 3 days
Absence	246	21	Imprisonment for max. of 4 weeks and min. of 3 days
Disorderly conduct	457	25	Imprisonment for max. of 4 weeks and min. of 3 days
Petty theft	303	14	Imprisonment for max. of 4 weeks and min. of 3 days and a few whipped
Disobedience	309	28	Imprisonment with hard labor
Trespass	33	—	Imprisonment with solitary confinement

SOURCE: Colthurst, Colthurst Journal, 243.

TABLE 4
Convictions of Barbadian Employers from August 1, 1837, to September 30, 1837

Offense	Number of Convictions	Number of Acquittals, etc.	Punishment for Conviction
Withholding of allowances	21	—	Fine
Assaults on apprentices	31	5	Fine

Source: Colthurst, Colthurst Journal, 243.

TABLE 5
Flogging by Order of Special Magistrates, Jamaica, 1836

	April	May	June	Total Number
Alley, W. H.	—	37	—	37
Baines, T. J.	—	40	176	216
Baynes, E. D.	167	39	418	624
Bell, W. A.	40	110	32	182
Bourne, Stephen	10	20	39	69
Brownson, W. H.	—	—	25	25
Carnaby, William	50	40	35	125
Chamberlayne, R., Jr.	20	—	—	20
Cocking, Ralph	78	—	117	195
Cooper, Richard S.	—	—	39	39
Daughtrey, John	45	—	12	57
Davies, Thomas	126	36	78	240
Dawson, J. K.	30	—	138	168
Dawson, H. W.	—	—	25	25
Dillon, T. A.	60	255	197	512
Dunne, Patrick	30	—	—	30
Ewart, David	—	—	—	—
Facey, Richard B.	—	55	—	55
Finlayson, Walter	20	—	50	70
Fishbourne, E. E.	120	260	265	645
Fyfe, Alexander Gordon	9	20	—	29
Gregg, G. D.	—	48	180	228
Gurley, John	30	—	30	60
Grant, J. W.	—	30	—	30
Gordon, George	4	39	—	63
Hamilton, Chemney	5	20	15	40
Harris, James	233	57	102	392
Hawkins, Charles	140	74	126	340
Higgins, G. O.	—	—	—	—
Hill, Richard	—	—	—	—
Hewitt, William	24	—	304	328
Hulme, J. R.	25	24	127	176
Jones, Thomas W.	35	44	130	209
Kelly, D. W.	25	—	20	45
Kent, Henry	—	20	—	20
Lambert, R. S.	188	162	272	624
Lloyd, Samuel	21	142	382	545
Lyon, Edmund B.	89	—	—	69
Marlton, W. F.	77	30	20	127
McLeod, A. N.	—	—	—	—
Moresby, Henry	359	690	472	1,521
Nolan, James	35	—	40	75
Odell, John	50	30	40	120
Oliver, T. M.	140	175	200	515
Palmer, A. L.	24	—	—	24
Pennell, R. C.	60	391	400	851
Philip, E. D.	80	20	110	210

TABLE 5
Flogging by Order of Special Magistrates, Jamaica (*continued*)

	April	May	June	Total Number
Pryce, Samuel	—	125	227	352
Ramsey, William	—	—	—	—
Rawlinson, S.	219	25	250	494
Reynolds, John	—	—	—	—
Rennell, Robert	—	—	—	—
Sowley, W. H.	271	210	462	943
St. John, Richard	264	319	598	1,181
Thomas, J. R.	567	230	296	1,093
Thompson, R.	—	—	51	51
Waddington, H.	78	36	210	324
Walsh, H.	82	25	12	119
Welsh, Arthur	18	123	87	228
Willis, George	99	40	20	159
Woolfreys, John	—	—	—	—
TOTAL	4,122	4,071	6,834	15,037

Source: Great Britain, Colonial Office, *Papers Presented to Parliament, by Her Majesty's Command*, pt. 5: Jamaica, *Accounts and Papers of the House of Commons*, vol. 49 (1838), 272.

TABLE 6
Apprehensions and Summonses, Barbados
Table showing the number of persons brought before the magistrates' courts by arrest warrant or summons for offenses and how their cases were disposed of in the magistrates' courts

	Number Discharged for Lack of Prosecution by Complaining Party or for Lack of Evidence	Number of Cases Dismissed on Merits	Number of Persons Summarily Convicted	Number of Persons Committed for Trial in Superior Courts
Offenses against the person	200	1,186	2,562	51
Predial larceny	132	51	1,181	—
Offenses against property other than predial larceny*	232	353	922	76
Offenses against master and servants acts, including acts relating to indentured "coolies"	10	14	147	—
Other offenses	141	575	4,381	15
Total number of persons summoned or apprehended	715	2,179	9,193	142

Source: Barbados Blue Book, 1892, BB15.
*These offenses included those against property and injuries to the subjects of property.

TABLE 7
Distribution of Barbadian Population by Parish, 1844

Name of Parish	Area in Square Miles	Inhabitants per Square Mile	Percentage of Jamaican Population
Christ Church	22.3	632	11.53
St. Andrew	13.7	438	8.33
St. George	16.9	602	6.99
St. James	12.1	471	4.67
St. John	13.5	632	5.53
St. Joseph	9.4	718	4.90
St. Lucy	13.6	510	5.67
St. Michael (Bridgetown population)	—*	—	15.84
St. Michael (rural area excluding Bridgetown)	15.0	1,070†	12.26
St. Peter	13.0	642	6.82
St. Philip	23.5	546	10.50
St. Thomas	13.3	639	6.96

Source: Schomburgk, *History of Barbados*, 88.
*This space was blank in the source.
† This figure excluded Bridgetown.

TABLE 8
Population Density (Persons per Square Mile)
in West Indian Islands at Selected Dates

Island	1841–44	1881
Antigua	215	205
Barbados	735	1,033
Dominica	74	92
Grenada	217	319
Jamaica	86	132
Montserrat	230	315
St. Kitts and Nevis	214	289
St. Lucia	90	165
St. Vincent	182	270
Trinidad	37	86

Source: Roberts, *Population of Jamaica*, 56.

TABLE 9

Comparative Criminal Statistics, 1841–1844, Barbados

NUMBER OF PRISONERS IN CONFINEMENT IN COURSE OF THE YEAR

Felons

	Tried				Untried			
	Whites		Black and "Coloured"		White		Black and "Coloured"	
Year	M	F	M	F	M	F	M	F
1841	10	1	351	91	7	—	117	29
1842	26	—	482	117	13	—	94	16
1843	3	—	55	5	4	—	53	4
1844	11	—	138	12	—	—	7	2

Year	Total Tried Felons	Total Untried Felons	Total Felons
1841	453	153	606
1842	625	123	748
1843	63	61	124
1844	161	9	170

Misdemeanors

	Tried				Untried			
	White		Black and "Coloured"		White		Black and "Coloured"	
Year	M	F	M	F	M	F	M	F
1841	47	4	529	192	8	—	35	16
1842	96	8	691	362	4	—	33	6
1843	65	3	928	438	—	—	73	19
1844	45	3	948	377	1	—	5	—

Year	Total Tried Misdemeanors	Total Untried Misdemeanors	Total Misdemeanors
1841	772	59	831
1842	1,157	43	1,200
1843	1,434	92	1,526
1844	1,373	6	1,379

Debtors

	White		Black and "Coloured"		Total Debtors	Grand Total
Year	M	F	M	F		
1841	23	—	134	58	215	1,652
1842	25	1	126	50	202	2,150
1843	25	—	148	96	269	1,919
1844	20	4	141	77	242	1,791

GREATEST NUMBER OF PRISONERS AT ANY ONE TIME

	Common Jail of Bridgetown				District A				District C				District E			
	White		Black and "Coloured"		Whites		Black and "Coloured"		Whites		Black and "Coloured"		Whites		Black and "Coloured"	
Year	M	F	M	F	M	F	M	F	M	F	M	F	M	F	M	F
1841	3	—	132	37	—	—	—	—	—	—	—	—	—	—	—	—
1842	14	3	137	57	4	—	38	—	1	—	42	—	1	—	19	19
1843	11	—	172	49	—	—	—	—	—	—	16	—	—	—	15	10
1844	9	2	139	38	—	—	26	—	—	—	33	—	1	—	16	10

Year	Total in Common Jail of Bridgetown	Total in District A	Total in District C	Total in District E
1841	172	—	—	—
1842	211	42	43	39
1843	232	—	16	25
1844	188	26	33	27

Punishments for Offenses in Prison

	Whipping	Irons	Stocks		Solitary confinement		Other punishments	
Year	M	M	M	F	M	F	M	F
1841	—	49	18	—	—	1	1	—
1842	—	51	25	—	13	6	22	—
1843	—	56	12	—	2	4	—	—
1844	—	131	17	—	42	0	27	—

Cases of Sickness

	White		Black and "Coloured"	
Year	M	F	M	F
1841	19	—	119	—
1842	40	—	248	19
1843	35	—	241	23
1844	31	—	249	17

Deaths

	Whites		Black and "Coloured"	
Year	M	F	M	F
1841	—	—	1	—
1842	—	—	5	—
1843	1	—	3	1
1844	—	—	2	—

Source: Schomburgk, *History of Barbados,* 137–39.

TABLE 10
Prisoners Committed in 1844 and 1845, Barbados

	1844					1845				
	White		Black and "Coloured"			Whites		Black and "Coloured"		
	M	F	M	F	Total	M	F	M	F	Total
Total prisoners committed during year	75	7	1,241	468	1,791	87	4	1,163	509	1,763
Under eighteen years of age	—	1	125	66	—	1	—	181	117	—
Above eighteen years of age	75	6	1,116	402	—	86	4	982	392	—
Prisoners who could not read	4	—	338	71	—	4	—	828	304	—
Prisoners who could read	71	7	903	397	—	83	4	335	205	—

Source: Schomburgk, History of Barbados, 137–39.

FIGURE I.
Inmates Receiving Corporal Punishment or Solitary Confinement in Glendairy Prison, 1879–1898

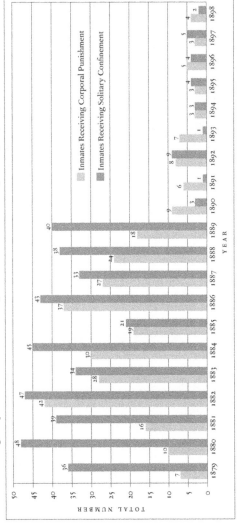

Source: Barbados Blue Books, 1898.

TABLE 11

Male Imprisonment, Barbados, 1896–1901

Year	Commitments	Percent Able to Read and Write	Percent Able to Read Only	Percent Illiterate
1896	1,353	44	3	53
1897	1,321	41	7	52
1898	1,475	41	6	53
1899	1,500	44	5	51
1900	1,708	47	4	49
1901	1,815	44	5	51

Source: Annual Colonial Report, Barbados, 1901–1902, 39.

TABLE 12

Female Imprisonment, Barbados, 1896–1901

Year	Commitments	Percent Able to Read and Write	Percent Able to Read Only	Percent Illiterate
1896	1,399	33	11	56
1897	1,450	33	12	55
1898	1,534	38	11	56
1899	1,675	32	9	59
1900	1,755	36	14	50
1901	1,996	36	7	57

Source: Annual Colonial Report, Barbados, 1901–1902, 40.

TABLE 13

Abstract of Cases of Assault by Employers against Apprenticed Laborers, Barbados, January 1–May 31, 1836

Case Number	Date	Name of Complainant	Name of Defendant	Substance of Complaint	Decision
DISTRICT A—RURAL DIVISION					
1	18 Jan.	Adam	J. T. Seal	That the complainant is a field-man; that Mr. Seal this morning was attending the mill, and that Seal beat him cruelly; that he ran off when defendant threw two large stones at him which struck him; that Seal a second time attacked him, and struck him with a stone.	Fined 40s.
2	26 Jan.	Richard	J. H. Whitehall	That complainant was beaten in a most severe manner yesterday by Mr. Whitehall; that he cut him severely with a horse-crupper, and gave him several severe kicks and cuffs.	ditto
3	9 Feb.	Sarah	Susanna Lucas	That defendant struck her yesterday a violent blow over the eye.	Fined 10s.
4	11 Feb.	Quaco	John Packer	That complainant being cook, and occasionally in the boiling-house, he was there yesterday afternoon when defendant came home, who asked him where he had been? On complainant telling him, he struck him several blows and kicked him.	Fined 30s.
5	16 Feb.	John	Wm. H. Green	That defendant had given him a pass, that he [might] obtain employment and pay him wages; that he had got business, and therefore came to defendant's house to tell him the same; that on entering the gate-door Mr. Duke, defendant's brother-in-law, ordered him away, and immediately kicked and cuffed him severely. During this time defendant came and ill-used complainant in a more violent manner than Mr. Duke; and that as defendant is master of complainant, he seeks redress now for assault and battery.	ditto

Case Number	Date	Name of Complainant	Name of Defendant	Substance of Complaint	Decision
6	11 March	Sam Abraham	Wm. Connell	That last evening defendant took occasion to find fault with complainant when waiting on him, and in the act of bringing him a knife and fork; that complainant was not rude to defendant, who beat him severely with his fist, and struck him with a whip, seized him by the throat and threw him down.	ditto
7	17 March	Jacob	John Packer	That on Monday afternoon complainant was cutting off the rotten canes, when defendant accosted him in a violent manner, struck him on the back of the neck with a cane, gave him a cuff in the face and kicked him.	ditto
8	22 March	Jem. Green	Jas. Williams	That on Wednesday evening last complainant went to defendant to ask him for the amount due him for working at extra hours; at that[,] defendant abused him, ordered him away, and struck him two severe blows on the back of the neck.	Fined 20s.
9	8 April	Celia	F. Callendar	That yesterday morning she was ordered to milk the cattle as usual; she obeyed and took the milk into the house to be measured; this was done by Sarah Dummett, who said something to her about bread; that she then accused the complainant of being drunk. This she denied, and was on her way out of the house to sell her milk, when the defendant seized her violently by the throat, and attempted to drag her into the house, &c.	ditto
10	21 April	Trist. Shandy	Robert Mayers	That without provocation, on Tuesday last, defendant struck complainant more than five times with a horsewhip, and last Saturday week struck him three blows with his fist.	Fined 2d. 50s.

11	23 April	John Thomas	Geo. T. Robert	That about three weeks ago he was sent by his mistress to get meat for the house, but he did not return, and the next day was brought home, when defendant tied him by the hands to a beam in the kitchen with a rope, in such a manner that he scarcely could touch the ground with his toes flat. Defendant then came and beat him till he got into fits again. N.B.—This is the worst case that has come before me since my arrival in the island. I should have sent this case to the sessions, but the boy is a very bad character and a runaway.	Fined [£]5
12	9 April	Richard	Henry Allamby	On Friday afternoon complainant was at work in the field; defendant came there and ordered two apprentices of the estate to take possession of complainant's house; turning to complainant he said to him, "Did not I, sir, forbid Renn from coming into this place?" Complainant answered he had not; defendant immediately knocked him down and kicked him, &c.	Fined 40s.
13	11 April	Sarah	Cath. Brown	Complainant being sick on Saturday last, went to lay down on her bed, and her daughter, a young girl, came and lay by her side, as required by complainant; shortly after defendant came in and gave complainant, without any provocation, two slaps on her jaws; that complainant is a very weak old woman, and unable to do her quantity of work as hitherto; that on Monday morning last, while complainant was at work in the field, defendant came to her and struck her on the back with a stone, &c.	Fined 30s.
14	13 April	Jack Nell	Geo. F. Harte	That yesterday morning he was employed in packing trash, and while so doing he discovered a snake in it; and that being much afraid of reptiles he immediately came from the trash-heap and went into the boiling-house to call Mr. Deane, the book-keeper, to catch it for him. On his entering the same, one of the men, aware of complainant's alarm, put something round his neck, which he supposed was the snake; but complainant knowing what was done to him was in joke, made a blow as if to strike the man, when defendant came into boiling-house and flogged complainant with a horsewhip.	Fined 50s.

TABLE 13

Abstract of Cases of Assault by Employers against Apprenticed Laborers, Barbados, January 1–May 31, 1836 (*continued*)

Case Number	Date	Name of Complainant	Name of Defendant	Substance of Complaint	Decision
DISTRICT A—TOWN DIVISION					
15	13 Jan.	Edward Jack	James King	That the complainant is the apprenticed labourer of the defendant, and that he struck him twice; once on the lip and once on the back of the head.	Fined 5s.
16	18 Jan.	Nancy	Wm. Healis	That the defendant gave her a cuff and beat her on the head with a chain. She is employed by the accused.	Fined [£]2
17	1 Feb.	Blossom	Bash A. Walsh	That complainant is apprenticed labourer to defendant, and that she directed her to scour the house, when she replied she was not able; and she then boxed her face, and gave her four kicks.	Fined 10s.
18	2 Feb.	Adam	Geo. Thompson	That complainant is apprenticed labourer to defendant; that last Sunday, in consequence of being sick, he was absent from his business; on Monday he and his master had some words about it, and defendant struck him four blows with his fist.	Fined [£]2
19	9 Feb.	Francis	Wm. Christie	That the complainant is employed by the defendant; that he was sweeping the back shop last Sunday morning, when Mr. Christie called him, and said Jemmy had told him he had refused to sweep before the front door; upon which defendant caught him by the shirt and beat him, first with his fist and then with the handle of the broom. N.B.—This small fine is awarded in consequence of the insolent conduct of the complainant.	Fined 5s.
20	2 March	Joseph Thorn	Henry Dyrrell	That the complainant is employed by the defendant, and that he was struck by him several times with his fist, and also with the key of a boot-tree, and was abused very much.	Fined 30s.
21	23 March	Isabella	Benj. Burney	That from the jealous feelings of his wife defendant struck her several times.	Fined [£]3

No.	Date	Defendant	Complainant	Offence	Sentence
22	27 April	Jack Langhan	Arch. Lamont	That yesterday evening, in consequence of the fire getting too hot and burning some bread, he was struck four times by the defendant. N.B.—From the insolent and irregular conduct on the part of the complainant this mitigated fine is awarded.	Fined 10s.
23	28 April	B. Charles	Arch. Lamont	That yesterday complainant was sent to bring three coppers' worth of plantain leaves, which from their being short for the purpose required, the defendant got a horsewhip, and gave him half-a-dozen stripes with it; shortly afterwards he came back and gave him another half-dozen.	Fined 15s.
24	28 April	James	J. B. Grissett	That a piece of wood yesterday slipped from complainant, and in consequence defendant beat him with a strap, which had a buckle upon it, and gave him two kicks, but left no mark.	Fined 10s.
25	30 April	Hugh	Wm. Cragg	That complainant is apprenticed labourer to defendant, and in consequence of complainant not picking up stones properly, the defendant horsewhipped him, and gave him about nine stripes.	Fined [£]1

DISTRICT B

No.	Date	Defendant	Complainant	Offence	Sentence
26	14 Jan.	Jno. Thomas	James Williams	Assault and battery	Fined [£]2 N.B.— 14 days given
27	26 Jan.	James	Budding Dash	ditto	Fined [£]1
28	1 March	Isaac	Rob. Jackman	ditto	Fined [£]2

DISTRICT C

No.	Date	Defendant	Complainant	Offence	Sentence
29	18 Jan.	Jenny Bess	Thomas Kerr	Committing an assault on complainant	ditto
30	4 Feb.	Jas., Henry, and Ben.	M. B. Gooding and J. R. Gooding	Having inflicted unlawful punishment on complainants	J. R. Gooding fined [£]1
31	8 Feb.	John Joseph	W. P. Rodgers	Having committed an assault on complainant	Fined [£]1
32	17 Feb.	Joseph	Geo. Boryne	Inflicting unlawful punishment on complainant	Fined 6s. 3d.
33	9 March	Townsend	Eyan Wood	Having committed an assault on complainant	Fined [£]3
34	14 March	Solomon	Jno. Tempro	Having struck complainant	Fined [£]1
35	15 March	Georgiana	S. Gunnidge	Having inflicted unlawful punishment on complainant	Fined [£]2

TABLE 13

Abstract of Cases of Assault by Employers against Apprenticed Laborers, Barbados, January 1–May 31, 1836 (*continued*)

Case Number	Date	Name of Complainant	Name of Defendant	Substance of Complaint	Decision
36	29 March	Queen Anne	T. N. Gooding	ditto	Fined [£]5
37	3 May	Fanny	R. A. Rogers	For striking complainant several times with a rope	Fined [£]2
38	6 May	Hestor	J. B. Seale	For inflicting corporal punishment 3d of May on complainant with a piece of hoop	ditto
39	6 May	Peter	J. B. Seale	Charged with inflicting corporal punishment on 3d May on complainant's person with two twigs	Fined [£]1
40	16 May	R. Charity	S. Massiah	Charged with maltreating complainant three weeks ago	Fined [£]5
41	16 May	Loveless	Jno. H. Baker	Charged with maltreating complainant 10th instant [of the current month]	Fined [£]2
42	17 May	Clysta	B. Thorne	Charged with beating defendant with a stick 10th instant [of the current month]	ditto
43	17 May	R. Charity	S. Massiah	Charged with inflicting corporal punishment on complainant's person with a horsewhip four times on 11th instant	Complainant discharged from service of employer.
44	19 May	Rebecca	Ralph Olton	Charged with inflicting corporal punishment on complainant's person on 17th instant [of the current month]	Defendant, as police officer, has made a breach of the law, consequently is dismissed from the service, & to lo[se?] his pay, should his Excellency approve.
45	23 May	W. Gittens	Jos. Connell	Charged with having tied and whipped complainant with a horsewhip	Fined [£]5
46	24 May	Betty Maine	Wm. Young	For beating her with a briar, and leaving sundry marks of the assault	Fined 50s.
47	25 May	Mazow	Jas. Fleming	For beating, inflicting sundry bruises on, and cutting his head	Fined [£]5

No.	Date				
48	26 May	Jacob Maule	J. H. Lord	For violent assault and battery	Abstained from inflicting penalty; sent with defendant's recognizance of two others, Thomas Briggs, esq., and ___ Heath, esq., to appear at court of grand sessions, the former in [£]100, two latter [£]50 each.
49	26 May	Jacob Maule	J. H. Lord	ditto	Complainant discharged from service of employer.
50	30 May	Jack	Mr. Rent	Assault and battery	Fined [£]2 10s.

DISTRICT D

No.	Date				
51	18 Jan.	S. Williams	Edward Worm	For beating him	Fined 10s.
53	28 Jan.	H. Criss and Ph. Grace	Joshua Birch	For causing them to be flogged	ditto
54	26 Feb.	Nanny Buck	John Drayton	For beating her. N.B.—Complaint admitted by prisoner. No marks visible on plaintiff.	Fined [£]3
55	14 March	Harriet	Mrs G. F. Gilkes	For assaulting her	Fined 50s.

DISTRICT E

No.	Date				
56	11 Jan.	J. Thomas	J. E. Armstrong	For beating him	Fined [£]5
57	11 Jan.	Ann	J. E. Armstrong	For whipping her	ditto
58	12 Jan.	Jimmy	Thos. Walton	For whipping him	Fined [£]1
59	29 Feb.	M. Phillis	Wm. Agard	For striking her	Fined [£]3
60	29 March	Butcher	James Cozier	For beating him	Fined £2 10s.
61	19 April	Jno. Francis	Jas. Whitehead	For beating him (second offense)	Complainant to be discharged from defendant's service
62	16 May	Geo. James	Wm. Corbin	For beating him	Fined [£]2

TABLE 13
Abstract of Cases of Assault by Employers against Apprenticed Laborers, Barbados, January 1–May 31, 1836 (*continued*)

Case Number	Date	Name of Complainant	Name of Defendant	Substance of Complaint	Decision
DISTRICT F:					
63	11 Jan.	Jno. Nelson	M'Clean	Assault and battery. N.B.—The most equivocating trial I ever investigated.	Fined [£]3
64	25 Jan.	Henry	Dr. Walton	Assault and battery	Fined [£]1
65	28 Jan.	C. William	A. A. M'Clean	ditto	Fined £2
66	28 April	M. George	T. E. Grogan	ditto	ditto
67	21 Jun.	Polly Anne	A. Ashurst	That complainant is apprenticed laborer to defendant, and that she beat her on the head with a rock. This case was omitted [from] the month of January, for District A, Town Division.	ditto

Source: CO 28/117, National Archives, Kew, United Kingdom.

TABLE 14
Jamaican Immigration, 1858–1901

Year	No. of "Coolies" Arriving	Percentage of Births during the Year	No. of "Coolies" Receiving Colonization Bounty*	No. of "Coolies" Returning to India	Mortality Rate	Value of Government Bills of Exchange Taken to India
1858	—	no record	274	126	no record	—
1860	592	"	—	—	"	—
1861	1,521	"	—	—	"	—
1862	1,982	"	—	—	"	—
1863†	540	"	—	—	"	—
1867	1,625	"	—	—	6.22	—
1868	—	"	—	—	12.11	—
1869	1,393	0.28	—	—	8.54	—
1870	906	2.78	340	—	7.14	—
1871	1,354	0.85	1,215	925	3.43	£7,229 2 0
1872	1,188	1.78	1,179	420	2.45	£3,855 0 0
1873	1,518	2.27	402	—	3.60	—
1874	1,356	1.55	23	—	2.86	
1875	1,250	1.85	20	356	3.55	£2,027 4 0
1876	748	1.97	9	251	2.84	£1,376 16 0
1877	—	2.28	1,088	316	2.79	£4,689 12 0
1878	895	0.93	15	237	2.89	£2,136 9 0
1879	167	1.10	560	416	3.10	£3,898 3 4½
1880	747	1.34	493	376	2.34	£4970 16 0
1881	504	2.15	717	403	3.78	£7,348 11 4
1882	—	2.23	698	448	4.56	£4,049 5 0
1883	896	1.82	602	415	2.25	£5,540 12 0¼
1884	680 [Chinese]	2.13	1,000	78	1.85	£1,189 14 0
1885	601	1.91	931	471	2.74	£7,300 9 11¼
1886	—	2.62	418	161	3.33	£2,875 6 3
1887	—	1.11	13	—	2.66	—
1888	—	1.10	366	573	2.28	£7,818 14 9
1889	—	"	6	—	2.66	—
1890	—	"	—	567	"	£4,297 9 0
1891	2,136 "	Nil	—	—	1.50	—
1892	—	1.62	—	375	2.49	£2,681 5 0
1893	484 "	5.97	—	—	1.94	—
1894	—	2.14	—	—	1.83	—
1895	698	3.40	—	348	2.34	£3,139 19 9
1896	—	1.90	—	—	2.27	—
1897	—	.44	—	—	1.91	—
1898	—	.65	—	—	1.90	—
1899	615	2.85	—	—	1.72	—
1900	661	.08	—	—	3.53	—
1901	—	3.50	—	—	4.17	—

Source: Jos. C. Ford and A. A. C. Finlay, *Handbook of Jamaica for 1903, Comprising Historical, Statistical and General Information Concerning the Island* (London: Edward Stanford; Jamaica: Government Printing Office), 204.

*Colonial bounties were sums of money given to Indian immigrant laborers who had served a full ten-year term of indentureship in the Caribbean. These bounties were to be paid to the laborers in lieu of a return passage (to India).

† Cessation of immigration until 1867.

NOTES

INTRODUCTION. *Colonial Body Politics*

1. Duffield, "From Slave Colonies to Penal Colonies." Other noteworthy studies by Trotman that touch on the subject of punishment include "Women and Crime in Late Nineteenth Century Trinidad."

2. Turner, "11 O'clock Flog"; Altink, "Slavery by Another Name"; Dalby, *Crime and Punishment in Jamaica*; Boa, "Experiences of Women Estate Workers"; Boa, "Discipline, Reform, or Punish? Attitudes towards Juvenile Crimes and Misdemeanours in the Post-emancipation Caribbean, 1838–88," in Heuman and Trotman, *Contesting Freedom*, 65–86. The importance of Turner's 1999 article may be demonstrated by the fact that it was reprinted in Frey and Wood's *From Slavery to Emancipation in the Atlantic World* in the same year and in 2001 in Shepherd's *Working Slavery, Pricing Freedom*.

3. See, for example, Green's "Abandoned Lower Class of Females" and "Local Geographies of Crime and Punishment."

4. For a discussion of this, see news reports from March 2005 and the following works published since the riot occurred: Cooke and Wozniak, "PRISM Applied to a Critical Incident Review"; Logan and Johnstone, *Managing Clinical Risk*, 172–73; Janet P. Stamatel and Hung-En Sung, *Crime and Punishment around the World*, vol. 2, *The Americas*, 31–40.

5. The destruction of Glendairy Prison by inmates in 2005 brought issues of punishment, human rights, and the experiences of the criminal to the fore when it was revealed that conditions in the prison had been intolerable. The commission appointed to investigate the destruction of the prison found that the prison had been overcrowded and that staff had abused inmates. See "New Boss Found Morale Low," Nationnews.com (Barbados), November 2, 2007. In addition, the plight of the prisoner was seen as particularly harrowing when inmates were rehoused in temporary spaces at Harrison Point in St. Lucy, where conditions were noted to be subhuman. See "Records Destroyed," Nationnews.com (Barbados), July 13, 2007.

6. More than anyone else, Diana Paton has led the way in producing work that ex-

plores the subject of punishment in the British West Indies—with particular attention being paid to Jamaica—in the pre- and post-emancipation periods. Some of Paton's works include *No Bond but the Law* and her introduction to the 2001 edition of James Williams's *A Narrative of Events.*

7. Paton, *No Bond but the Law,* 3, 5, 6.

8. Ibid., 10.

9. See ibid., 154, 241n149.

10. Grosz, *Volatile Bodies*; Butler, *Gender Trouble*; Canning, "Body as Method?"

11. Grosz, *Volatile Bodies,* 141.

12. Ibid., 87.

13. Scott, "Gender."

14. Schomburgk, *The History of Barbados,* v.

15. Knight, *The Caribbean,* 51.

16. G. K. Lewis, *The Growth of the Modern West Indies,* 226.

17. Ibid.

18. "Almost pure sugar plantation": ibid. For a discussion of pens and pen-keeping in Jamaica, see, for example, Shepherd, *Livestock, Sugar, and Slavery.*

19. Lewis, *The Growth of the Modern West Indies,* 229.

20. Knight, *The Caribbean,* 89.

21. W. A. Green, *British Slave Emancipation,* 3.

22. Beckles, "Black Women and the Political Economy of Slavery," 3.

23. Another important demographic factor that differentiated these two islands was the relative size of their white populations. Unlike Jamaica with its high rate of planter absenteeism, Barbados was noteworthy for its large resident planter class, a phenomenon that also helped to consolidate the strength of this class of elites. The planters, along with other white groups, including middle-class and poor whites, helped to form a "relatively stable" white population that was "proportionally larger than that of any [of] the other true sugar colonies." Lambert, *White Creole Culture, Politics and Identity,* 20.

24. William Carr, on the twentieth day (February 16, 1866) of the investigation into the suppression of the Morant Bay Rebellion, in Great Britain, Jamaica Royal Commission, *Report of the Jamaica Royal Commission, 1866,* pt. 1, 508.

25. *Negro Apprenticeship in the Colonies,* 1, 2.

26. W. A. Green, *British Slave Emancipation,* 129–30.

27. Enclosure in No. 44, Captain Pringle's Instructions, 12 September 1837, in Great Britain, Colonial Office, *Papers Presented to Parliament, by Her Majesty's Command,* pt. 5: Jamaica, *Accounts and Papers of the House of Commons,* vol. 49 (1838), 136.

28. Ibid., 139.

29. G. M. Hall, *Social Control in Slave Plantation Societies,* 79.

30. Ibid., 77, 79.

31. Hay and Craven, introduction to *Masters, Servants, and Magistrates in Britain and the Empire,* 1–58.

32. Ibid., 10.

33. Adelson, *Making Bodies, Making History*, xiii.

34. The apprenticeship period may be considered legally and socially ambiguous in the sense that the apprentices were neither fully freed nor fully enslaved. They occupied a liminal position on the plantation and within the wider society in terms of their status as workers and citizens. As a case in point, apprentices were still required to work for their former slave masters on the plantations on which they had been enslaved, even as they were being prepared to be wage laborers instead of slaves. Moreover, the change in their legal appellation—from "slave" to "apprentice"—did not result in a change in their physical, bodily locations—particularly when one notes the positions occupied by truly free citizens.

35. "Systems of rules": this definition of "discipline" was taken from the *Concise Oxford Dictionary* (Oxford: Oxford University Press, 1999).

36. Because hair-cropping was a potent way of marking the bodies of women to show that they had been punished, this is included under public punishments.

CHAPTER 1. *Six-Legged Women and Derby's Dose*

1. Trevor Burnard, *Mastery, Tyranny, and Desire*, 131.

2. George Metcalf, introduction to Long, *The History of Jamaica*, vol. 1, 2nd ed.

3. Edward Long, *The History of Jamaica*, vol. 2, 351–52.

4. Ibid., 352

5. Ibid., 365.

6. Ibid., 364.

7. Ibid., 353.

8. For an account of this idea, see Metcalf, introduction to Long, *The History of Jamaica*, vol. 1, 2nd ed.

9. Richard Ligon, *A True and Exact History of the Island of Barbadoes*, 45.

10. Ibid., 44.

11. Ibid., 51.

12. Ibid.

13. Ibid.

14. Morgan, *Laboring Women*, 12, 49.

15. Bush, "'Sable Venus,' 'She Devil' or 'Drudge'?," 761.

16. This idea that the colonial Caribbean was organized socio-racially is borrowed from Franklin W. Knight and can be found in his important work *The Caribbean* (see esp. pp. 122–25).

17. This us-versus-them ideology meant that so-called differences between individuals were highlighted and exploited and any similarities between those outside the group were obscured.

18. The scope of this work does not permit me to discuss how the labor laws in the seventeenth-century Caribbean evolved to the point whereby blackness and enslavement became intertwined. Rugemer, "The Development of Mastery and Race," provides a comprehensive and cogent treatment of this topic. Rugemer traces how the language in

the laws changed, a linguistic evolution that also reflected the creation of "black slavery" and white mastery. What is also evident in Rugemer's sophisticated treatment of this subject is how blackness and whiteness, as social identities, were *created* in the British Caribbean. Additionally, Jenny Shaw provides a well-written and insightful account of the thorniness of difference in the early Caribbean by focusing on the experiences of Irish indentured servants in her important text *Everyday Life in the Early English Caribbean*.

19. Rugemer, "The Development of Mastery and Race," 433.

20. *Acts of Assembly, Passed in the Island of Jamaica, from 1681, to 1737*, 2.

21. Ibid., 50–51.

22. The Act of Assembly of the Island of Jamaica to Repeal Several Acts," 10.

23. Ligon, *A True and Exact History*, 43, 44.

24. Shaw, *Everyday Life in the Early English Caribbean*, 19–21. Shaw provides a sophisticated analysis of how difference functioned in the seventeenth-century, English-speaking Caribbean. Her work is particularly important because of the wealth of details that it provides, along with its thorough investigation into the similarities and differences in experiences between the Irish and Africans.

25. Ibid., 24.

26. Quoted in ibid., 95.

27. For a discussion of how European indentured servants might be considered a "proto-peasantry" that provided the blueprint for the slave system in the Caribbean, see Beckles, "Black Men in White Skins"; Beckles, "Plantation Production and White 'Proto-slavery.'"

28. Williams, *From Columbus to Castro*, 103–4.

29. For a compelling analysis of this demographic shift and how it was related to the economic exigencies of the developing societies, see Williams, *From Columbus to Castro*, esp. pp. 104–5.

30. Although the enslaved could be manumitted by purchasing their freedom, slavery was based on the ideology that blacks were slaves in perpetuity. Moreover, the idea of *partus sequitur ventrem*, which held that a slave child followed its mother's status, was in contrast to indenture, which lasted for a defined, contractual period. In addition, the indentured child was not the property of his or her mother's owner.

31. Douglas Hay and Paul Craven noted, for example, that "in 1664 Jamaica had both an act 'For the better ordering and governing of Negro slaves,' and another, 'For the good governing of servants,' with very different terms." Hay and Craven, introduction to *Masters, Servants, and Magistrates in Britain and Empire*, 23.

32. Schaw, *Journal of a Lady of Quality*, 12.

33. Goveia, *The West Indian Slave Laws*, 20.

34. Craton, *Empire, Enslavement, and Freedom in the Caribbean*, 151.

35. Stedman, *Narrative of a Five Years Expedition*, 102–3.

36. Thistlewood, "Notes on Plantation Life, 1755–1759," in Hall, *In Miserable Slavery*, 73.

37. V. Brown, "Spiritual Terror and Sacred Authority," 26.

38. Ibid.

39. Ibid.

40. Morrissey, *Slave Women in the New World*, 151.

41. Ibid., 152.

42. Lewis, *Journal of a West India Proprietor*, 388–89

43. Prince, *The History of Mary Prince*, 55.

44. Ibid., 57.

45. Bush, *Slave Women in Caribbean Society*, 44.

46. Manzano, "Autobiography of a Slave," 51.

47. Thistlewood, "Notes on Plantation Life, 1755–1759," in Hall, *In Miserable Slavery*, 72. Egypt Susanah and Mazerine were whipped because they had refused to go to Mr. Cope and Mr. McDonald that night when summoned (91n2).

48. Although Diana Paton noted that there were changes in punishment in Jamaica, which she tied to the changing climate in Britain, I argue that in spite of these changing sensibilities, punishment continued to be carried out in a tendentious fashion, even after slavery. Thus, punishment remained a critical marker between blacks and whites.

CHAPTER 2. *The Persistence of Corporeality*

1. Although W. A. Green makes the point that "punishments were mitigated during apprenticeship, and in some colonies the whip was entirely abandoned," the argument made here is that on the whole, punishments meted out to the apprentices specifically, and blacks in general, were overwhelmingly corporeal and that their form and function spoke to ideas about the perceived inferiority of blacks and the black body. See W. A. Green, *British Slave Emancipation*, 135–36, for his assessment of punishment during the apprenticeship period. Henrice Altink also makes the point that although the Abolition Act made it illegal for female apprentices to be whipped, they tended to be whipped in workhouses based on the spurious arguments made by prison personnel that female apprentices were not protected by the Abolition Act when they were confined but instead were governed by the Act for Making Further Provision for the Building, Repairing and Regulating of Gaols, Houses of Correction, Hospitals and Asylums. See Altink, "Slavery by Another Name," 46.

2. See Levy, *Emancipation, Sugar, and Federalism*, for a detailed account of the tussle that ensued between Barbadian and imperial legislators over the colony's Abolition Act. Chapters 2 and 3 are particularly helpful in that they often refer to the plethora of correspondence exchanged between the Colonial Office and Barbados. Most notably, Levy's narrative also affords us the opportunity to see the importance of key figures—like Governor Lionel Smith, James Stephen, and colonial secretaries Lord Stanley and Thomas Spring-Rice—and the role of bodies like the Barbados Council, local proprietors, and soon-to-be apprentices and how they influenced the final iteration of the apprenticeship system.

3. W. A. Green, *British Slave Emancipation*, 122.

4. For a good analysis of the stipendiary magistrates, their duties, and the problems that they faced in the execution of their duties, see also W. A. Green, *British Slave Emancipation*, 136–44; W. L. Burn, *Emancipation and Apprenticeship in the British West Indies*.

5. An Act for the Abolition of Slavery in This Island, in Consideration of Compensation and for Promoting Industry of the Manumitted Slaves, in *Papers in Explanation of the Measures Adopted by His Majesty's Government for Giving Effect to the Act for the Abolition of Slavery throughout the British Colonies*, Pt. 2: *Jamaica—(continued) Barbadoes, British Guiana and Mauritius. 1833–1835*, 273, microfilm, University of Toronto Library.

6. "The Sligo Papers," 17.

7. Ibid.

8. This idea is developed later in this chapter. See also appendix, table 13.

9. Colthurst, *Colthurst Journal*, 55.

10. This study does not argue that only whites owned plantations and thus were the only group who would be punished for this particular infraction. Instead, it argues that whites made up the majority of plantation owners and employers of apprentices, so this clause is significant.

11. W. A. Green, *British Slave Emancipation*, 136–37.

12. For a detailed discussion of the onerous position into which stipendiary magistrates were placed, see ibid., 136–42.

13. Colthurst, *Colthurst Journal*, 70.

14. The term "relatively" is used here to describe these types of punishments because fines could very well represent a material hardship to the apprentices who would have few economic resources.

15. Article reprinted from the *Eclectic Review*, April 1838, in *Anti-Slavery Crisis*, 4–5.

16. Burn, *Emancipation and Apprenticeship in the British West Indies*, 180.

17. Ibid., 179.

18. Quoted in ibid., 181.

19. *A Statement of Facts, Illustrating the Administration of the Abolition Law*, 4.

20. Burn, *Emancipation and Apprenticeship*, 202.

21. Lord Stanley during the passage of the Abolition Act in the House of Commons, quoted in Bevan, *The Operation of the Apprenticeship System in the British Colonies*, 2.

22. Ibid.

23. *An Abstract of the British West Indian Statutes*, 5. It should be noted that this act was initially rejected by the Colonial Office and was not allowed until 1831. However, the controversy it elicited had little to do with concern over the harshness of punishment that could be given to slaves. Instead it surrounded religious restrictions in the original act that the Colonial Office found objectionable. See W. A. Green, *British Slave Emancipation*, 122.

24. *An Abstract of the British West Indian Statutes*, 6.

25. For more information on corporal punishments in the British army, particu-

larly the nineteenth-century campaign against flogging, see Dinwiddy, "The Early Nineteenth-century Campaign against Flogging in the Army."

26. "An Abstract of the British West Indian Statutes," 9.

27. See Beckles, "Female Enslavement and Gender Ideologies," esp. pp. 174–78. For more on Lambert's analysis of these pro-natalist policies, see chapter 7 of this book.

28. Beckles, "Female Enslavement and Gender Ideologies," 177.

29. This was particularly true of middle-class and wealthy white women as working-class white women were not automatically regarded as decorous, although, in the socio-racial hierarchy, they were definitely considered superior to all black women.

30. One only has to look at Thomas Thistlewood's diary entries (Hall, *In Miserable Slavery*) to glimpse the different rules that governed white male sexuality in the slave colony of Jamaica and see that there was a gendered interpretation of morality and virtue. Not only did Thistlewood, as a white slave-owning male, have full license to the bodies of black women as laborers, he also had unrestricted access to them sexually. Throughout the diary, Thistlewood chronicles his many sexual exploits with female slaves and even one sexual liaison with the wife of one of his friends. In spite of the latter case, scholars like Trevor Burnard have shown that white female sexuality was strictly proscribed in Jamaica during the period of slavery, a proscription that was reflected in societal attitudes about white women's roles as sexual beings and in legislation against miscegenation. For a look at how white women who showed autonomous sexual license were treated, see Burnard, "A Matron in Rank, a Prostitute in Manners." The idea that morality and purity were tied only to white women in the colonial Caribbean, a region that depended upon the creation of ideological and tangible boundaries to keep the races socially apart, may be compared to how sexuality and gender were apprehended in eighteenth-century England. John Tosh makes the argument that in eighteenth-century Britain, there was a contradictory apprehension of manliness and male sexuality. He notes that "public teaching on manliness was almost unanimous in enjoining purity on young men, and in casting a veil over sex within marriage," even as there was "the incontrovertible evidence of large-scale prostitution." See Tosh, *Manliness and Masculinities in Nineteenth-Century Britain*, 33. By way of comparison, the evidence does not suggest that white planters and overseers in Barbados and Jamaica were encouraged to be sexually intemperate, nor was there the contradictory idea that they practiced different forms of public and private sexuality that rested on virtue and purity.

31. Moore, "The Culture of the Colonial Elites," 102.

32. James Williams's narrative is integral to an understanding of the apprenticeship system in the British Caribbean as it played a prominent role in anti-slavery debates in Britain. The controversy surrounding this narrative has been presented in terms of knowledge claims, truth, who gets to speak, and for what reason. For instance, although noting its "political importance," Diana Paton points out that the "circumstances of its production" make it a "complicated text." See Paton, introduction to Williams, *A Narrative of Events, Since the First of August, 1834* (2001), xiii–xv. The narrative, although

Williams's, was birthed through the efforts of the abolitionist Joseph Sturge, who took Williams to England to have his narrative "produced." The text itself was made possible by the fact that Williams told his story to the white amanuensis Dr. Archibald Palmer. Ibid., xxx–xxxii. Although this has been a point of criticism, with the argument being made that the degree of interpolation by the amanuensis may undermine the degree to which the narrative may be Williams's own, it might also be argued that the very fact of the white amanuensis could in itself be a coup of sorts. For a former slave to have a white man pen his narrative turns the idea of the *servus a manu* (the Latin phrase meaning a slave who takes dictation) on its head. Thus, even if the degree of Williams's ability to own the manuscript can be debated, the fact of him being able to assert his humanity and mock the ideas upon which the ownership of black bodies rested cannot. See also Dhanda, review of Williams, *Narrative of Events* (2001); Paton, "From His Own Lips."

33. Franklin W. Knight uses the term "pyramidal illustration" to explain the social organization of West Indian societies. See Knight, *The Caribbean*, 124.

34. Smith and Smith, *To Shoot Hard Labour*, 73.

35. Ibid., 80.

36. Ibid.

37. Smith, quoted in Mindie Lazarus-Black, *Legitimate Acts and Illegal Encounters*, 110–11.

38. Also see Trotman *Crime in Trinidad*, 183–212, where he examines the different legal and punitive methods employed by legislators and planters to keep a pool of cheap, easily accessible labor, namely indentured immigrants and non-plantation labor, on hand for the exigencies of the plantation economy.

39. Lazarus-Black, *Legitimate Acts and Illegal Encounters*, 114. Although I am drawing on Michel Foucault's concept of "punishment-body" relations, I have deliberately transposed the two words, punishment and body, by placing "body" in the premier spot. This transposition is meant to highlight the central role of the body in punishments in nineteenth-century Barbados and Jamaica. This placement also reinforces a central tenet of this thesis, which is that the body remained an important locus for the exercise of punishment and as a visual reminder of the power relations in Barbados and Jamaica.

40. Ibid.

41. Ibid., 102.

42. London Anti-Slavery Society, *The Permanent Laws of the Emancipated Colonies*, 42.

43. Foucault, *Discipline and Punish*, 8.

44. Levy, *Emancipation, Sugar, and Federalism*, 49, 50.

45. Ibid., 50, table 3.3.

46. Ibid., 51, table 3.4. Ninety-five persons had been remanded to the Town Hall jail for this reason. The numbers remanded for petty theft and "disobedience" were even greater, 156 and 101, respectively.

47. Appendix, 195, "Enclosure in Sir Lionel Smith's Despatch of the 6 August 1836,"

32, Papers Relative to the Abolition of Slavery in the British Colonies, 1836, microfilm, University of Toronto Library.

48. Ibid.

49. *Colonial Laws as Examined by a Committee of the House of Commons*, 8.

50. Smith served as governor of the Windward Islands from 1833 to 1836 and of Jamaica from 1836 to 1839. Bell and Morrell, *Select Documents on British Colonial Policy*, 407.

51. "No. 595, Copy of a Despatch from Governor Sir Lionel Smith, K.C.B., to Lord Glenelg, 26 July 1836," CO 28/117, National Archives, Kew, United Kingdom.

52. Ibid.

53. See appendix, tables 1 and 3, for the crimes for which apprentices were punished in Jamaica and Barbados, respectively.

54. "No. 3, Abstract of Cases of Assaults committed by Employers against Apprenticed Labourers in the Island of Barbados between 1 January and 31 May 1836, as Extracted from the Journals of the Special Magistrates," enclosure in "No. 595, Copy of a Despatch from Governor Sir Lionel Smith, K.C.B., to Lord Glenelg, 26 July 1836."

55. Ibid.

56. See appendix, table 13.

57. "No. 3, Abstract of Cases of Assaults," 368.

58. Ibid., 369.

59. Ibid., 365.

60. Cicely Jones gives a persuasive account of how white women could be both victim and oppressor within the plantation economy. See Jones, "Contesting the Boundaries of Gender, Race and Sexuality."

61. "No. 3, Abstract of Cases of Assaults," 368.

62. "No. 5, Enclosure in No. 539, Special Justice Gilmore D'Ames Gregg to the Marquis of Sligo, July 1836," in Great Britain, Colonial Office, *Papers Presented to Parliament, by Her Majesty's Command*, pt. 4, 1837, 116.

63. Act for the Abolition of Slavery in This Island, 273.

64. "Circulars to Special Magistrates, Circular, No. 815, Enclosure in No. 1, 16th May 1837," in Great Britain, Colonial Office, *Papers Presented to Parliament, by Her Majesty's Command*, pt. 5: Jamaica, *Accounts and Papers of the House of Commons*, 15 November 1837–16 August 1838, vol. 49 (1838), 9.

65. Lord Stanley during the passage of the Abolition Act in the House of Commons, quoted in Bevan, *The Operation of the Apprenticeship System*, 2.

66. Act for the Abolition of Slavery in This Island, 273. It must also be noted that this injunction had a pernicious impact on black female apprentices. In this regard, Henrice Altink, "Slavery by Another Name," showed convincingly that the rates of women being confined in houses of corrections and workhouses actually *increased*. Altink's findings confirm a central idea of this book, that in the period after slavery, corporal punishments, in whatever form they were manifested, continued to mark the black workers, distinct from the white plantocrats.

67. Altink, "Slavery by Another Name," 40.

68. Sharpe, *On the Abolition of the Negro Apprenticeship*, 15–18.

69. Burn, *Emancipation and Apprenticeship*, 188.

70. "Enclosure 15, in No. 528, Copy of a Letter from Patrick Dunne, Esq., Special Justice, to the Marquis of Sligo, 29 June, 1836," in Great Britain, Colonial Office, *Papers Presented to Parliament, by Her Majesty's Command*, pt. 4 (1), 14 July 1837.

71. Williams, *Narrative of Events* (1837), 2.

72. Ibid., 7.

73. The treadmill had been introduced into the colonial prisons as a means of compulsory labor. See "Remarks on the Colonial Prisons," Enclosure 1, in (W.); Copy of a Letter from Samuel Hoare, Chairman to the Committee of the Prison Discipline Society, to Sir George Grey, Bart, &c. &c., 23 March, 1837, Great Britain, Colonial Office, *Papers Presented to Parliament, by Her Majesty's Command*, pt. 4 (1), 14 July 1837, 21.

74. "Remarks on the Colonial Prisons."

75. "No. 3, Abstract of Cases of Assaults committed by Employers against Apprenticed Labourers in the Island of Barbados between 1 January and 31 May 1836, as Extracted from the Journals of the Special Magistrates," enclosure in "No. 595, Copy of a Despatch from Governor Sir Lionel Smith, K.C.B., to Lord Glenelg, 26 July 1836," 365; "No. 56, in Enclosure 6, Narrative of Events since the 1st of August 1834, by James Williams, an Apprenticed Labourer in Jamaica," in *Accounts and Papers of the House of Commons*, "Slavery," Session 15 November 1837–16 August 1838, vol. 49 (1838), 159–60.

76. "No. 56, in Enclosure 6, Narrative of Events since the 1st of August 1834, by James Williams, an Apprenticed Labourer in Jamaica," 160.

77. Williams, *Narrative of Events* (1837), 7.

78. *Accounts and Papers of the House of Commons*, 15 November 1837–16 August 1838, vol. 49 (1838), 197.

79. Ibid.

80. *A Statement of Facts, Illustrating the Administration of the Abolition Law*, 17.

81. Ibid., 18.

82. Ibid., 19.

83. For instance, Thomas Thistlewood recorded that the driver on his pen, Quashe, was paid "2 bitts" for flogging other slaves, for which he was commended by Thistlewood. Hall, *In Miserable Slavery*, 259. By comparison, Dick, another driver on Thistlewood's plantation, was flogged "for not making the Negroes work," whereas Jimmy was flogged "for not exerting himself in flogging Dick." Ibid., 257. Paton also makes a similar argument in chapter 2 of *No Bond but the Law*, her groundbreaking work that examines disciplinary and punitive practices in Jamaica from 1780 to 1870. Paton cites the example of a leader in the Spanish Town Baptist Church who found it difficult to carry out his role as a constable. This constable and church leader was also reported to have frequently remonstrated with his overseer "about the oppressions which he practised." Quoted in Paton, *No Bond but the Law*, 61.

84. *Accounts and Papers of the House of Commons*, 15 November 1837–16 August 1838, vol. 49 (1838), 204.

85. Ibid., 203.

86. Ibid., 205.

87. Trotman, *Crime in Trinidad*, 131.

88. *Accounts and Papers of the House of Commons*, vol. 49 (1838), 160.

89. Ibid., 213

90. Sturge and Harvey, *The West Indies in 1837*, 204–5.

91. "Repayment of time" refers to the practice whereby apprentices who had been imprisoned had to repay to their employer—in the form of labor—the time that they had been absent from work. James A. Thome and J. Horace Kimball noted that apprentices were obligated to repay this time on Saturdays, the apprentices' off days. Thus, if an apprentice was "committed for ten working days," he or she was obliged to "give the master ten successive Saturdays." Thome and Kimball, *Emancipation in the West Indies*, 81.

92. Colthurst, *The Colthurst Journal*, 243.

93. Table 3 in this book.

94. "No. 103, Copy of a Despatch from Lord Glenelg to Governor Sir E. J. M. Mac-Gregor, Bart, 31 January 1838," in Great Britain, Colonial Office, *Papers Presented to Parliament, by Her Majesty's Command*, pt. 5, "Barbados and British Guiana, 1838," 72.

95. Ibid.

96. CO 323/53, National Archives, Kew, United Kingdom.

97. Duffield, "From Slave Colonies to Penal Colonies," 25–45.

98. Ibid., 35.

99. Ibid., 37.

100. Ibid., 38.

101. Buckley, *The British Army in the West Indies*, 205–6.

102. Ibid.

103. There was a long-running joke reputedly told among slaves, that when they took property from their owners that they were not actually stealing since they too were owned by their masters. A corollary to that was that, in effect, what was their masters' was theirs too.

104. Duffield, "From Slave Colonies to Penal Colonies," 37, 39. What is noteworthy about these crimes is that they were all forms of stealing and would have been labeled as offenses against property.

105. Duffield, "From Slave Colonies to Penal Colonies," 35.

106. Matthew Lewis, *Journal of a West India Proprietor*, 179.

107. Duffield, "From Slave Colonies to Penal Colonies," 26.

108. Matthew Lewis, *Journal of a West India Proprietor*, 227.

109. Duffield, "From Slave Colonies to Penal Colonies," 36.

110. "Copy of a Despatch from Governor Sir Lionel Smith, K.C.B., to Lord Glenelg,

27 July 1836," Great Britain, Colonial Office, *Papers Presented to Parliament, by Her Majesty's Command*, pt. 4, 14 July 1837, 354.

111. "No. 585, Copy of a Despatch from Lord Glenelg to Governor Sir E. J. Murray MacGregor, Bart., 30 November 1836," in Great Britain, Colonial Office, *Papers relative to the West Indies, 1840*, 356.

112. Ibid.

113. "Copy of a Circular Despatch Addressed by Lord Glenelg to the Governors of the West India Colonies &c. 25 May 1837," Great Britain, Colonial Office, *Papers Presented to Parliament, by Her Majesty's Command*, pt. 4 (1), 14 July 1837, 19.

114. "Enclosure in No. 544, No. 1, Letter from J. Rowe, Chief Justice, to C. H. Darling, Esq., Dated 15 October 1836," Great Britain, Colonial Office, *Papers Presented to Parliament, by Her Majesty's Command*, pt. 4 (1), 14 July 1837, 136.

115. See also Dalby, *Crime and Punishment in Jamaica*, 35–36.

116. Duffield, "From Slave Colonies to Penal Colonies," 29.

117. Ibid., 26.

118. It must be pointed out that transportation continued to be used as a form of punishment after emancipation and arguably applied in an unsystematic fashion. For example, during the Surrey Assizes in Jamaica on August 2, 1847, a number of cases were heard and judgments of transportation issued. There was the case of John Williams, for example, who was sentenced to transportation for ten years for a felonious assault on Ann Taylor. At the Surrey Assizes on August 3, 1847, John Saunders Haywood was placed on trial for horse stealing, and because it was not his first offense he was sentenced to transportation for ten years. By way of comparison, also at the Surrey Assizes on August 3, William Francis was found guilty of killing William Brown. For this crime he was sentenced to twelve months hard labor in the General Penitentiary in Jamaica. *Morning Journal* (Kingston), August 3 and 4, 1847. Dalby notes too that in 1844 alone twenty-two persons were sentenced to transportation, although it was not known how many of these sentences were actually carried out. Dalby, *Crime and Punishment in Jamaica*, 79.

119. See "An Act to Substitute in Certain Cases Other Punishment in Lieu of Transportation" (passed May 24, 1854), in *Laws of Barbados*, vol. 1, 459–60.

120. "Enclosure 1, in No. 43, Legislative Summary," in Great Britain, Parliament, *Papers relating to the Late Disturbances in Barbados*, 92.

CHAPTER 3. *The Entanglements of Freedom*

1. Austin, *How to Do Things with Words*, 6.

2. For insight into how "social relations" are "ensconced in legal rules," see, for example, López, *White by Law*, especially pp. 123–24.

3. Austin, *How to Do Things with Words*, 6.

4. I borrow the subheading from the term "performative sentence" used in ibid.

5. London Anti-Slavery Society, *The Permanent Laws of the Emancipated Colonies*, 42–43.

6. "Copy of a Circular Despatch, Addressed by Lord Glenelg to the Governors of the West India Colonies, & c.," in *Papers relative to the West Indies, 1839*, pt. 1, 1.

7. Ibid.

8. "Enclosure 1, in No. 12, an Act to Authorise the Appointment of Rural Constables in This Island, Copy of a Despatch from Governor E. J. M. MacGregor, Bart., to Lord Glenelg, dated 8 July 1838," in *Papers relative to the West Indies, 1839*, pt. 2, 27.

9. "Skin for skin" and "join their colour," two of the rallying cries used during the Morant Bay Rebellion, tend to disprove the hypothesis of the legislators. The kidnapping of black constables at the estate in Stony Gut shows that the notion of race and the office of the black constabulary could be co-opted and eventually used in ways they were not intended to be used. The role of maroons and black constables in the suppression of this rebellion also helps to show the flimsiness of so-called racial allegiances. (Maroons were runaway slaves who had established communities in mountainous regions of Jamaica.) For reference to the rallying cries, "colour for colour" and "skin for skin," see, for example, Heuman, "Tale of Two Jamaican Rebellions," 1–8.

10. "Enclosure 1, in No. 12, an Act to Authorise the Appointment of Rural Constables in this Island, in Copy of a Despatch from Governor E. J. M. MacGregor, Bart., to Lord Glenelg, dated 8 July 1838," in *Papers relative to the West Indies, 1839*, pt. 2, 27.

11. Ibid., 28.

12. London Anti-Slavery Society, *The Permanent Laws of the Emancipated Colonies*, 30.

13. Great Britain, Colonial Office, *Papers relative to the West Indies, 1841–42, Jamaica—Barbados*, 21.

14. CO 137/256, August, 2, 1841, National Archives, Kew, United Kingdom.

15. "Copy of a Circular Despatch Addressed by Lord Glenelg to the Governors of British Guiana, Trinidad, and St. Lucia, and Mauritius, 15 September 1838," in *Papers relative to the West Indies, 1839*, pt. 1, 6.

16. Ibid.

17. "Enclosure 4, in No. 12," in Great Britain, Colonial Office, *Papers relative to the West Indies, 1839*, pt. 2, 33–36.

18. Ibid., 33.

19. Ibid. The "alteration" in question refers to the substitution of the phrase "any house or other place" for "any house kept or purporting to be kept for the reception, lodging, or entertainment of travellers."

20. "Enclosure 4, in No. 12," in Great Britain, Colonial Office, *Papers relative to the West Indies, 1839*, pt. 2, 34.

21. *Laws of Jamaica*, 1839–40, 58–63.

22. In discussing the place of obeah and myalism in Jamaican conflict, Paton notes that these two practices are hard to define, although she does acknowledge their metaphysical orientation. She states that obeah and myalism make up "a very broad system of beliefs and practices that does not correspond to any of the realms into which scholars are accustomed to dividing social life. These beliefs and practices cannot be categorized as medicine, law, religion, magic, or judicial practice; they encompassed all these

areas of life but were not confined to any of them, or even to all them collectively." Paton, *No Bond but the Law*, 183. Like Paton, Handler and Bilby also acknowledge that the term "obeah" has been used by various groups to refer to a variety of practices and beliefs. They note that for whites, "obeah" became "a catch-all term for a range of supernatural-related ideas and behaviors that were not of European origin and which they heavily criticized and condemned." Handler and Bilby, "On the Early Use and Origin of the Term 'Obeah,'" 87. An early reference to myalism may be found in Tregelles, *Edwin Octavius Tregelles*. Tregelles, like the white slave owners in Barbados and Jamaica who lumped a variety of ideas and practices under the term "obeah," did not have a full comprehension of myalism. Tregelles defined myalism as "an African fiendish superstition, the opposite to Obeeism, which it is supposed to counteract" (227). For a detailed discussion of obeah, see Moore and Johnson, "Afro-Creole Belief System I: Obeah, Duppies and Other 'Dark Superstitions,'" in *Neither Led nor Driven*, 14–50. Moore and Johnson delineate a complex practice that, although reviled, criminalized, and simultaneously feared by white elites, was embraced by blacks for varied uses in romantic, economic, health-related, and judicial matters, among other things. "Myal/Revival" is given similarly detailed treatment in "Afro-Creole Belief System II," chapter 3 of the same book (51–58). Relying on the work of a varied group of scholars, including anthropologists and historians like Robert J. Stewart, Diane Austin-Broos, Philip D. Curtin, and Monica Schuler, Moore and Johnson conclude that myalism was a melding of elements of black American Baptist faith and African beliefs.

23. *Laws of Jamaica*, 1842.

24. Ibid.

25. Dalby, *Crime and Punishment in Jamaica*, 51.

26. *Laws of Jamaica*, 1842.

27. Ibid., 41.

28. Ibid., 44.

29. "Extract of a Despatch from Governor Sir E. J. Murray MacGregor to the Marquis of Normandy, July 10, 1839," in *Papers relative to the West Indies, 1840*, pt. 2, 16.

30. Ibid.

31. Ibid., 24–25.

32. Ibid., 33.

33. Ibid.

34. "Enclosure in No. 19, Copy of a Despatch from Governor Sir E. J. Murray MacGregor to Lord John Russell," in *Papers relative to the West Indies, 1840*, pt. 2, 44.

35. Ibid., 45–46.

36. Wright, *Draft of a Criminal Code*. Although the Jamaican legislature passed Wright's criminal code in 1879, it was not enforced and was eventually repealed. In its stead, James Stephens's 1878 code was implemented. In spite of this, Wright's 1877 draft says much about the apprehension of crime and punishment in nineteenth-century Jamaica. Moreover, that Stephens's criminal code was drafted in response to the 1877 draft code suggests that it warrants consideration in Jamaica's history of punishment.

For more on this point, see Friedland's "Codification in the Commonwealth" and "R. S. Wright's Model Criminal Code."

37. Wright, *Draft of a Criminal Code*, 7.

38. Ibid., 80. The use of a light rod or cane on juveniles may also be interpreted as a way of "keeping boys in their place." There is the sense that those so punished were being infantilized and reminded of who was in authority. See also Trotman, *Crime in Trinidad*, 175–76.

39. Wright, *Draft of a Criminal Code*, 79. The cat-o'-nine-tails was a whip with nine tails or strands. In Barbados and Jamaica in the 1800s, cat-o'-nine-tails were made from a variety of materials, including leather and wire. The importance of space and place in differentiating between whipping and flogging was also established in this code. Perhaps in an attempt to concretize the gravity of the crimes committed by those flogged, floggings were to be executed only within that most serious of spaces—the jail. By way of comparison, offenders could be whipped in the confines of the jail, at a police office, or at a reformatory. Ibid., 80.

40. Wright, *Draft of a Criminal Code*, 103.

41. Ibid., 100.

42. Ibid., 125.

43. "Obeah and Myalism Acts Amendment Law, 1892," in *Laws of Jamaica*, 1892.

44. "Obeah and Myalism Acts Further Amendment Law, 1893," in *Laws of Jamaica*, 1893.

45. "Law 21 of 1893, a Law to Amend Sections 52 and 53 of the Act to Consolidate and Amend the Law relating to Offences against the Person," in *Laws of Jamaica*, 1893.

46. "Law 8 of 1896, Juvenile Offenders Law," in *Laws of Jamaica*, 1896.

47. "Law 38 of 1896," in *Laws of Jamaica*, 1896.

48. Bryan, *The Jamaican People*, 24.

49. Great Britain, Jamaica Royal Commission, *Report of the Jamaica Royal Commission, 1866*, pt. 1, 808–9.

50. Beckles, *History of Barbados*, 140.

51. Ibid., 138.

52. Table 3, "Summary Convictions," in *Barbados Blue Book*, 1898, 1, 2, 4.

53. Ibid., 1–2.

54. Archer and Ferguson, *Laws of Barbados*, vol. 2, 1894–1906, 236–37.

55. "Law 4 of 1900," in *Laws of Jamaica*, February 1900.

56. Verene Shepherd, *Transients to Settlers*, 53.

57. Jamaica experimented with various forms of immigrant labor, but Barbados did not. In this book, these two different labor situations are viewed distinctly, particularly because of what they meant in terms of discipline and punishment. Jamaica's response to its labor shortage, the introduction of foreign workers, is analyzed more as a rupture within the social fabric, whereas the labor situation in Barbados is examined in terms of constraints placed on the "native" laborers.

58. For an account of Indian immigration to Jamaica, see Shepherd, *Transients to Set-*

tlers, 22–42. Here Shepherd also examines the different debates about the labor problem in Jamaica. For a more general account of the supposed exodus of blacks from the plantations in the post-emancipation period, see Hall, "The Flight from the Estates Reconsidered," 55–63.

59. For a useful, although general account of indentured migration, see W. A. Green, *British Slave Emancipation*, 261–93. Here Green estimates that between 1834 and 1865 Jamaica received approximately 25,094 immigrants (284, table 17). An 1881 census estimated that East Indians made up 1.9 percent of Jamaica's population, and Chinese made up .02 percent. Brown, *Jamaica Exhibition, 1891*, 5. Other sources break down the figure for East Indian immigrants differently. For example, the periodical publication of the British Colonial Land and Emigration Commission, *Colonization Circular*, no. 31 (1872), 53, shows the total number of immigrants introduced from the East Indies from the January 1, 1845, to December 31, 1871, as 14,469. See also table 17, in *Colonization Circular*, no. 31 (1872), 53, for the numbers of East Indian indentured workers who migrated to Jamaica.

60. *Colonization Circular*, no. 31 (1872), 55. W. A. Green notes that this extension was granted by the Duke of Newcastle, secretary for the colonies in 1863. Green, *British Slave Emancipation*, 281.

61. *Colonization Circular*, no. 31 (1872), 46.

62. Ibid., 53.

63. Shepherd, *Transients to Settlers*, 53.

64. Great Britain, Colonial Office, *Papers relative to the Affairs of the Island of Jamaica*, 5.

65. Ibid., 7.

66. Verene Shepherd notes that between 1845 and 1916 an estimated thirty-seven thousand indentured laborers of East Indian descent migrated to Jamaica. Shepherd, *Transients to Settlers*, 53.

67. *Morning Journal* (Kingston, Jamaica), August 3 and 4, 1847.

68. "Enclosure 1, in No. 1, to the Duke of Newcastle, Secretary for the Colonies, 14 June 1862, Copy of the Correspondence in relation to the Removal of Mr. G. W. Gordon from the Magistracy in Jamaica, and the Circumstances Connected with the Morant Bay Lock-Up Case," in *Accounts and Papers of the House of Commons*, 1 February–10 August 1866, vol. 51, 7, microfilm, University of Toronto Library.

69. For instance, Michele Johnson points out that in the 1894–95 report of Philip C. Cork, the protector of immigrants, Cork opined that "jealousy amongst Coolies" was to blame for the incidence of uxoricide. Johnson, "Century of Murder in Jamaica," 35.

70. Sohal, "The East Indian Indentureship System in Jamaica," 143.

71. Johnson, "Century of Murder in Jamaica," 34–40; Mohapatra, "Restoring the Family"; Trotman, *Crime in Trinidad*, 170.

72. Quoted in Bryan, *The Jamaican People*, 194.

73. W. A. Green, *British Slave Emancipation*, 281.

74. Schuler, *Alas, Alas, Kongo*, 58–59.

75. The existence of this "power order" is akin to the gender order discussed in chapter 7.

76. Quoted in Adelson, *Making Bodies, Making History*, 21.

77. Ibid., 22.

78. Walton Look Lai points out that the final introduction of the contract that bound the indentured laborer to a specific plantation for a five-year term, at an official rate of daily wages, was not introduced until 1862. He asserts that up until then there was much variance in the indenture contracts. See Look Lai, *Indentured Labour, Caribbean Sugar*, 52. He points out that "the shipment of Indians between 1845 and 1848 to Trinidad, British Guiana, and Jamaica entered the West Indies under the strict labor regulations of 1838. Promised a free return passage after five years in the region, they were not permitted to make other than verbal one-month contracts or written one-year contracts after arrival. No regulations existed for the control of their physical movements after this period, and as a result, desertion and widespread vagrancy became common among these immigrants, unaccustomed as most of them were to regular agricultural labor of the kind being offered to them, and more often than not being the victims of various kinds of abuse and ill-treatment on the plantations to which they had been assigned." Ibid., 55.

79. Shepherd, *Transients to Settlers*, 69.

80. Sohal, "The East Indian Indentureship System in Jamaica," 102.

81. Ibid.

82. Verene Shepherd cites work by Pieter Emmer on Suriname and Hugh Tinker on Mauritius to substantiate this argument. Both Emmer and Tinker note that those who employed Indian indentured workers were seldom convicted for crimes under the labor laws. See Shepherd, *Transients to Settlers*, 78.

83. Kale, "Casting Labor," 57–58, 60.

84. Des Voeux, *Experience of a Demerara Magistrate*, 91–92.

85. *Colonization Circular*, no. 31 (1872), 46.

86. Ibid.

87. Ibid., 47.

88. This linking of these seemingly disparate conditions, slavery and freedom to criminality and lawfulness, is a recognition of the fact that the status of the indentured laborer, who was contractually tied to a plantation and an employer, was like that of the apprentice, half-slave, half-free. At the same time, in stressing the status of indentured migrants as *bonded* laborers, there is also the contention that they were always on the verge of lawlessness—as the laws that regulated their behavior were the same ones that governed them as employees. Thus, in shirking employment laws the indentured laborer not only contravened laws at work, he or she ran the risk of being seen as going against laws governing conduct in the wider society.

89. Trotman, *Crime in Trinidad*, 139.

90. Ibid., 140

91. Sohal, "The East Indian Indentureship System in Jamaica," 112.

92. "Swift and brutal": Heuman, "Tale of Two Jamaican Rebellions," 3.

93. For an insightful look at the law and punishment and how they worked in society, see Treviño, *The Sociology of Law*.

94. Heuman, "Tale of Two Jamaican Rebellions," 3.

95. Because the Morant Bay Rebellion has been covered extensively in the secondary literature, I give only a brief overview of the events that led up to it. The majority of my discussion is limited to what the reprisals meant in the context of a society that had promised justice and equality for all. Notable works that deal with the Morant Bay Rebellion include Heuman, *Killing Time*; Heuman, "Tale of Two Jamaican Rebellions"; Semmel, *Jamaican Blood and Victorian Conscience*; W. A. Green, *British Slave Emancipation*, 381–405; Don Robotham, *Notorious Riot*.

96. For a discussion of the tensions between government officials and workers in 1859 and the role that Baptist missionaries played in publicizing the hardships experienced by the Jamaican working classes, see Holt, *The Problem of Freedom*, 264–65.

97. W. A. Green, *British Slave Emancipation*, 388.

98. Holt, *Problem of Freedom*, 299–300.

99. Heuman, *Killing Time*, 1–4.

100. Hutton, "The Defeat of the Morant Bay Rebellion," 31.

101. Despatches from the Secretary of State, Inclosure in No. 2, Memorandum of passages referred to in the preceding Despatch (November 1865), in Great Britain, Foreign Office, *Papers relating to the Disturbances in Jamaica*, pt. 1, 241.

102. Scarry, *The Body in Pain*, 61.

103. Heuman, *Killing Time*, 7.

104. Bakan, *Ideology and Class Conflict in Jamaica*, 82.

105. Hutton, "Defeat of the Morant Bay Rebellion," 31.

106. "Enclosure 37 in No. 1., Governor Eyre to Major-General O'Connor (October 22, 2865), Despatches from Governor Eyre," in Great Britain, Foreign Office, *Papers relating to the Disturbances in Jamaica*, 24.

107. Harvey and Brewin, *Jamaica in 1866*, 12, 13.

108. Ibid., 14–15.

109. Ibid., 80.

110. Despatches from the Secretary of State, Inclosure in No. 2, Memorandum of passages referred to in the preceding Despatch (November 1865), 241. A copy of Captain L. B. Hole's letter can also be found in Inclosure 62 No. 1 in this same document, 37.

111. Great Britain, Jamaica Royal Commission, *Report of the Jamaica Royal Commission, 1866*, part 2, 1120.

112. Burns, *History of the British West Indies*, 672.

113. Harvey and Brewin, *Jamaica in 1866*, 83.

114. See Thomas Faughnan's autobiography, where the author, citing a rumor, noted that one of the aims of the black men who participated in the Morant Bay Rebellion was to take the wives of the white men. Faughnan, *Stirring Incidents in the Life of a British Soldier*, 330–31.

CHAPTER 4. *Confined Spaces, Constrained Bodies*

I would like to thank Mary Hawkesworth of Rutgers University for introducing me to Thomas Hobbes's *Leviathan* and for helping me to formulate the ideas that are presented in this chapter.

1. Great Britain, Jamaica Royal Commission, *Report of the Jamaica Royal Commission, 1866*, pt. 2, 508.

2. For a detailed analysis of emigration from Barbados in the nineteenth and early twentieth century, see Roberts, "Emigration from the Island of Barbados." Under the tenantry system, planters allocated parcels of land to laborers who were required to work for the planter. See Beckles, *History of Barbados*, 115.

3. For a thought-provoking analysis that explores the relationship between land and constrained labor, see Domar, "The Causes of Slavery or Serfdom." Domar asserts that, where there is an abundance of land, elites need to control labor. By contrast, where land is not plentiful, there is no need to control labor because workers are dependent on the largesse of landowners. As this chapter demonstrates, Domar's argument can be challenged when one examines the case of nineteenth-century Barbados. With the majority of the arable land in the hands of white colonial elites, Barbadian subalterns had little recourse but to labor on plantations for wages that were widely known to be the lowest in the region. In spite of this, planters still attempted to control an already disadvantaged populace. It was not enough for Barbadian colonial elites to close off or at least constrict internal avenues for socio-economic advancement. Legislation like the 1836 Emigration Act ensured that external outlets were also closed, thus guaranteeing plantocrats an almost infinite supply of readily available and easily exploitable labor.

4. The argument that land and labor resources were used as tools to control the laboring classes in the British West Indies is not new. One of the most notable proponents of this thesis is O. Nigel Bolland. In his aptly titled "Systems of Domination after Slavery: The Control of Land and Labour in the British West Indies after 1838," Bolland cogently illustrates how in the aftermath of slavery the "wage/rent system" was used in various parts of the British Caribbean, including Barbados and Antigua, to "extract" labor from the former slaves.

5. Also see Levy, *Emancipation, Sugar, and Federalism*, 134–35, for a discussion of this phenomenon in the 1870s in Barbados. The labor advantage enjoyed by Barbadian planters was well known in the metropole. It was noted that during debates regarding the compensation that was to be given to the territories at the abolition of slavery, the imperial government had been reluctant to give more money to Barbadian planters in return for them foregoing the apprenticeship system because they were already thought to enjoy "an advantage over the other colonies as a result of [their] abundant labour supply." For this latter point, see Beckles, *History of Barbados*, 93.

6. Beckles, *History of Barbados*, 95.

7. Ward, *Poverty and Progress in the Caribbean*, 32–33. Beckles, *History of Barbados*,

96, notes that Barbados's sugar exports were said to have increased from 17,234 tons in 1835 to 23,679 tons in 1838.

8. Beckles, *History of Barbados*, 95.

9. Schomburgk, *History of Barbados*, 88. Also see pages 86–87, where Schomburgk examines the 1844 census of Barbados. In the table on page 86 he shows how many males and females were engaged in agriculture by using the age eighteen as a cutoff point.

10. Ibid. Michael Craton, quoting Claude Levy, notes that at the time of emancipation, Barbados's total population was about 101,000, "of whom 82,000 had been slaves." By 1864 the population had expanded to 162,000, of whom 66.4 percent were black, 24.4 percent "coloured" (mixed-race), and 10.2 percent white. Forty-two thousand members of this population were labeled as agricultural workers, 36,500 of whom were said to be over fifteen years of age, 16,000 males and 20,500 females. See Craton, "Continuity not Change," 205.

11. Campbell, *The Maroons of Jamaica*, provides an insightful and detailed account of Maroon communities in Jamaica.

12. Roberts, *The Population of Jamaica*, 56.

13. For instance, Bolland makes the point that the number of freeholds in Jamaica increased from about 2,000 in 1838 to 27,379 in 1845, and sixteen years later they had increased to about 50,000. Bolland, "Systems of Domination after Slavery," 111.

14. "Speech of His Excellency Governor Pope Hennessy, C.M.G., to both Houses of the Legislature of Barbados, in Enclosure in No. 64, Governor Hennessy, C.M.G. to the Earl of Carnarvon, March 11, 1876," in Great Britain, Parliament, *Papers relating to the Late Disturbances in Barbados*, 131. The idea that Barbadian planters had a greater command over the bodies of the peasantry was still being expressed some twenty years after full emancipation. As a case in point, in an 1858 dispatch from Governor Hincks of Barbados to Sir E. Bulwer Lytton, Hincks contended that "in Barbados, owing to the scarcity of land and the density of the population, the tenure has not yet deprived the planters of an adequate supply of labourers. In all the other Colonies the effect has been to drive the labourers from the plantations." "Correspondence between the Colonial Office and the Governors of the West Indian Colonies and the Mauritius, with respect to the Condition of the Labouring Population of such Colonies, both Native and Immigrant, and the Supply of Labour," *Accounts and Papers of the House of Commons*, vol. 21 (1859), session 2, microfilm, University of Toronto Library.

15. Levy, *Emancipation, Sugar, and Federalism*, 80.

16. To develop this point further, it may be argued that the introduction of indentured laborers in the seventeenth century was one of the first variables that served to transform the Barbadian landscape, in a geographical and social sense. At this time, the physical landscape was altered, through deforestation, to accommodate the exigencies of the tobacco, cotton, and then sugar-based economies. For more information on how the natural landscape was changed as a result of human encroachment, see chapter 2 of Gragg, *Englishmen Transplanted*, esp. pp. 13–28. There were also changes in the social landscape that were less tangible, as laws were created that restricted the physical and

social mobility of indentured servants by tying them to the land. This management of the landscape and bodies occurred in tandem, and at times the two even helped to reproduce each other.

17. "Copy of a Despatch from Governor Sir Lionel Smith, K.C.B. to Lord Glenelg, 26 July 1836," in Papers Relative to the Abolition of Slavery in the British Colonies, 377, microfilm, University of Toronto Library.

18. In his dispatch to Glenelg, Smith noted that emigration agents purchased the legal term of apprenticeship from the laborers, who were also made to sign contracts that they would offer their services for three years. These agreements were made without any condition of remuneration being offered to the laborers. Enclosure in No. 601, CO 28/11, 26 July 1836, National Archives, Kew, United Kingdom.

19. "An Act to Regulate the Emigration of Labourers from This Island," 84, CO 30/22, National Archives, Kew, United Kingdom.

20. Ibid. This image of irresponsible black working classes was not without precedent, of course, but the paternalism, racism, and classism that fueled its deployment obscured the alternative idea that these laborers could have viewed emigration as a way to provide for their left-behind families. Historical and contemporary studies that show how migrant workers not only support their left-behind families but also help to build their home economies can provide a valuable theoretical model to show how emigrant labor in the nineteenth century could have had a similar function. V. Newton, *The Silver Men*, 104–6, notes that remittances sent from laborers in Panama benefited both the home country and the families that the migrants had left behind. This is not to say that some of the men and women who were able or who wanted to take advantage of the offer to migrate to regions like British Guiana would not have used it to flee from paternal, maternal, familial, or spousal responsibilities. See also "Enclosure in No. 601, Smith's letter to Glenelg, 26th July 1836," CO 28/117, National Archives, Kew, United Kingdom.

21. "Correspondence Relating to the 1836 Act to Regulate the Emigration of Labourers from This Island," 84–85, CO 30/22, National Archives, Kew, United Kingdom; "Correspondence from Smith to Glenelg, 26 July 1836," 278, CO 28/117, National Archives, Kew, United Kingdom. It is not clear what Smith meant by this assertion, but when one considers that poor whites were the main beneficiaries of state support, one could conclude that Smith did not want left-behind families to use the resources that were normally the preserve of poor whites.

22. Ibid.

23. "Enclosure in No. 1, Copy of a Despatch from Governor Sir E. J. Murray MacGregor, Bart. to Lord John Russell, February 4, 1841," in Great Britain, Colonial Office, *Papers relative to the West Indies, 1841–42, Jamaica—Barbados*, 55.

24. I have not found similarly restrictive legislation for other types of workers.

25. "Enclosure in No. 1, Copy of a Despatch from Governor Sir E. J. Murray MacGregor, Bart. to Lord John Russell, February 4, 1841," in Great Britain, Colonial Office, *Papers relative to the West Indies, 1841–42, Jamaica—Barbados*, 63.

26. Ibid., 64, 66.

27. These answers were in response to the questions for the quarterly report from January 1 to March 31, 1840. "Enclosure in No. 6, 24th May 1841, Copy of a Despatch from Mr. President Brathwaite, to Lord John Russell," in *Papers relative to the West Indies, 1841–42, Jamaica—Barbados*, 74, 76, 81.

28. Ibid., 92.

29. Ibid., 126.

30. Foucault, *Discipline and Punish*, 203.

31. P. L. Applewhaite, the police magistrate for St. Philip, in his report for 1840 noted that agricultural production had improved because laborers were more contented as it had been proved that "they cannot better their condition by transporting themselves from their native land." CO 28/140, "Reports of the Police Magistrates with the President of the Council to Russell, 17 June 1841," National Archives, Kew, United Kingdom, 1.

32. Joseph P. Evelyn, police magistrate for Christ Church, blamed the emigration agents for "seeking to sow discord and dissatisfaction amongst the labouring population." Ibid., 2.

33. L. Brown and Inniss, "The Slave Family in the Transition to Freedom," 264.

34. Schomburgk, *History of Barbados*, 472.

35. Ibid., 76.

36. Beckles, *History of Barbados*, 113. While on their way to Jamaica in 1866, Thomas Harvey and William Brewin noted that their company on board the RMS *La Plata* included "a very mixed and interesting company, including planters belonging to six or seven British colonies," from whom they were able to get information about the state of the colonies. Harvey and Brewin heard, for instance, that there had been a "continuous and on the whole large loss of labourers by emigration" from Barbados, an allegation that supports the argument that, in spite of the legislative restrictions, Barbadians displayed agentic behavior and left the island in search of better working conditions. Harvey and Brewin, *Jamaica in 1866*, 1.

37. Richardson, "Freedom and Migration in the Leeward Caribbean," 391.

38. Ibid., 391, 399–400.

39. Beckles, *History of Barbados*, 109.

40. Ibid.

41. Ibid., 110. The restrictive nature of the Barbadian plantation economy remained well into the twentieth century as the Contract Law was not repealed until June 1937. See Beckles, *History of Barbados*, 112.

42. Ibid., 110.

43. Passed on July 8, 1890, the full title of this act was "An Act to Consolidate and Amend the Acts relating to Poor Apprentices." Archer and Ferguson, *Laws of Barbados*, 1:373.

44. Ibid., 373–74.

45. Hobbes, *Leviathan*, 181.

46. Ibid., 159.

47. Foucault, *Discipline and Punish*, 195–200.

48. Ibid., 197.

49. "Simple idea in legislative architecture": I paraphrase Jeremy Bentham's assessment of the Panopticon. See Jeremy Bentham, preface to "Panopticon, or, The Inspection-House, & C.," in *The Panopticon Writings*, 31.

50. Ibid.

51. One of the major reasons for the proposal of this act, to stem the rise of indigent families and orphaned children, seems hollow when one considers that a similar emigration act had not been drawn up to prevent planters from migrating and leaving behind mulatto offspring.

52. This system of "less eligibility" also made itself felt in what can be defined as the minutiae of prison life, as a case of prison diet in nineteenth-century India showcases. In giving his report on the state of the prisons in a select number of British colonies, E. C. Wines noted, "Prison dietaries in India have been arranged with a view to giving all that is really required for health and strength, and withholding everything that would place the prisoner in a better condition than the poor and honest in his own walk of life." According to Wines, a similar philosophy guided practices in prisons in Jamaica. He noted that the Jamaican prison diet was designed to "keep the prisoners in good health, but without pampering them." Wines, *Report on the International Penitentiary Congress of London*, 125. It would not be too far-fetched to assume that the same feeling was held in Barbados.

53. Levy, *Emancipation, Sugar, and Federalism*, 62–63. Pringle had been appointed by the British government to inspect prisons in the West Indies after abuses in the Jamaican prison system had been reported by members of the Anti-slavery committee, including Sturge, Harvey, and John Scoble, and in the wake of the publication of James Williams's narrative. See also "Copy of a Despatch from Lord Glenelg to Governor Sir Lionel Smith, K.C.B., 25 August 1837," in Papers Relative to the Abolition of Slavery in the British Colonies, 134. Pringle's task was to investigate prison discipline and administration in the British West Indies. His appointment saw the imperial government taking a more aggressive role in the administration of institutions that had previously been left primarily in the hands of the colonial governments.

54. Ibid., 63.

55. Pringle, *Report of Captain J. W. Pringle*, pt. 2, 6, 3.

56. Ibid., 3.

57. Ibid.

58. This confluence of the religious with the punitive was not unusual and was done quite seamlessly. For instance, in the latter part of the nineteenth century full religious services were conducted in the jail on Sunday mornings, and short services were held every weekday before inmates started their work. *Barbados Blue Books*, 1882, 4.

59. Even in 1882 the association of punishment with a specific set of auxiliary professions remained. The seemingly easy ability of officials to go from one role to another

may be illustrated in the case of the personnel who supervised the confined at the District D Juvenile Prison. The keeper for this prison was also the sergeant at the attached police station, while the overseer was a schoolmaster. A casual reading of this suggests that discipline had a long reach within society. Whether at work or at school, the lives of the boys within the prison would have been dominated by discipline. See *Barbados Blue Books*, 1882, 4.

60. Pringle, *Report of Captain J. W. Pringle*, pt. 2, 9.

61. Ibid., 11–12.

62. "Enclosure in No. 579, No. 1," in Great Britain, Colonial Office, *Papers Presented to Parliament, by Her Majesty's Command*, pt. 4, 14 July 1837, 349.

63. Ibid., 350.

64. Look Lai, *Indentured Labour, Caribbean Sugar*, 127–35.

65. Pringle, *Report of Captain J. W. Pringle*, pt. 2, 17.

66. See the first section of table 9, showing the number of prisoners in confinement in the course of a year.

67. There is not necessarily a direct correlation between the size of a country's general population and the demographic makeup of its incarcerated population. One only has to look at the racial makeup of the incarcerated population in the United States in the twenty-first century. In 2006, for example, statistics from the U.S. Department of Justice showed that out of a total of 1,502,200 prisoners sentenced under state or federal jurisdiction, blacks accounted for 534,200, nearly 36 percent, while whites accounted for 478,000, about 32 percent. When these figures are read against data from the 2000 census, their significance is underscored as blacks made up just 12.3 percent of the total population, whereas whites accounted for 75.1 percent.

68. Pringle, *Report of Captain J. W. Pringle*, pt. 2, 4.

69. Ibid., 10. Schomburgk noted that these visits took place every Saturday, with the keeper and turnkey present. He also noted that convicted prisoners were not allowed to receive food, clothing, or letters from their relatives or friends. Schomburgk, *History of Barbados*, 135.

70. Pringle, *Report of Captain J. W. Pringle*, 10.

71. "Rules and Regulations for the Common Gaol, and District Houses of Correction, of Barbados, Approved and Confirmed by the Governor-in-Council on the 11th day of January, 1870," Barbados National Archives, St. James, Barbados.

72. Carpenter, *Female Life in Prison*, 90.

73. Great Britain, Colonial Office, *Further Papers relating to the Improvement of Prison Discipline*, 60.

74. Ibid.

75. Ibid.

76. *Barbados Blue Book*, 1882, 3.

77. In 1882, for example, "The actual net profits arising from the labour of the Convicts amounted to £340 10 7½. The estimated value of the labour performed outside the

Prison [was] £1,057 5 4. That of other labour £345 0 0, equal to £1,402 5 4. The saving to the Treasury effected by the Bakery which [was] worked by convicts [was] calculated as £869 15 3." Ibid.

78. *Barbados Blue Book*, 1882, 6.

79. Ibid.

80. *Annual Colonial Report, Barbados*, 1900 (London: Printed for His Majesty's Stationery Office, 1901), 21.

81. Ibid., 39.

82. *Barbados Blue Book*, 1898, 17.

83. Levy, *Emancipation, Sugar, and Federalism*, 130. Moreover, in the latter half of the nineteenth century, the British Caribbean grappled with a host of economic and social problems. Sugar production was low, and beet sugar had made such significant inroads into the world market that by 1884 its producers were supplying 53.4 percent of the world's total sugar market. This crisis within the economy had a severe impact on the laborers, as their livelihood depended heavily on the profitability of sugar. Also, after 1856 the cost of food in Barbados increased. See Levy, *Emancipation, Sugar, and Federalism*, 137.

84. See Levy, *Emancipation, Sugar, and Federalism*, 130.

85. Ibid., 135.

86. Hamilton, *Barbados and the Confederation Question*, 8.

87. Ibid., 8–9.

88. One of the best historical accounts of the Confederation Crisis in Barbados was written by Bruce Hamilton. See Hamilton, *Barbados and the Confederation Question*.

89. "Minutes of Proceedings of the Honourable House of Assembly", *Official Gazette* (Bridgetown, Barbados), February 17, 1876, CO 32/3.

90. Ibid.

91. Great Britain, Colonial Office, *Further Papers relating to the Improvement of Prison Discipline*, 66.

92. "Minutes of Proceedings of the Honourable House of Assembly, for Session of 1875–76," *Official Gazette*, February 17, 1876, CO 32/3.

93. CO 321/9, No. 37, 22nd March 1876, National Archives, Kew, United Kingdom.

94. See "Enclosure 2 in No. 36, Message from the Governor to the Legislative Council," in Great Britain, Parliament, *Papers relating to the Late Disturbances in Barbados*, 84.

95. "Enclosure 1 in No. 43, Legislative Summary," in Great Britain, Parliament, *Papers relating to the Late Disturbances in Barbados*, 92.

96. Hamilton, *Barbados and the Confederation Question*, 94.

97. My findings so far are insufficient to paint a true and complete picture of Hennessy's influence on penal and punitive reforms in Barbados.

98. *Barbados Blue Book*, 1882, 4, 8.

99. *Laws of Barbados*, vol. 1, 347.

100. Ibid.

101. *Barbados Blue Books*, 1892.

102. *Annual Colonial Report, British Guiana*, 1899–1900, 25; Trotman, "Women and Crime in Late Nineteenth Century Trinidad," 255.

103. *Annual Colonial Report, Barbados*, 1901–1902, 38.

104. See Paton, *No Bond but the Law*, esp. pp. 110–12 and 192.

105. *Annual Colonial Report, Barbados*, 1901–1902, 38.

106. *Barbados Blue Book*, 1883. In 1883 the lower portion of Glendairy Prison consisted of forty separate cells and six associated rooms. Three men were confined in each cell, and twelve or less were housed in the larger rooms.

CHAPTER 5. *Enclosing Contagion*

1. Thus far I have found no evidence of a similar emigration act in Jamaica.

2. Bernault, "Shadow of Rule," 73.

3. Wilton, "The Constitution of Difference"; Sibley, *Geographies of Exclusion*; Popke, "Managing Colonial Alterity."

4. Sibley, *Geographies of Exclusion*, 74.

5. Pile, "Human Agency and Human Geography Revisited," 135.

6. Rapoport, "Vernacular Architecture," 289.

7. In this section of the chapter I concentrate primarily, although not exclusively, on evidence from Captain J. W. Pringle's visit to the British West Indies in 1837 as his findings represented an important intervention in decoding and reporting on the nature of penal spaces in Jamaica. The importance of Pringle's contribution to the ongoing discourse on penal confinement in the entire British Caribbean cannot be overstated. Pringle's visit produced one of the most comprehensive accounts of penal spaces in Jamaica specifically and the British West Indies in general, and it helped to reframe the debates relating to these spaces. The importance of his findings may be underscored further when one notes that he visited a large number of penal spaces, recorded the location of these spaces, and assessed whether the locations were conducive to the inmates' social and moral rehabilitation. He also produced firsthand accounts of how jails and houses of correction were organized spatially and described the internal workings of these spaces and their impact on the confined.

8. "Copies of Acts Passed by the Legislature of the Island of Jamaica, Session 5 February–27 August 1839," vol. 35, 2, microfilm, University of Toronto Library.

9. "No. 512, Copy of a Despatch from the Marquis of Sligo to Lord Glenelg, 15 May 1836," in Great Britain, Colonial Office, *Papers Presented to Parliament, by Her Majesty's Command*, pt. 4 (1), 36.

10. Ibid.

11. "Enclosure in No. 554, No. 2, 11 August 1836," in Great Britain, Colonial Office, *Papers Presented to Parliament, by Her Majesty's Command*, pt. 4, 174.

12. "Enclosure No. 43, Copy of a Despatch from Governor Sir Lionel Smith, K.C.B., to Lord Glenelg, 13 October 1837," in Papers Relative to the Abolition of Slavery, microfilm, University of Toronto Library.

13. "Appendix No. 181, An Act for the More Effectual Protection of Persons and Property, and to Appoint Constables, and for Other Purposes—Passed 15 June 1836" in Papers Relative to the Abolition of Slavery in the British Colonies, appendix, 1. As Diana Paton points out, hard labor could include prisoners being made to clean the streets, build roads, or provide agricultural labor to estates owned by private citizens. See Paton, *No Bond but the Law*, 99.

14. "Appendix No. 181, An Act for the More Effectual Protection of Persons and Property, and to Appoint Constables, and for Other Purposes—Passed 15 June 1836" in Papers Relative to the Abolition of Slavery in the British Colonies, appendix, 1.

15. Pringle, *Report of Captain J. W. Pringle*, pt. 1, 3, 4.

16. Ibid.

17. Ibid.

18. Ibid., part I, appendix, 15, 11.

19. Evans, *The Fabrication of Virtue*, 119.

20. Great Britain, Colonial Office, *Prison Discipline*, 5.

21. Paton, *No Bond but the Law*, 21.

22. Tomlinson, "Design and Reform," 110.

23. "No. 9, Report of the Inspectors of Prisons, April 5, 1849," in Great Britain, Colonial Office, *Papers relative to the Affairs of the Island of Jamaica*, 150.

24. "Enclosure 1 in No. 2, Report of the Commissioners on the Prison Enquiry, 1873," in Great Britain, Colonial Office, *Further Papers relating to the Improvement of Prison Discipline*, 11.

25. Ibid., 21.

26. Ibid., 21, 23.

27. "Governor Norman, Jamaica No. 3534, No. 39, 4 February 1885," Crime and Prisons Report 84, CO 137/520, National Archives, Kew, United Kingdom.

28. Bryan, *The Jamaican People*, 26.

29. "Governor Norman. Jamaica No. 3534, No. 39, 4 February 1885," Crime and Prisons Report 84, 13, CO 137/520, National Archives, Kew, United Kingdom.

30. Forsythe, *The Reform of Prisoners, 1830–1900*, 9, 12.

31. "Enclosure 1, in No. 2, Report of the Commissioners on the Prison Enquiry, 1873," in Great Britain, Colonial Office, *Further Papers relating to the Improvement of Prison Discipline*, 13–14.

32. Ibid., 15.

33. CO 137/525 Jamaica, Crime and Prison Discipline 1885, Minutes, National Archives, Kew, United Kingdom.

34. "The Director of Prisons to the Colonial Secretary, 10 November 1885," CO 137/525, National Archives, Kew, United Kingdom.

35. Flannigan, *Antigua and the Antiguans*, 239.

36. *Report of Captain J. W. Pringle*, pt. 1, 7–8, 32.

37. Thome and Kimball, *Emancipation in the West Indies*, 91.

38. *Report of Captain J. W. Pringle*, pt. 1, 45.

39. Ibid., 31, 34–35.

40. Ibid., 5.

41. It must be acknowledged that the fact that white prisoners were not chained may not have been evidence of racial privileging but may stem from the reality that, as minorities with light skin, it would have been easier to recognize and recapture them compared to black prisoners who, it could be asserted, would have had a better chance of disappearing within the majority demographic landscape.

42. *Report of Captain J. W. Pringle on Prisons*, pt. 1, 20, 21.

43. Ibid., 6.

44. Ibid., 8.

45. Paton, *No Bond but the Law*, 110–12, 192.

46. *Report of Captain J. W. Pringle on Prisons*, pt. 1, 8.

47. For a discussion of the relationship between the construction of time and the nature of spaces, see Rapoport, "Vernacular Architecture," 292–93.

48. Rapoport, "Vernacular Architecture," 293.

49. *Report of Captain J. W. Pringle on Prisons*, pt. 1, 8.

50. "Copy of a Circular Despatch, addressed by Lord Glenelg to the Governors of the West India Colonies, &c., 29 June 1838," in *Papers Relative to the West Indies*, pt. 1, 1–2.

51. "Enclosure 1, in No. 13," in *Papers Relative to the West Indies, 1839*, pt. 1, 67–70.

52. "Copy of a Circular Despatch, addressed by Lord Glenelg to the Governors of the West India Colonies, &c., 29 June 1838," in *Papers Relative to the West Indies*, pt. 1, 3.

53. See Curtin, *Two Jamaicas*.

54. Ibid., 161.

55. "Enclosure in No. 576," in Great Britain, Colonial Office, *Papers Presented to Parliament, by Her Majesty's Command*, pt. 4 (91), 14 July 1837, 348.

56. Burns, *History of the British West Indies*, 651.

57. "An Act to Provide for the Regulation of the Gaols, Houses of Correction, and Other Prisons in This Island," in *Laws of Jamaica*, 1839, 116–30.

58. For information about Pringle's life and work, see Jackson, "John W. Pringle." See also Rose, "The Military Background of John W. Pringle."

59. Pringle had been appointed by the British government to inspect prisons in the West Indies after abuses in the Jamaican prison system had been reported by members of the British anti-slavery society. See Levy, *Emancipation, Sugar, and Federalism*, 62–63. See also "Copy of a Despatch from Lord Glenelg to Governor Sir Lionel Smith, K.C.B., 25 August 1837," in Papers Relative to the Abolition of Slavery in the British Colonies, 134.

60. Great Britain, Colonial Office, *Further Papers Relating to the Improvement of Prison Discipline*, 1.

61. Ibid.

62. "No. 9, Report of the Inspectors of Prisons, April 5, 1849," in Great Britain, Colonial Office, *Papers relative to the Affairs of the Island of Jamaica*, 153.

63. See James Williams's testimony where he revealed that he and other inmates, when imprisoned in the dungeon, were also deprived of light and food. In this respect, one can see the similarities between confinement in dungeons in the apprenticeship period and the more modern form of confinement in the jails in the late nineteenth century. See page 3 of Williams, *Narrative of Events* (1837), for this account, and see chapter 2 of this book for an analysis of this form of punishment.

64. *Barbados Blue Book*, 1882, 7.

65. Ibid., 2–3; Burton, *Clocks and Watches 1400–1900*, 77. The telltale clock was invented by John Whitehurst. Its purpose, according to Burton, was "to keep check on night watchmen." These clocks "were in narrow or long tapering cases made of oak and had 12- or 24-hour dials which rotated." According to Burton, when a night watchman visited the place where the clock was located, he pulled a plunger that depressed pegs on the dial, an action that produced a record of the time that he had visited. The clock was also known as "night-watchman's clock." Figures in Burton's *Clocks and Watches 1400–1900* include one showing a telltale clock.

66. Foucault, *Discipline and Punish*, 195.

67. *San Fernando (Trinidad) Gazette*, May 26, 1883.

68. Ibid.

CHAPTER 6. *The Punished Black Body and the Public's Gaze*

1. I use the term "public works" here to mean any type of labor that took prisoners outside of their spaces of penal confinement—even if this work was then performed in some other enclosed space—and thereby forced prisoners to confront a world outside of the prison.

2. Braithwaite, *Crime, Shame, and Reintegration*, 81.

3. For a detailed discussion of public punishments, see Foucault, *Discipline and Punish*, esp. pp. 3–31 and 42–69. See also Ignatieff, *A Just Measure of Pain*, chap. 2 (esp. pp. 20–24), for a treatment of public punishment during the eighteenth and nineteenth centuries.

4. See Ignatieff, *A Just Measure of Pain*, 20–24, for discussion of how the dependence on a ritualized spectacle of punishment was a fundamental flaw in punitive practice in Britain.

5. I draw again on the work of Braithwaite to argue that some types of public punishment in Barbados and Jamaica were infused primarily with a shaming element. The theory held that by stigmatizing the crime and the criminal, criminals and would-be criminals would be less inclined to flout societal laws. Following Braithwaite's theory, this stigmatization is deemed to work best when it leads to criminals' reintegration into the community rather than when they are ostracized totally from the community. See Braithwaite, *Crime, Shame, and Integration*.

6. I borrow the term "spectacular terror" from Vincent Brown, "Spiritual Terror and Sacred Authority in Jamaican Slave Society," 24. In using the word "terror" to categorize punishments like public flogging and hanging, I emphasize their dramatic and sen-

sational characteristics. I wish to call attention also to the fact that these punishments tended to be multisensory: that not only were they arresting visually, they engaged other senses as well. Further, these acts were accompanied usually by language and verbal exchanges that were similarly striking and even sometimes by other punitive acts that were meant to capture the attention of observers. As a case in point, the state reprisals in the wake of the Morant Bay Rebellion not only included public hangings and public floggings—villages were also burnt. Thus, one could argue, the sight, sound, and scent of burning buildings and other objects would have created arresting and memorable imagery as much as the hangings, floggings, and shootings of alleged rebels that also characterized the state reprisals.

7. Foucault, *Discipline and Punish*, 3–6. Executed in March 1757 for his nonfatal stabbing of Louis XV, Damiens was elaborately tortured, torn apart, and burned.

8. Braithwaite, *Crime, Shame, and Reintegration*, 81.

9. Colthurst, *Colthurst Journal*, 100.

10. "Rules and Regulations for the Common Gaol, and District Houses of Correction, of Barbados, Approved and Confirmed by the Governor-in-Council on the 11th day of January, 1870," 3, Barbados National Archives, St. James, Barbados.

11. Archer and Ferguson, *Laws of Barbados*, 1:136.

12. Wines, *Report on the International Penitentiary Congress of London*, 126. Wines was also paraphrasing assertions made by H. B. Shaw, the inspector-general of the prisons in Jamaica, who put forward this idea in his presentation at the International Penitentiary Congress. See Pears, *Prisons and Reformatories at Home and Abroad*, 578–82, for Shaw's presentation.

13. Wines, *Report on the International Penitentiary Congress of London*, 126.

14. Quoted in Damousi, *Depraved and Disorderly*, 93.

15. *St. Lucian*, August 12, 1865.

16. Anderson, *Between Slavery and Freedom*, 136.

17. Ibid.

18. Des Voeux, *My Colonial Service in British Guiana*, 309–10.

19. *Barbados Blue Book*, 1882, 7.

20. Ibid., 1882, 14.

21. Thanks to Michele Johnson of York University in Toronto for pointing this out.

22. Colthurst, *Colthurst Journal*, 100. A "quadroon" was the offspring of a white and a mulatto.

23. Ibid.

24. Ibid.

25. Foucault, *Discipline and Punish*, 43.

26. Judges 16:19 (King James Version).

27. *Barbados Blue Book*, 1883.

28. *Barbados Blue Book*, 1892, 3.

29. Coleridge, *Six Months in the West Indies*, 257.

30. "Enclosure 1, in No. 2, Report of the Commissioners on the Prison Enquiry,

1873," in Great Britain, Colonial Office, *Further Papers relating to the Improvement of Prison Discipline*, 10.

31. For an analysis of how social conventions were inverted in the colonial Caribbean during carnival, Jonkonnu, and other celebrations, see R. D. E. Burton, *Afro-Creole*, esp. pp. 65–83, where he discusses the characteristics of Jonkonnu in Jamaica between 1800 and 1834, and pp. 156–220, where he examines what he refers to as the "carnival complex." For more on how the ritual of punishment was inverted, see Ignatieff, *A Just Measure of Pain*, 23. Here Ignatieff looks at the crowd's support of the criminal, rather than the actions of the criminal, as an example where the act of punishment was transformed from "a solemn act of the state to a popular bacchanal."

32. Ignatieff, *A Just Measure of Pain*, 21.

33. Ibid.

34. *Concise Oxford Dictionary* (Oxford: Oxford University Press, 1999).

35. See Scarry, *The Body in Pain*, 27–59.

36. Ibid., 28.

37. Brown, "Spiritual Terror and Sacred Authority," 26–28.

38. Paton, "Punishment, Crime, and the Bodies of Slaves."

39. Ibid., 928–29.

40. Ibid., 940.

41. Bleby, *Death Struggles of Slavery*, 29–30.

42. Even though hanging did not show up often in the data on punishment, its occurrence is still important as it offers the opportunity to look at how the punished—in life and death—were regarded in the British West Indies. In the 1892 Report on Gaols and Prisoners in Barbados, for instance, there was only one case of a prisoner—a male—being hanged. See *Barbados Blue Book*, 1892.

43. Paton, "Punishment, Crime, and the Bodies of Slaves," 939, 941.

44. Despatches from the Secretary of State. Enclosure in No. 2 Memorandum of passages referred to in the preceding Despatch. The Right Hon. Edward Cardwell, M.P. to Governor Eyre (November 23, 1865), 241, microfilm, University of Toronto Library.

45. Great Britain, Jamaica Royal Commission, *Report of the Jamaica Royal Commission*, 755.

46. "Enclosure 64, in No. 1, Captain Hole to Brigadier-General Nelson, Despatches from Governor Eyre," in Great Britain, Foreign Office, *Papers relating to the Disturbances in Jamaica*, 38.

47. "Governor Eyre to the Right Hon. Edward Cardwell, M.P. Despatches from Governor Eyre," in Great Britain, Foreign Office, *Papers relating to the Disturbances in Jamaica*, 4.

48. "No. 6, Copy of a Despatch from Governor Sir J. Peter Grant, K.C.B., to the Right Hon. the Earl of Carnarvon (October 24, 1866)," in Great Britain, Colonial Office, *Further Correspondence Relative to the Affairs of Jamaica*, 11, 12, 16.

49. "Enclosure No. 8, the Attorney General to the Colonial Secretary (November 8, 1866), Copy of a Despatch from Governor Sir J. Peter Grant, K.C.B., to the Right Hon.

the Earl of Carnarvon," in Great Britain, Colonial Office, *Further Correspondence Relative to the Affairs of Jamaica*, 16.

50. Ibid.

51. Ibid., 17.

52. Ibid.

53. It should be pointed out that Ford stated that sailors were not present, but Augustus Walter Hewitt Lake, another witness, stated that sailors were present, and these were the ones who had flogged Marshall and hoisted up to the courthouse. Ibid.

54. Great Britain, Colonial Office, *Further Correspondence Relative to the Affairs of Jamaica*, 18.

55. Ibid., 21–22.

56. "Minute—Mr. Ramsay's Case, Enclosure in No. 9, Mr. Ramsay to the Colonial Secretary, October 25, 1866," in Great Britain, Colonial Office, *Further Correspondence Relative to the Affairs of Jamaica*, 24.

57. Colthurst, *Colthurst Journal*, 106.

58. "Copy of a Despatch from Governor Sir E. J. M. McGregor, Bart., to Lord Glenelg, 21 December 1837," in *Accounts and Papers of the House of Commons*, "Slavery," Session 15 November 1837–16 August 1838, 68, microfilm, University of Toronto Library.

59. Dalby, *Crime and Punishment in Jamaica*, 82.

60. Williams, *Narrative of Events* (1837), 4.

61. For one example, although it refers to the period before emancipation, see Flannigan, *Antigua and the Antiguans*, 146, which says that the insurrectionists who participated in the 1831 rebellion in Antigua were punished by public floggings.

62. "Enclosure No. 8, The Attorney General to the Colonial Secretary," in Great Britain, Colonial Office, *Further Correspondence Relative to the Affairs of Jamaica*, 20. Margaret Minott's last name is spelled "Minot" and "Minott" in the documents. To be consistent and avoid confusion I have chosen to spell her surname as "Minott."

63. "Enclosure in No. 10, Mr. S. D. Lindo to the Attorney General, December 1, 1866," in Great Britain, Colonial Office, *Further Correspondence Relative to the Affairs of Jamaica*, 28.

64. Ibid., 28–29.

65. Ibid., 31.

CHAPTER 7. *The Difference That Gender Makes*

1. Bush, *Slave Women in Caribbean Society*, 14–15.

2. Hilary Beckles, in writing about "masculinities" in the British West Indies during slavery, draws upon R. W. Connell's concept of the "gender order" to argue that there were "competing masculinities" in the slave economies of the British Caribbean. These masculinities, according to Beckles's theorization, were not created equally—"some were hegemonic, some marginalised." Beckles, "Black Masculinity in Caribbean Slavery," 227.

3. The subhead is a phrase borrowed from the introduction of Sawicki, *Disciplining Foucault*, 10.

4. Foucault, *Discipline and Punish*. It may even be argued that women like Lescombat (p. 58), Marie Françoise Salmon (p. 62), and Marie Le Goff (p. 66) are treated as mere addenda in this work. Generally speaking, when Foucault writes about *the criminal* he uses the male personal pronouns "he" and "his." Also noticeably absent in Foucault's work is a sustained critique of the gendered dimensions of punishment. This inattention to how ideas about the sexed body impinged on the birth of the prison and the evolution of punishment could be attributed to the fact that the original work, *Surveiller et Punir: Naissance de la prison*, first appeared in 1975 and reflected the sensibilities of that time.

5. Scott, "Gender."

6. Ibid.

7. See Barriteau, "Theorizing Ruptures in Gender Systems," 26.

8. Lambert, *White Creole Culture, Politics and Identity*, 44.

9. Sturge and Harvey, *West Indies in 1837*, 219.

10. Pringle, *Report of Captain J. W. Pringle*, pt. 2, 15. This appears to be an abridged version of the list, not a comprehensive one.

11. "Enclosure 1, in No. 508, Copy of a Letter from Thomas J. Baines, Special Justice, to his Excellency the Marquis of Sligo, 9 February 1836, and Copy of a Letter from Andrew Cooke, Esq. To Major J. Baines, Special Justice, 6 February 1836," in Great Britain, Colonial Office, *Papers Presented to Parliament, by Her Majesty's Command*, pt. 4 (1), 30–32.

12. "Enclosure 2, in No. 509, Copy of a Despatch from Lord Glenelg to the Marquis of Sligo, 11 June, 1836," in ibid., 33.

13. This evidence was heard during a convening of justices by order of the custos of St. Thomas in the East to inquire into the state of the house of correction in that parish and into the cause of the deaths that occurred there between April 1835 and February 1836. See "Enclosures 1 and 2 in No. 514," ibid., 39–40.

14. For instance, Pringle points out that the population of Jamaica in 1835 stood at approximately 350,000, with the apprentices accounting for 311,692 of this total, while whites and free persons were about 39,308 combined. See Pringle, *Report of Captain J. W. Pringle*, 3. In August 1838, Barbados was reported to be inhabited by 83,000 blacks, 15,000 whites, and 12,000 "coloureds." For this last point, see Beckles, *History of Barbados*, 104.

15. Bush, "White 'Ladies,' Coloured 'Favourites' and Black 'Wenches,'" 249.

16. *San Fernando Gazette*, May 26, 1883.

17. Sturge and Harvey, *West Indies in 1837*, 176.

18. Ibid., 169

19. Ibid., 205.

20. Williams, *Narrative of Events (1837)*, 7–8.

21. Ibid., 8. On the importance of white abolitionist women and the concerted appeals

that were made to their "nature," see, for example, Association for the Universal Abolition of Slavery, *An Appeal to the Christian Women of Sheffield*; Bourne, *Slavery Illustrated
in its Ill-effects upon Women*; Dublin Ladies' Association, Hibernian Anti-slavery Society, *Second Appeal from the Dublin Ladies' Association*.

22. Pringle, *Report of Captain J. W. Pringle*, pt. 1, 48.

23. Ibid., 59.

24. Ibid., 204.

25. Ibid., 217.

26. Ibid., 233.

27. Sturge and Harvey, *West Indies in 1837*, 139.

28. Trotman, "Capping the Volcano," 124–25.

29. "Jamaica Crime and Prison Discipline 1885, Minutes," CO 137/525, National Archives, Kew, United Kingdom.

30. "No. 516, Copy of a Despatch from the Marquis of Sligo to Lord Glenelg, 4 June
1836," in Great Britain, Colonial Office, *Papers Presented to Parliament, by Her Majesty's
Command*, pt. 4 (1), 14 July 1837, 41–42.

31. *Negro Apprenticeship in the Colonies*, 17–18.

32. Although it is noted that wars are coded as male, Nira Yuval-Davis has shown
that women have been key participants in them. See her *Gender and Nation*, especially
chap. 5, "Gendered Militaries, Gendered Wars," pp. 93–115.

33. "No. 1, Governor Eyre to the Right Hon. Edward Cardwell, M.P.," in Great Britain, Foreign Office, *Papers relating to the Disturbances in Jamaica*, 3.

34. "Testimony of Mrs. Eleanor Shortridge on the Fifth Day of the Investigation into
the Morant Bay Rebellion," in Great Britain, Jamaica Royal Commission, *Report of the
Jamaica Royal Commission*, 39.

35. "No. 3, Copy of a Despatch from Governor Sir J. Peter Grant, K.C.B., to the
Right Hon. the Earl of Carnarvon (October 9, 1866)," in Great Britain, Colonial Office,
Further Correspondence Relative to the Affairs of Jamaica, 6.

36. Ibid., 7.

37. Ibid., 9.

38. "No. 1. Governor Eyre to the Right Hon. Edward Cardwell, M.P.," in Great
Britain, Foreign Office, *Papers relating to the Disturbances in Jamaica*, 1. The evidence
strongly suggests that these women, children, and unprotected persons were only white.
Indeed, Captain Hole, writing to Brigadier-General Nelson, delineated a dichotomy
between the white victim under assault and the black marauding rebel. He noted that
on October 17, 1865, a number of "Europeans" were rescued from the village of Betty's
Hope in Manchioneal. "Inclosure 62 in No. 1, Captain Hole to Brigadier-General Nelson
(October 17, 1865), Despatches from Governor Eyre," in Great Britain, Foreign Office,
Papers relating to the Disturbances in Jamaica, 37.

39. "No. 3, Copy of a Despatch from Governor Sir J. Peter Grant, K.C.B., to the
Right Hon. the Earl of Carnarvon (October 9, 1866)," in Great Britain, Colonial Office,
Further Correspondence Relative to the Affairs of Jamaica, 7.

40. Lambert, *White Creole Culture, Politics and Identity*, 131.

41. This is the term that Lambert uses to refer to the notion held by whites that blacks were particularly threatening. Blacks were thought to be threatening not only in terms of their perceived capabilities to do violence to whites but also through sexual encounters that could result in miscegenation. Ibid., 133.

42. Faughnan, *Stirring Incidents in the Life of a British Soldier*, 320.

43. Great Britain, Jamaica Royal Commission, *Report of the Jamaica Royal Commission*, 16.

44. Ibid., 17.

45. Ibid., 16.

46. "Captain Henry Francis Luke, Friday 26th January 1866, the Third Day of Testimony," in Great Britain, Jamaica Royal Commission, *Report of the Jamaica Royal Commission*, 23.

47. Hutton, "The Defeat of the Morant Bay Rebellion," 30, 31. Also see Semmel, *Jamaican Blood and Victorian Conscience*, for an account of the Morant Bay Rebellion. On pp. 16–17 Semmel refers to the comments that were allegedly made by Captain Hole.

48. "An Act to Consolidate and Amend the Law of This Island relating to Larceny and Other Similar Offences, 17 February 1868," in Archer and Ferguson, *Laws of Barbados*, vol. 1, 40–74.

49. Ibid., 74–92.

50. Ibid., 114–36.

51. Ibid., 124.

52. Wright, *Draft of a Criminal Code*, 8, 20.

53. Levy, *Emancipation, Sugar, and Federalism*, 50.

54. The Barbadian version of the Act for the Better Prevention of Contagious Diseases was passed on July 30, 1868, and amended on August 14, 1869. Archer and Ferguson, *Laws of Barbados*, vol. 2, 277–86, 295–97.

55. Acton, *Prostitution Considered in its Moral, Social, and Sanitary Aspects*, 83.

56. Archer and Ferguson, *Laws of Barbados*, vol. 2, 279, 280, 281.

57. Ibid., 285–86.

58. Bryan, *The Jamaican People*, 108–9.

59. Ibid.

60. Ibid., 105.

61. It should be noted that Philippa Levine's findings challenge the idea that the colonial versions of the Contagious Diseases Act were "modelled on the allegedly parent legislation of the 'mother' country." Instead she argues that "colonial legislation around the venereal diseases often predated and differed, in profound ways, from that promulgated in Britain." Levine, "What Difference Did Empire Make?," 71.

62. Walkowitz, *Prostitution and Victorian Society*, 71, 70.

63. "An Act to Consolidate and Amend the Law of This Island Relating to Offenses against the Person," 150.

64. Wright, *Draft of a Criminal Code*.

65. "The Director of Prisons to the Colonial Secretary, 10 November 1885," CO 137/525, National Archives, Kew, United Kingdom.

66. Of course, the most obvious reason why men and women were separated was to prevent sexual contact between them, but at the same time it is argued that female and male criminals were seen as different from each other in *kind*, even if not in the types of crimes committed.

67. "The Director of Prisons to the Colonial Secretary, 10 November 1885," CO 137/525, National Archives, Kew, United Kingdom.

68. Quoted in Luddy, "Abandoned Women and Bad Characters," 496.

69. *Barbados Blue Book*, 1882, 14.

70. Ibid., 8.

EPILOGUE. FINAL THOUGHTS ON WHAT IT MEANS
TO PUNISH BLACK BODIES

1. G. M. Hall, *Social Control in Slave Plantation Societies*, 79, 77. It is important to note that this position does not negate the fact that some white bodies were "more inviolate" than other white bodies. What is critical to note, however, is that whites, as a *class*, were seen as superior to blacks.

BIBLIOGRAPHY

ARCHIVES

Barbados National Archives, Black Rock, St. James, Barbados
National Archives, Kew, Surrey, United Kingdom
U.K. Parliamentary Papers, University of Toronto Library

PRINTED PRIMARY SOURCES

An Abstract of the British West Indian Statutes, for the Protection and Government of Slaves. London: J. Ridgway, 1830.

Acton, William. *Prostitution Considered in Its Moral, Social, and Sanitary Aspects in London and other Large Cities and Garrison Towns, with Proposals for the Control and Prevention of Its Attendant Evils*. 2nd ed. 1870. Reprint, London: Frank Cass, 1972.

The Act of Assembly of the Island of Jamaica to Repeal Several Acts, and Clauses of Acts, Respecting Slaves, and for the Better Order and Government of Slaves . . . Commonly Called the Consolidated Act. London, 1788.

Acts of Assembly, Passed in the Island of Jamaica, from 1681, to 1737, Inclusive. London, 1743.

Anderson, John. *Between Slavery and Freedom: Special Magistrate John Anderson's Journal of St. Vincent during the Apprenticeship*. Edited by Roderick A. McDonald. Philadelphia: University of Pennsylvania Press, 2001.

Archer, C. V. H., and W. K. Ferguson. *Laws of Barbados: Revised and Consolidated*. 6 vols. Barbados: Advocate Company, 1944–46.

Barbados Blue Book. Annual.

Bleby, Henry. *Death Struggles of Slavery: A Narrative of Facts and Incidents, Which Occurred in a British Colony, during the Two Years Immediately Preceding Negro Emancipation*. 3rd ed. 1886. Reprint, Coconut Grove, Fla.: Dewar's Limited Editions, 1973.

Bourne, George. *Slavery Illustrated in Its Effects upon Women and Domestic Society*. Boston: Isaac Knapp, 1837.

Brown, Adam. *Jamaica Exhibition, 1891: Trade Statistics.* CIHM/ICMH Microfiche Series 7783. Ottawa: Canadian Institute for Historical Microreproductions, 1980.

Candler, John. "A Good Friend in our Midst. 1850." *Jamaican Historical Review* 3.2 (March 1951).

Carpenter, Mary. *Female Life in Prison, by a Prison Matron,* vol. 1. 2nd ed. London: Hurst and Blackett, 1862.

Coleridge, Henry Nelson. *Six Months in the West Indies.* New York: Negro Universities Press, 1970.

Colonial Laws as Examined by a Committee of the House of Commons in the Year 1836, Exhibiting Some of the Principal Discrepancies between those Laws, and the Imperial Act of Abolition. London: J. Haddon, 1837.

Colthurst, John Bowen. *The Colthurst Journal: Journal of a Special Magistrate in the Islands of Barbados and St. Vincent, July 1835–September 1838.* Edited by Woodville K. Marshall. Millwood, N.Y.: KTO Press, 1977.

Des Voeux, George William. *Experiences of a Demerara Magistrate, 1863–1869.* Georgetown, British Guiana: Daily Chronicle, 1948.

———. *My Colonial Service in British Guiana, St. Lucia, Trinidad, Fiji, Australia, New-Foundland, and Hong Kong with Interludes,* vol. 1. London: John Murray, 1903.

Faughnan, Thomas. *Stirring Incidents in the Life of a British Soldier: An Autobiography.* Toronto: Hunter, Rose, 1879.

Flannigan, Mrs. *Antigua and the Antiguans: A Full Account of the Colony and Its Inhabitants from the Time of the Caribs to the Present Day,* vol. 1. London: Saunders and Otley, 1844.

Ford, Jos. C., and A. A. C. Finlay. *The Handbook of Jamaica for 1903, Comprising Historical, Statistical, and General Information Concerning the Island.* London: Edward Stanford; Kingston, Jamaica: Government Printing Office, 1903.

Great Britain, Colonial Office. *Further Correspondence Relative to the Affairs of Jamaica.* London: George Edward Eyre and William Spottiswoode, 1867.

———. *Further Papers relating to the Improvement of Prison Discipline in the Colonies.* London: Harrison and Sons, 1876.

———. *Papers Presented to Parliament, by Her Majesty's Command, in Explanation of the Measures Adopted by Her Majesty's Government, for Giving Effect, to the Act for the Abolition of Slavery throughout the British Colonies.* London: House of Commons, 1835–38.

———. *Papers relative to the Affairs of the Island of Jamaica.* London: William Clowes and Sons, 1849.

———. *Papers relative to the West Indies, 1839.* London, 1839.

———. *Papers relative to the West Indies, 1840.* London: William Clowes and Sons, 1841.

———. *Papers relative to the West Indies, 1841–42, Jamaica—Barbados.* London: William Clowes and Sons, 1842.

————. *Prison Discipline: Digest and Summary of Answers from Colonial Governors to Circular Despatches Sent out by the Secretary of State on the 16th and 17th January 1867.* London: George Edward Eyre and William Spottiswoode, 1867.

Great Britain, Foreign Office. *Papers relating to the Disturbances in Jamaica*, part I. London: Harrison and Sons, 1866.

Great Britain, Jamaica Royal Commission. *Report of the Jamaica Royal Commission, 1866.* 2 parts. London: George Edward Eyre and William Spottiswoode, 1866.

Great Britain, Parliament. *Papers relating to the Late Disturbances in Barbados.* London: George Edward Eyre and William Spottiswoode, 1876.

Hall, Douglas, ed. *In Miserable Slavery: Thomas Thistlewood in Jamaica, 1750–86.* Kingston, Jamaica: University of the West Indies Press, 1999. First published 1989.

Harvey, Thomas, and William Brewin. *Jamaica in 1866: A Narrative Tour through the Island, with Remarks on its Social, Educational and Industrial Condition.* London: A. W. Bennett, 1867.

Laws of Barbados. 2 vols. London: William Clowes and Sons, 1875.

Laws of Jamaica, 1834–1900. 2 vols. Spanish Town, Jamaica: For William J. Pearson, n.d.; Government Printing Establishment, n.d.

Lewis, Matthew Gregory. *Journal of a West India Proprietor, Kept during a Residence in the Island of Jamaica.* New York: Negro Universities Press, 1969. First published 1834.

Pears, Edwin, ed. *Prisons and Reformatories at Home and Abroad: Being the Transactions of the International Penitentiary Congress Held in London July 3–13, 1872, including Official Documents, Discussions, and Papers Presented to the Congress.* London: Longmans, Green, 1872.

Prince, Mary. *The History of Mary Prince, a West Indian Slave, Related by Herself.* Edited by Moira Ferguson. Ann Arbor: University of Michigan Press, 1993.

Pringle, J. W. *Report of Captain J. W. Pringle on Prisons in the West Indies.* 2 parts. London, 1838.

Sinclair, A. C., and Laurence R. Fyfe. *The Handbook of Jamaica for 1884–85: Comprising Historical, Statistical and General Information Concerning the Island; Compiled from Official and Other Reliable Records.* 4 vols. in 8. London: Edward Stanford; Kingston, Jamaica: Government Printing Establishment, 1884.

"The Sligo Papers, an Official View: Excerpts from the Letter Books of Howe Peter Browne, 2nd Marquis of Sligo." *Jamaica Journal* 17.3 (August–October 1984): 11–17.

Smith, Keithlyn B., and Fernando B. Smith. *To Shoot Hard Labour: The Life and Times of Samuel Smith, an Antiguan Workingman, 1877–1982.* Scarborough, Ontario: Edan's Publishers, 1986.

Stedman, John Gabriel. *Narrative of a Five Years' Expedition against the Revolted Negroes of Surinam.* Baltimore: Johns Hopkins University Press, 1988.

Sturge, Joseph, and Thomas Harvey. *The West Indies in 1837.* London: Dawsons of Pall Mall, 1968.

Thome, James A., and J. Horace Kimball. *Emancipation in the West Indies: A Six Months' Tour in Antigua, Barbadoes, and Jamaica in the Year 1837.* 1838. Reprint, New York: Arno Press and New York Times, 1969.

Tregelles, Edwin Octavius. *Edwin Octavius Tregelles: Civil Engineer and Minister of the Gospel.* Edited by Sarah E. Fox. London: Hodder and Stoughton, 1892.

Verney, Thomas. "A Vagabond in Paradise: Thomas Verney in Barbados." *History Today* 45.8 (August 1995): 40–46.

Williams, James. *A Narrative of Events, since the First of August, 1834, by James Williams, an Apprenticed Labourer in Jamaica.* London: J. Rider, 1837.

———. *A Narrative of Events, since the First of August, 1834, by James Williams, an Apprenticed Laborer in Jamaica.* Edited by Diane Paton. Durham: Duke University Press, 2001.

Wines, E. C. *Report on the International Penitentiary Congress of London, Held July 3–13, 1872.* Washington, D.C.: Government Printing Office, 1873.

Wright, R. S. *Draft of a Criminal Code and a Code of Criminal Procedure for the Island of Jamaica, with an Explanatory Memorandum.* London: George Edward Eyre and William Spottiswoode, 1877.

SECONDARY SOURCES

Adelson, Leslie A. *Making Bodies, Making History: Feminism and German Identity.* Lincoln: University of Nebraska Press, 1993.

Alper, Benedict S., and Jerry F. Boren. *Crime: International Agenda: Concern and Action in the Prevention of Crime and Treatment of Offenders, 1846–1972.* Lexington, Mass.: D.C. Heath, 1972.

Altink, Henrice. "Slavery by Another Name: Apprenticed Women in Jamaican Workhouses in the Period 1834–8." *Social History* 26.1 (January 2001): 40–59.

Anti-Slavery Crisis: Policy of Ministers, with a Postscript on the Debate and Division in the House of Commons, on the 29th and 30th March. London: William Ball, 1838.

Association for the Universal Abolition of Slavery. *An Appeal to the Christian Women of Sheffield.* Sheffield, England: R. Leader, 1837.

Austin, J. L. *How to Do Things with Words.* 2nd ed. Cambridge, Mass.: Harvard University Press, 1975.

Bakan, Abigail. *Ideology and Class Conflict in Jamaica: The Politics of Rebellion.* Montreal: McGill-Queen's University Press, 1990.

Barriteau, Violet Eudine. "Theorising Ruptures in Gender Systems and the Project of Modernity in the Twentieth-century Caribbean." In *The Culture of Gender and Sexuality in the Caribbean*, edited by Linden Lewis, 25–52. Gainesville: University Press of Florida, 2003.

Beckles, Hilary McD. "Black Masculinity in Caribbean Slavery." In *Interrogating Caribbean Masculinities: Theoretical and Empirical Analyses*, edited by Rhoda E. Reddock, 225–43. Kingston, Jamaica: University of the West Indies Press, 2004.

———. "'Black Men in White Skins': The Formation of a White Proletariat in West

Indian Slave Society." *Journal of Imperial and Commonwealth History* 15.1 (1986): 5–21.

———. "Black Women and the Political Economy of Slavery." In *Centering Woman: Gender Discourses in Caribbean Slave Society* (Kingston, Jamaica: Ian Randle, 1999), 2–21.

———. "Female Enslavement and Gender Ideologies in the Caribbean." In *Identity in the Shadow of Slavery*, edited by Paul E. Lovejoy, 163–82. London: Continuum, 2000.

———. *A History of Barbados: From Amerindian Settlement to Nation-State*. Cambridge: Cambridge University Press, 1990.

———. "Plantation Production and White 'Proto-slavery': White Indentured Servants and the Colonisation of the English West Indies, 1624–1645." *Americas* 41.3 (1985): 21–45.

———. "A 'Riotous and Unruly Lot': Irish Indentured Servants and Freemen in the English West Indies, 1644–1713." *William and Mary Quarterly*, third series, 47.4 (1990): 503–22.

Beckles, Hilary McD., and Verene Shepherd, eds. *Caribbean Freedom: Society and Economy from Emancipation to the Present*. Kingston, Jamaica: Ian Randle Publishers; London: James Currey Publishers, 1993.

Bell, Kenneth N., and W. P. Morrell. *Select Documents on British Colonial Policy 1830–1860*. Oxford: Clarendon Press, 1928.

Bentham, Jeremy. *The Panopticon Writings*. Edited by Miran Božovič. London: Verso, 1995.

Bernault, Florence. "The Shadow of Rule: Colonial Power and Modern Punishment in Africa." In *Cultures of Confinement: A History of the Prison in Africa, Asia and Latin America*, edited by Frank Dikötter and Ian Brown, 55–94. Ithaca, N.Y.: Cornell University Press, 2007.

Bevan, William. *The Operation of the Apprenticeship System in the British Colonies: A Statement, the Substance of Which Was Presented and Adopted at the Meeting of the Liverpool Anti-Slavery Society, December 19th, 1837, with References to Official Documents, Authentic Narratives, and Additional Subsequent Information*. Liverpool: D. Marples, T. Taylor; London: Hamilton, Adams, 1838.

Boa, Sheena. "Experiences of Women Estate Workers during the Apprenticeship Period in St. Vincent, 1834–38: The Transition from Slavery to Freedom." *Women's History Review* 10.3 (2001): 381–407.

Bolland, O. Nigel. "Systems of Domination after Slavery: The Control of Land and Labour in the British West Indies after 1838." In Beckles and Shepherd, *Caribbean Freedom*, 107–23.

Braithwaite, John. *Crime, Shame, and Reintegration*. Cambridge: Cambridge University Press, 1989.

Brown, Laurence and Tara Inniss. "The Slave Family in the Transition to Freedom: Barbados, 1834–1841." *Slavery and Abolition* 26.2 (August 2005): 257–69.

Brown, Vincent. "Spiritual Terror and Sacred Authority in Jamaican Slave Society." *Slavery and Abolition* 24.1 (April 2003): 24–53.

Bryan, Patrick. *The Jamaican People, 1880–1902: Race, Class and Social Control*. Kingston, Jamaica: University of the West Indies Press, 1991.

Buckley, Roger Norman. *The British Army in the West Indies: Society and the Military in the Revolutionary Age*. Gainesville: University Press of Florida, 1998.

Burn, W. L. *Emancipation and Apprenticeship in the British West Indies*. London: Jonathan Cape, 1937.

Burnard, Trevor. *Mastery, Tyranny, and Desire: Thomas Thistlewood and His Slaves in the Anglo-Jamaican World*. Chapel Hill: University of North Carolina Press, 2004.

———. "'A Matron in Rank, a Prostitute in Manners': The Manning Divorce of 1741 and Class, Gender, Race and Law in Eighteenth-century Jamaica." In *Working Slavery, Pricing Freedom: Perspectives from the Caribbean, Africa and the African Diaspora*, edited by Verene A. Shepherd, 133–52. New York: Palgrave, 2001.

Burns, Allan. *History of the British West Indies*. London: George Allen & Unwin, 1954.

Burton, Eric. *Clocks and Watches 1400–1900*. New York: Frederick A. Praeger, 1967.

Burton, Richard D. E. *Afro-Creole: Power, Opposition, and Play in the Caribbean*. Ithaca: Cornell University Press, 1997.

Bush, Barbara. "'Sable Venus', 'She Devil' or 'Drudge'? British Slavery and the 'Fabulous Fiction' of Black Women's Identities, c. 1650–1838." *Women's History Review* 9.4 (2000): 761–89.

———. *Slave Women in Caribbean Society, 1650–1838*. Bloomington: Indiana University Press, 1990.

———. "White 'Ladies', Coloured 'Favourites', and Black 'Wenches': Some Considerations on Sex, Race and Class Factors in Social Relations in White Creole Society in the British Caribbean." *Slavery and Abolition* 2.3 (December 1981): 245–62.

Butler, Judith. *Gender Trouble: Feminism and the Subversion of Identity*. New York: Routledge, 1990.

Campbell, Mavis C. *The Maroons of Jamaica 1655–1796: A History of Resistance, Collaboration, and Betrayal*. Massachusetts: Bergin & Garvey, 1988.

Canning, Kathleen. "The Body as Method? Reflections on the Place of the Body in Gender History." *Gender & History* 11.3 (1999): 499–513.

Cooke, David J., and Ed Wozniak. "PRISM Applied to a Critical Incident Review: A Case Study of the Glendairy Prison Riot and Its Aftermath in Barbados." *International Journal of Forensic Mental Health* 9.3 (2010): 159–72.

Craton, Michael. "Continuity not Change: The Incidence of Unrest among Ex-slaves in the British West Indies, 1838–1876." In Beckles and Shepherd, *Caribbean Freedom*, 192–206.

———. *Empire, Enslavement, and Freedom in the Caribbean*. Kingston, Jamaica: Ian Randle, 1997.

Curtin, Philip D. *The Image of Africa: British Ideas and Action, 1780–1850.* Madison: University of Wisconsin Press, 1964.

———. *Two Jamaicas: The Role of Ideas in a Tropical Colony 1830–1865.* New York: Atheneum, 1975.

Dalby, Jonathan. *Crime and Punishment in Jamaica: A Quantitative Analysis of the Assize Court Records, 1756–1856.* Mona, Jamaica: Social History Project, Dept. of History, University of the West Indies, 2000.

Damousi, Joy. *Depraved and Disorderly: Female Convicts, Sexuality and Gender in Colonial Australia.* Cambridge: Cambridge University Press, 1997.

Dhanda, Karen S. Review of James Williams, *A Narrative of Events, Since the First of August, 1834, by James Williams, An Apprenticed Laborer in Jamaica,* edited by Diane Paton (Durham: Duke University Press, 2001). H-LatAm, 2003, https://networks.h-net.org/node/23910/reviews/54407/dhanda-paton-narrative-events-first-august-1834-james-williams.

Dikötter, Frank, and Ian Brown, eds. *Cultures of Confinement: A History of the Prison in Africa, Asia and Latin America.* Ithaca: Cornell University Press, 2007.

Dinwiddy, J. R. "The Early Nineteenth-century Campaigns against Flogging in the Army." *English Historical Review* 97.383 (April 1982): 308–31.

Domar, Evsey D. "The Causes of Slavery or Serfdom: A Hypothesis." *Journal of Economic History* 30.1 (1970): 18–32.

Dublin Ladies' Association, Hibernian Anti-slavery Society. *Second Appeal from the Dublin Ladies' Association.* Cork: George Ridings, 1837.

Duffield, Ian. "From Slave Colonies to Penal Colonies: The West Indian Convict Transportees to Australia." *Slavery and Abolition* 7.1 (May 1986): 25–45.

Dumm, Thomas L. *Michel Foucault and the Politics of Freedom.* Thousand Oaks, Calif.: Sage, 1996.

Evans, Robin. *The Fabrication of Virtue: English Prison Architecture, 1750–1840.* Cambridge: Cambridge University Press, 1982.

Fanon, Frantz. *Black Skin, White Masks.* Translated by Richard Philcox. New York: Grove Press, 1952.

———. *The Wretched of the Earth.* Translated by Constance Farrington. New York: Grove Press, 1963.

Forsythe, William James. *The Reform of Prisoners, 1830–1900.* New York: St. Martin's Press, 1987.

Foucault, Michel. *Discipline and Punish: The Birth of the Prison.* Translated by Alan Sheridan. New York: Vintage Books, 1995.

———. "Of Other Spaces." *Diacritics* 16.1 (Spring 1986): 22–27.

Frey, Sylvia R., and Betty Wood. *From Slavery to Emancipation in the Atlantic World.* New York: Routledge, 1999.

Friedland, Martin L. "Codification in the Commonwealth: Earlier Efforts." *Criminal Law Forum* 2.1 (1990): 145–59.

————. "R. S. Wright's Model Criminal Code." *Oxford Journal of Legal Studies* 1.3 (1981): 307–46.

Garland, David. "Review Essay: Foucault's 'Discipline and Punish': An Exposition and Critique." *American Bar Foundation Research Journal* 11.4 (1986): 847–80.

Goveia, Elsa. *The West Indian Slave Laws of the Eighteenth Century*. Barbados: Caribbean Universities Press, 1970.

Gragg, Larry. *Englishmen Transplanted: The English Colonisation of Barbados 1627–1660*. Oxford: Oxford University Press, 2003.

Green, Cecilia A. "'The Abandoned Lower Class of Females': Class, Gender, and Penal Discipline in Barbados, 1875–1929." *Comparative Studies in Society and History* 53.1 (2011): 144–79.

————. "Local Geographies of Crime and Punishment in a Plantation Colony: Gender and Incarceration in Barbados, 1878–1928." *New West Indian Guide/Nieuwe West-Indische Gids* 86.3–4 (2012): 263–90.

Green, William A. *British Slave Emancipation: The Sugar Colonies and the Great Experiment 1830–1865*. Oxford: Oxford University Press, 1991.

Grosz, Elizabeth. *Volatile Bodies: Toward a Corporeal Feminism*. Bloomington: Indiana University Press, 1994.

Hall, Douglas. "The Flight from the Estates Reconsidered: The British West Indies, 1838–1842." In Beckles and Shepherd, *Caribbean Freedom*, 55–63.

Hall, Gwendolyn Midlo. *Social Control in Slave Plantation Societies: A Comparison of St. Domingue and Cuba*. Baltimore: Johns Hopkins University Press, 1971.

Hall, Neville A. T. *Slave Society in the Danish West Indies: St. Thomas, St. John, and St. Croix*. Edited by Barry W. Higman. Baltimore: Johns Hopkins University Press, 1992.

Hamilton, Bruce. *Barbados and the Confederation Question, 1871–1885*. London: Chiswick Press, 1956.

Handler, Jerome S., and Kenneth M. Bilby. "On the Early Use and Origin of the Term 'Obeah' in Barbados and the Anglophone Caribbean." *Slavery and Abolition* 22.2 (2001): 87–100.

Haralambos, Michael, and Martin Holborn. *Sociology: Themes and Perspectives*. London: Collins Educational, 1991.

Harris, Cheryl I. "Whiteness as Property." *Harvard Law Review* 106.8 (1993): 1709–91.

Hay, Douglas, and Paul Craven. Introduction to *Masters, Servants, and Magistrates in Britain and the Empire, 1562–1955* (Chapel Hill: University of North Carolina Press, 2004), 1–58.

Heuman, Gad. "*The Killing Time*": *The Morant Bay Rebellion in Jamaica*. Knoxville: University of Tennessee Press, 1994.

————. "A Tale of Two Jamaican Rebellions." *Jamaican Historical Review* 19 (1996): 1–8.

Heuman, Gad, and David V. Trotman, eds. *Contesting Freedom: Control and Resistance in the Post-emancipation Caribbean*. Oxford, England: Macmillan Education, 2005.

Hobbes, Thomas. *Leviathan; Or the Matter, Forme and Power of a Commonwealth Ecclesiastical and Civil.* Edited by Michael Oakeshott. New York: Touchstone, 1997.

Holt, Thomas C. *The Problem of Freedom: Race, Labour, and Politics in Jamaica and Britain, 1832–1938.* Baltimore: Johns Hopkins University Press, 1992.

Hutton, Clinton. "The Defeat of the Morant Bay Rebellion." *Jamaican Historical Review* 19 (1996): 30–38.

Ignatieff, Michael. *A Just Measure of Pain: The Penitentiary in the Industrial Revolution, 1750–1850.* New York: Pantheon Books, 1978.

Jackson, Patrick N. Wyse. "John W. Pringle (c. 1793–1861) and Ordnance Survey Geological Mapping in Ireland." *Proceedings of the Geologists' Association* 108 (1997): 153–56.

Johnson, Michele A. "A Century of Murder in Jamaica 1880–1980." *Jamaica Journal* 20.2 (1987): 34–40.

Jones, Cecily. "Contesting the Boundaries of Gender, Race, and Sexuality in Barbadian Plantation Society." *Women's History Review* 12.2(2003): 195–232.

Kale, Madhavi. "Casting Labor: Empire and Indentured Migration from India to the British Caribbean, 1837–1845." PhD diss., University of Pennsylvania, 1992.

Knight, Franklin W. *The Caribbean: The Genesis of a Fragmented Nationalism.* New York: Oxford University Press, 1990.

Lambert, David. *White Creole Culture, Politics and Identity during the Age of Abolition.* Cambridge: Cambridge University Press, 2005.

Lazarus-Black, Mindie. *Legitimate Acts and Illegal Encounters: Law and Society in Antigua and Barbuda.* Washington, D.C.: Smithsonian Institution Press, 1994.

Levine, Philippa. "What Difference Did Empire Make? Sex, Gender, and Sanitary Reform in the British Empire." In *National Healths: Gender, Sexuality, and Health in a Cross-cultural Context,* edited by Michael Worton and Nana Wilson-Tagore, 71–81. London: UCL Press, 2004.

Levy, Claude. *Emancipation, Sugar, and Federalism: Barbados and the West Indies, 1833–1876.* Gainesville: University Presses of Florida, 1980.

Lewis, Gordon K. *The Growth of the Modern West Indies.* New York: Monthly Review Press, 1968.

Lewis, Michael. Review of Daniel V. Botsman, *Punishment and Power in the Making of Modern Japan. American Historical Review* 11.2 (2006): 450–51.

Ley, David. "Social Geography and the Taken-for-granted World." *Transactions of the Institute of British Geographers,* new series, 2.4 (1977): 498–512.

Ligon, Richard. *A True and Exact History of the Island of Barbadoes.* 1673. Reprint, London: Frank Cass, 1970.

Logan, Caroline, and Lorraine Johnstone, eds. *Managing Clinical Risk: A Guide to Effective Practice.* New York: Routledge, 2012.

London Anti-Slavery Society. *The Permanent Laws of the Emancipated Colonies.* London: London Anti-Slavery Society, 1838.

Long, Edward. *The History of Jamaica; Or, General Survey of the Antient and Modern State of that Island: With Reflections on its Situation, Settlements, Inhabitants, Climate, Products, Commerce, Laws, and Government*, vol. 1. 2nd ed. London: Frank Cass, 1970.

————. *The History of Jamaica; Or, General Survey of the Antient and Modern State of that Island: With Reflections on its Situation, Settlements, Inhabitants, Climate, Products, Commerce, Laws, and Government*, vol. 2. London: Printed for T. Lowndes, 1774.

Look Lai, Walton. *The Chinese in the West Indies, 1806–1995: A Documentary History*. Kingston, Jamaica: Press, University of the West Indies, 1998.

————. *Indentured Labour, Caribbean Sugar: Chinese and Indian Immigrants to the British West Indies, 1838–1918*. Baltimore: Johns Hopkins University Press, 1993.

López, Ian F. Haney. *White by Law: The Legal Construction of Race*. New York: New York University, 1996.

Luddy, Maria. "'Abandoned Women and Bad Characters': Prostitution in Nineteenth-Century Ireland." *Women's History Review* 6.4 (1997): 485–504.

Maimonides, Moses. *The Judaic-Law, as Opposed to the English Poor-Law*. Translated by J. W. Peppercorne. London: Pelham Richardson, n.d.

Manzano, Juan Francisco. "Autobiography of a Slave." In *The Cuba Reader: History, Culture, Politics*, edited by Aviva Chomsky, Barry Carr, and Pamela Marie Smorkaloff, 49–57. Durham: Duke University Press, 2003.

Mathurin, Lucille. *The Rebel Woman in the British West Indies during Slavery*. Kingston: Institute of Jamaica, 1975.

Miller, Marilyn Grace. "Imitation and Improvisation in Juan Francisco Manzano's *Zafira*," *Colonial Latin American Review* 17.1 (2008): 49–71.

Mohapatra, Prabhu P. "'Restoring the Family': Wife Murders and the Making of a Sexual Contract for Indian Immigrant Labour in the British Caribbean Colonies, 1860–1920." *Studies in History* 11.2 (1995): 227–60.

Moore, Brian L. "The Culture of the Colonial Elites of Nineteenth-Century Guyana." In *The White Minority in the Caribbean*, edited by Howard Johnson and Karl Watson, 95–115. Kingston, Jamaica: Ian Randle, 1998.

Moore, Brian L., and Michele A. Johnson. *Neither Led nor Driven: Contesting British Cultural Imperialism in Jamaica*. Kingston, Jamaica: University of the West Indies Press, 2004.

Morgan, Jennifer L. *Laboring Women: Reproduction and Gender in New World Slavery*. Philadelphia: University of Pennsylvania Press, 2004.

Morrissey, Marietta. *Slave Women in the New World: Gender Stratification in the Caribbean*. Lawrence: University Press of Kansas, 1989.

Negro Apprenticeship in the Colonies: A Review of the Report of the Select Committee of the House of Commons, Appointed to Inquire into "The Working of the Apprenticeship System in the Colonies, the Condition of the Apprentices, and the Laws and Regulations affecting them which have Been Passed." London: John Hatchard and Son, 1837.

Newton, Graeme R., ed. *Crime and Punishment around the World.* 4 vols. Santa Barbara, Calif.: ABC-CLIO, 2010.

Newton, Velma. *The Silver Men: West Indian Labour Migration to Panama, 1850–1914.* Kingston, Jamaica: Institute of Social and Economic Research, 1984.

Paton, Diana. "'From His Own Lips': The Politics of Authenticity in *A Narrative of Events since the First of August, 1834, by James Williams, an Apprenticed Labourer in Jamaica.*" In *Discourses of Slavery and Abolition: Britain and its Colonies, 1760–1838,* edited by Brycchan Carey, Markman Ellis, and Sara Salih, 108–22. New York: Palgrave Macmillan, 2004.

Paton, Diana. *No Bond but the Law: Punishment, Race, and Gender in Jamaican State Formation, 1780–1870.* Duke University Press, 2004.

———. "Punishment, Crime, and the Bodies of Slaves in Eighteenth-Century Jamaica." *Journal of Social History* 34.4 (2001): 923–54.

Perkins, Cyril Frances. *Busha's Mistress or Catherine the Fugitive: A Stirring Romance of the Days of Slavery in Jamaica.* Edited by Paul E. Lovejoy, Verene Shepherd, and David V. Trotman. Kingston, Jamaica: Ian Randle, 2003.

Pile, Steve. "Human Agency and Human Geography Revisited: A Critique of 'New Models' of the Self." *Transactions of the Institute of British Geographers* 18.1 (1993): 122–39.

Popke, E. Jeffrey. "Managing Colonial Alterity: Narratives of Race, Space and Labour in Durban, 1870–1920." *Journal of Historical Geography* 29.2 (2003): 248–67.

Rapoport, Amos. "Vernacular Architecture and the Cultural Determinants of Form." In *Buildings and Society: Essays on the Social Development of the Built Environment,* edited by Anthony D. King, 283–305. London: Routledge & Kegan Paul, 1980.

Richardson, Bonham C. "Freedom and Migration in the Leeward Caribbean, 1838–48." *Journal of Historical Geography* 6.4 (1980): 391–408.

———. *Panama Money in Barbados 1900–1920.* Knoxville: University of Tennessee Press, 1985.

Roberts, George W. "Emigration from the Island of Barbados." *Social and Economic Studies* 4.1 (1995): 245–88.

———. *The Population of Jamaica.* 1957. Millwood, N.Y.: Kraus Reprint, 1979.

Robotham, Don. *"The Notorious Riot:" The Socio-economic and Political Base of Paul Bogle's Revolt.* Mona, Jamaica: Institute of Social and Economic Research, University of the West Indies, 1981.

Rose, Edward P. F. "The Military Background of John W. Pringle in 1826, Founding Superintendent of the Geological Survey of Ireland." *Irish Journal of Earth Sciences* 17(1999): 61–70.

Rugemer, Edward B. "The Development of Mastery and Race in the Comprehensive Slave Codes of the Greater Caribbean during the Seventeenth Century." *William and Mary Quarterly* 70.3 (2013): 429–58.

Sawicki, Jana. *Disciplining Foucault: Feminism, Power, and the Body.* New York: Routledge, 1991.

Scarry, Elaine. *The Body in Pain: The Making and Unmaking of the World.* New York: Oxford University Press, 1985.

Schaw, Janet. *Journal of a Lady of Quality, 1774–1776.* Edited by E. W. and C. M. Andrews. New Haven: Yale University Press, 1923.

Schomburgk, Robert H. *The History of Barbados; Comprising a Geographical and Statistical Description of the Island; A Sketch of the Historical Events since the Settlement; and an Account of its Geology and Natural Productions.* London: Longman, Brown, Green and Longmans, 1848.

Schuler, Monica. *"Alas, Alas, Kongo": A Social History of Indentured African Immigration into Jamaica, 1841–1865.* Baltimore: Johns Hopkins University Press, 1980.

Scott, Joan W. "Gender: A Useful Category of Historical Analysis." *American Historical Review* 91 (December 1986): 1053–75.

Semmel, Bernard. *Jamaican Blood and Victorian Conscience: The Governor Eyre Controversy.* Boston: Houghton Mifflin, 1963.

Sharpe, Henry Edward. *On the Abolition of the Negro Apprenticeship, in a Letter to the Right Hon. the Lord Brougham.* London: John W. Parker, 1838.

Shaw, Jenny. *Everyday Life in the Early English Caribbean: Irish, Africans, and the Construction of Difference.* Athens: University of Georgia Press, 2013.

Shepherd, Verene. *Transients to Settlers: The Experience of Indians in Jamaica 1845–1950.* Leeds: Peepal Tree Press, 1993.

———. *Working Slavery, Pricing Freedom: Perspectives from the Caribbean, Africa and the African Diaspora.* New York: Palgrave Macmillan, 2001.

Sibley, David. *Geographies of Exclusion: Society and Difference in the West.* London: Routledge, 1995.

Sohal, Harinder Singh. "The East Indian Indentureship System in Jamaica, 1845–1917." PhD. diss., University of Waterloo, 1979.

Spierenburg, Pieter. "Punishment, Power, and History. Foucault and Elias." *Social Science History* 28.4 (2004): 607–36.

Stamatel, Janet P., and Hung-en Sung, eds. *Crime and Punishment around the World,* vol. 2, *The Americas.* Santa Barbara, ABC-CLIO, 2010.

A Statement of Facts, Illustrating the Administration of the Abolition Law, and the Sufferings of the Negro Apprentices, in the Island of Jamaica. London: John Haddon, 1837.

Sunder Rajan, Rajeswari. *Real and Imagined Women: Gender, Culture and Postcolonialism.* London: Routledge, 1993.

Tomlinson, Heather. "Design and Reform: The 'Separate System' in the Nineteenth-Century English Prison." In *Buildings and Society: Essays on the Social Development of the Built Environment,* edited by Anthony D. King, 94–119. London: Routledge & Kegan Paul, 1980.

Tosh, John. *Manliness and Masculinities in Nineteenth-Century Britain: Essays on Gender, Family, and Empire.* Harlow: Pearson Educational, 2005.

Treviño, A. Javier. *The Sociology of Law: Classical and Contemporary Perspectives.* New York: St. Martin's Press, 1996.

Trotman, David V. "Capping the Volcano: Riots and their Suppression in Post-emancipation Trinidad." In *Contesting Freedom. Control and Resistance in the Post-emancipation Caribbean*, ed. Gad Heuman and David V. Trotman, 118–41. Oxford: Macmillan Caribbean, 2005.

————. *Crime in Trinidad: Conflict and Control in a Plantation Society, 1838–1900*. Knoxville: University of Tennessee Press, 1986.

————. "Women and Crime in Late Nineteenth Century Trinidad." In Beckles and Shepherd, *Caribbean Freedom*, 251–59.

Turner, Mary. "The 11 O'clock Flog: Women, Work, and Labour Law in the British Caribbean. *Slavery and Abolition* 1.1 (1999): 38–58.

Walkowitz, Judith R. *Prostitution and Victorian Society: Women, Class, and the State*. Cambridge: Cambridge University Press, 1980.

Ward, J. R. *Poverty and Progress in the Caribbean, 1800–1960*. Hampshire, England: Macmillan, 1985.

Williams, Eric. *From Columbus to Castro: The History of the Caribbean, 1492–1969*. New York: Vintage Books, 1984.

Wilton, Robert D. "The Constitution of Difference: Space and Psyche in Landscapes of Exclusion." *Geoforum* 29.2 (1998): 173–85.

Yuval-Davis, Nira. *Gender and Nation*. Thousand Oaks, Calif.: Sage, 1997.

Index

Race in the Atlantic World, 1700–1900

CPSIA information can be obtained
at www.ICGtesting.com
Printed in the USA
LVHW032100120220
646728LV00003B/253